Globalizing Women

Themes in Global Social Change

Series Editor: Christopher Chase-Dunn
Consulting Editors: Janet Lippman Abu-Lughod
Giovanni Arrighi
Jonathan Friedman
Keith Griffin

Globalizing Women

Transnational Feminist Networks

Valentine M. Moghadam

The Johns Hopkins University Press
Baltimore and London

© 2005 The Johns Hopkins University Press
All rights reserved. Published 2005
Printed in the United States of America on acid-free paper
9 8 7 6 5 4 3 2

The Johns Hopkins University Press
2715 North Charles Street
Baltimore, Maryland 21218-4363
www.press.jhu.edu

Library of Congress Cataloging-in-Publication Data

Moghadam, Valentine M., 1952–
   Globalizing women : transnational feminist networks /
Valentine M. Moghadam.
      p. cm. — (Themes in global social change)
   Includes bibliographical references and index.
   ISBN 0-8018-8023-8 (hardcover : alk. paper)—
   ISBN 0-8018-8024-6 (pbk. : alk. paper)
      1. Feminists—Social networks. 2. Feminism—International
cooperation. 3. Women—Developing countries—Economic
conditions. 4. Women—Developing countries—Social
conditions. 5. Transnationalism. 6. Globalization.
7. International business enterprises. 8. Sexual division of
labor. I. Title. II. Series.
HQ1101.M64 2005
305.42—dc22   2004010123

A catalog record for this book is available from the British
Library.

To the memory of MSM, beloved sister

Contents

Preface

This book examines globalization as a gendered process, which means that I draw attention to the role of female labor in the global economy, the gender implications of the changing nature of the state in an era of globalization, and new forms of women's organizing and mobilizing. In particular, I analyze transnational feminist networks (TFNs), their relationship to globalization processes, their responses to such features of globalization as neoliberal capitalism and patriarchal fundamentalism, the ways that they engage with public policy at the national and international levels to accomplish their goals, and their organizational dynamics. I seek to show that transnational feminist networks are the organizational expression of the transnational women's movement and are guided by a set of emerging ideas and goals that may be referred to as global feminism.

Since 1985, transnational feminist networks have proliferated around a number of broad agendas or on specific issues and campaigns. For reasons that I explain in chapter 1, I have chosen to focus on three TFNs that formed in opposition to structural adjustment and neoliberal economic policy, developing a feminist critique and an alternative feminist economics framework; and on three TFNs that promote women's human rights in Muslim countries where fundamentalism emerged and the legal status of women became compromised. As such, this book is about how "globalization-from-above" has engendered "globalization-from-below," producing a dynamic and transnational women's movement that has been confronting neoliberal capitalism and patriarchal fundamentalism. In addition, I describe the weaknesses of feminist organizing, the financial constraints that transnational women's organizations can face, and the dilemmas of professionalization. Although a number of feminist studies have appeared that emphasize the exploitative effects of globalization on women (for example, Wichterich 1999 and Ehrenreich and Hochschild 2003), in this book I also examine how "globalizing women" are responding to and resisting growing inequalities, the exploitation of female labor, and patriarchal fundamentalisms.

Research Methods and Plan of the Book

In preparing this book I used several qualitative research methods. In addition to a survey of the relevant secondary sources, I used the participant-observation method and gathered interview and documentary data. Some background information on the process leading up to this book may be helpful.

In the early 1990s, in my capacity as a senior researcher with the WIDER Institute of the United Nations University, I began to encounter, at various international and regional conferences and at UN expert group meetings, representatives of organizations that I later called transnational feminist networks. At times, these women were representing their nongovernmental organizations at preparatory meetings and at the major UN conferences; other times, they were presenting papers at expert groups meetings to which they (and I) had been invited. I became intrigued by their activities and decided to study them more closely. I began by observing their interactions with UN officials and members of governmental delegations, reading their literature, and holding informal conversations with them. In 1995 I attended (and spoke at) an annual conference of one network, WIDE, in Brussels. The following year I published my first article on the subject, entitled "Feminist Networks North and South: DAWN, WIDE, and Women Living under Muslim Laws." At the 1997 annual meetings of the American Sociological Association, I helped to organize a panel that examined global feminism from a world-systems perspective, and three articles followed (Moghadam 1996a, 1998b, 1999, 2000a). At that point I decided to write a book and began to more systematically collect interview and documentary data. In the summer of 1998 I attended the annual conference of the Association of Women of the Mediterranean Region (AWMR); two years later I attended the annual meetings of WIDE and AWMR, and wrote a short article that compared and contrasted the meetings and networks (Moghadam 2000b). In the meantime, I conducted interviews in various locations with women associated with DAWN, WEDO, SIGI, and WLUML. This book draws heavily on the literature of transnational feminist networks, as well as on the interviews I have conducted over the years.

The book begins in a conceptual vein and moves on to describe the feminist networks in more detail. Chapter 1 provides an introduction and overview to my argument. Chapter 2 surveys globalization studies and then maps out my own gendered account of globalization. Chapter 3 shows how female labor incorporation, growing inequalities, and regional crises led to increased unionization and transnational activism among women. The focus of chapter 4 is on the nature and characteristics of women's organizations and the factors behind the emergence of transnational feminist networks in the mid-1980s. Chapters 5, 6, and 7 are more empirical accounts of the six case-study TFNs and describe the networks' activities, organizational structures, strengths, and weaknesses. In chapter 8, I summarize the argument and conclude with some reflections on the relationship between globalization and global feminism and the future of global governance.

Acknowledgments

This book would not have been possible without the support of two institutions, Illinois State University and the Woodrow Wilson International Center for Scholars. At Illinois State, I was centrally involved in two year-long seminar series on globalization (1997–98 and 2000–2001) that allowed me to test my ideas about globalization and the women's movement, present my work in progress, and learn from the many speakers—off-campus guests and ISU colleagues alike—who similarly took part in the seminar series. A University Research Grant allowed me to travel to Brussels and Cyprus in the summer of 2000 to attend the annual meetings of two transnational feminist networks, conduct interviews, and collect documents. During the academic year 2001–2002, a sabbatical leave enabled me to accept a fellowship at the Woodrow Wilson Center in Washington, D.C., which provided the time, space, and resources that I needed to complete the final research and to write the first draft of the book manuscript. I thank the Woodrow Wilson Center for its stimulating environment, and student intern Lisa Viscidi for her excellent research assistance and intellectual curiosity. I also wish to thank various friends and colleagues who read and commented on draft chapters, and in particular Ann Sisson Runyan, Mahnaz Afkhami, Miriam Cooke, Marieme Helie-Lucas, and Brigitte Holzner for their cogent and generous comments. I am also grateful for very helpful suggestions by an anonymous external reviewer. Needless to add, the analysis and any errors are mine.

Glossary of Acronyms and Terms

AAWORD	Association of African Women for Research and Development
ACP	Africa, Caribbean, Pacific countries (with special trade agreements with the European Union)
AFL-CIO	American Federation of Labor–Congress of Industrial Organizations (largest U.S. union)
Alt-WID	Alternative Women in Development
APEC	Asia Pacific Economic Cooperation
ARROW	Asia Pacific Research and Resource Organization for Women
AWID	Association for Women's Rights in Development
AWMR	Association of Women of the Mediterranean Region
AWSA	Arab Women's Solidarity Association
CEDAW	Convention on the Elimination of All Forms of Discrimination against Women; also: Committee on the Elimination of Discrimination against Women (UN)
CSW	Commission on the Status of Women (UN)
DAWN	Development Alternatives with Women for a New Era
ECE	Economic Commission for Europe (UN)
ECOSOC	Economic and Social Committee (UN)
EGCG	External Gender Consultative Group (World Bank)
encuentros	Latin American feminist meetings
EPZ	export-processing zone
EU	European Union
FAR	Feminists for Animal Rights
FDI	foreign direct investment
FIS	Front Islamique du Salut (Islamic Salvation Front, Algeria)
FSU	former Soviet Union

FWCW	Fourth World Conference on Women (aka the Beijing conference)
GATT	General Agreement on Tariffs and Trade
GDP	gross domestic product
Hamas	a Palestinian Islamist organization
HERA	Health, Empowerment, Rights, and Accountability
IAW	International Alliance of Women
ICFTU	International Confederation of Free Trade Unions
ICPD	International Conference on Population and Development (UN)
ICT	information and computer technologies
ICW	International Council of Women
IFBPW	International Federation of Business and Professional Women
IFI	international finance institution
IGO	intergovernmental organization
ILO	International Labor Organization; International Labor Office (UN)
IMF	International Monetary Fund
INGO	international nongovernmental organization
INSTRAW	Institute for Research and Training on Women (UN)
ISIS	International Women's Information and Communication Service
IWTC	International Women's Tribune Center
Jehadis	former Afghan Mujahideen and Northern Alliance
jihad	struggle, holy war
KARAT	Central and East European feminist network
maquila	a U.S.-Mexico border factory producing for the world market
MAI	Multilateral Agreement on Investment
MENA	Middle East and North Africa
MNC	multinational corporation
Mujahideen	Afghan Islamist rebel group of the 1980s and early 1990s
NAFTA	North American Free Trade Agreement
NGO	nongovernmental organization
NIEO	new international economic order

OECD	Organization for Economic Cooperation and Development
OECD/DAC/WID	OECD Development Assistance Committee for Women in Development
PLO	Palestine Liberation Organization
PSI	Public Services International (an international union)
RAWA	Revolutionary Association of Women of Afghanistan
SAP	structural adjustment policy
SEWA	Self-Employed Women's Association (India)
SIGI	Sisterhood Is Global Institute
SMO	social movement organization
TAN	transnational advocacy network
TCC	transnational capitalist class
TFN	transnational feminist network
TSA	transnational state apparatus
TSMO	transnational social movement organization
UNCED	UN Conference on Environment and Development
UNDP	United Nations Development Program
UNFPA	United Nations Fund for Population Activities
UNICEF	United Nations Children's Fund
UNIFEM	United Nations Development Fund for Women
WEDO	Woman's Environment and Development Organization
WICEJ	Women's International Coalition for Economic Justice
WID/WAD/GAD	women in development / women and development / gender and development (research paradigms)
WIDE	Women in Development in Europe
WIDF	Women's International Democratic Federation
WILPF	Women's International League for Peace and Freedom
WLP	Women's Learning Partnership for Peace, Development, and Rights
WLUML	Women Living under Muslim Laws
WSF	World Social Forum
WSSD	World Summit for Social Development (or Social Summit, UN)
WTO	World Trade Organization
YWCA	Young Women's Christian Association

Globalizing Women

CHAPTER ONE

Globalizing Women

An Introduction and Overview

> Women are taking the lead and making a huge contribution to defining
> the international agenda in terms of human rights, macroeconomics, con-
> flict/peace, and sustainable development. We have a valuable and unique
> perspective on these issues as women and as human beings. We recognize
> that feminism in one country is not sustainable—we need feminism on a
> global scale. [Women in Development Europe, 1995]

Central to women's experiences—and to analyses informed by socialist-feminism or feminist political economy—has been the sexual division of labor, the
separation of societies into public and private spheres, the organization of
economies into the spheres of production and reproduction, and the ways that
these have articulated with gender and class, as well as with ethnicity and race.
Feminist analyses, and women's activism, have been concerned with the broad
implications of the identification of women with the private sphere of the family, including their exclusion from the public sphere, their varied experiences
of marginalization, exploitation, and integration in the sphere of production,
and their undervalued location within the sphere of reproduction, whether as
paid or unpaid labor.[1] Although these experiences and analyses have preoccupied women and feminists throughout the world, it may be said that prior to
the mid-1980s the world's women had not yet developed a collective identity,
a collective sense of injustice, or common forms of organizing. The year 1985
was, in many ways, a watershed. The third United Nations world conference
on women, which took place in Nairobi, Kenya, and consisted of both an intergovernmental conference and a forum of nongovernmental organizations,

brought together women from across the globe who shared their experiences with and criticisms of new economic policies, conservative governments, and cultural-political movements that they deemed inimical to women's interests. Although the term *globalization* would not be used until years later, the emerging global state of affairs proved to be an impetus for novel forms of women's organizing and mobilizing.

This book examines transnational feminist networks (TFNs), their relationship to the globalization process, the ways that they engage with public policy at the national and international levels, and their organizational dynamics. The study is situated at the nexus of three bodies of literature and is intended as a contribution to all three. The first is the now extensive literature on globalization, which analyzes the complex and multidimensional processes that are said to have begun in the late twentieth century. This literature addresses globalization from different disciplinary, conceptual, and political vantage points, but it rarely investigates the gender dimension of globalization. Much of the literature emphasizes globalization as an economic process; some studies examine globalization in terms of the changing nature of the post–Cold War world order; other studies emphasize the cultural aspects and effects of globalization.[2] The literature does not, however, consider globalization as a gendered process.

A related body of studies has appeared on the growth of nongovernmental organizations, civil society and citizenship, global civil society, transnational advocacy networks, and global social movements.[3] This, too, is a rich literature, but attention to the women's movement or to women's organizations is limited to only a few studies. For example, the well-known volume by Keck and Sikkink examined transnational advocacy networks (TANs) organized around human rights, the environment, and violence against women. O'Brien, Goetz, Scholte, and Williams studied the ways in which global social movements—women's movements, unions, and environmental organizations—have engaged with multilateral economic institutions such as the World Bank, the International Monetary Fund, and the World Trade Organization. And the collection by Cohen and Rai on global social movements includes essays on feminist networking for conflict resolution and the advancement of women's human rights.[4]

A third literature focuses precisely on women's movements and women's organizations.[5] Much feminist theorizing of women's movements has focused on national-level factors such as the growth of the population of educated women with grievances about their second-class citizenship. More recent studies have begun to connect women's movements and organizations to international or global processes such as the role of international organizations or the United Nations Decade on Women, and they examine the ways that women's organizations have engaged with the world of public policy. For the most part, however, this literature has not explained the worldwide social movement of women in terms of globalization processes such as the feminization of labor, growing social inequalities, and increased access to the new information and computer technologies (ICTs) by educated and politically active women—which is the argument I make in this book. At the same time, we have seen increasing numbers of feminist studies on globalization and gender, some of which draw on postmodernist and postcolonialist thought and some of which may be described as Marxist-feminist or as constituting a materialist, structuralist, or feminist political economy approach.

This book offers an analysis of globalization as a multidimensional and gendered process (the subject of chapter 2) and of the transnational women's movement as a product of sociodemographic, economic, political, and cultural changes (discussed in chapters 3 and 4). I also describe the research, advocacy, and lobbying efforts of TFNs, their methods of organizing global networks of women, and the ways that they engage with states, international organizations, and global civil society to influence public policy and raise international awareness about women and gender issues (chapters 5, 6, and 7). In discussing Islamic fundamentalism and neoliberal capitalism as two key features of globalization that have resulted in transnational feminist responses, I bring together topics that are usually discussed separately. Conceptually, I draw on world-systems, Marxist, and feminist frameworks to analyze contemporary globalization processes and explain the emergence of a transnational women's movement in the late twentieth century. My explanation incorporates the concepts of gender, class, capital, and the state, all of which operate within a hierarchical world-system divided into core, periphery, and semiperiphery.[6] This book illuminates the links between globalization, inequalities, and women's movements and brings neglected feminist research and activism into clearer view.

The capitalist world-system has often produced antisystemic movements that cross borders and boundaries, while national-level class conflicts and political contradictions have similarly generated forms of collective action and social protest, including social movements and revolutions. But a key characteristic of the era of late capitalism, or globalization, is the proliferation of

transnational social movements, including the transnational women's movement and its organizational expression, the transnational feminist network.

What exactly are transnational feminist networks? They are structures organized above the national level that unite women from three or more countries around a common agenda, such as women's human rights, reproductive
health and rights, violence against women, peace and antimilitarism, or feminist economics. They are part of the family of political change organizations
operating above and across national borders that have been variously described as global civil society organizations, transnational advocacy networks,
and transnational social movement organizations—and which, along with international nongovernmental organizations, constitute the making of a transnational public sphere. As three scholars of social movements have noted:
"Globalization has in fact brought social movements together across borders
in a 'transnational public sphere,' a real as well as conceptual space in which
movement organizations interact, contest each other, and learn from each
other."[7]

Transnational feminist networks work with each other and with transnational human rights, labor, social justice, and environmental organizations to
draw attention to the negative aspects of globalization, to try to influence policy-making, and to insert a feminist perspective in transnational advocacy and
activism. Since 1985, when a number of now well-known TFNs emerged, feminist networks have proliferated around broad agendas or specific issues and
campaigns. The focus in this book is on those TFNs that address themselves
primarily to women's human rights and to economic policy. In particular, I
examine three feminist networks that formed in opposition to structural adjustment and neoliberal economic policy, developing a feminist critique and
an alternative feminist economics framework (chapter 5); and I examine three
feminist networks that promote women's human rights, especially in Muslim
countries where fundamentalism emerged and the legal status of women became compromised (chapters 6 and 7).

Why the focus on feminist economics and the human rights of women in
the Muslim world? I can offer three reasons. First, some of the best-known and
well-organized transnational feminist networks are precisely those oriented
principally toward economic policy (notably Development Alternatives with
Women for a New Era, or DAWN) and the human rights of women in the Muslim world (in particular, the network Women Living under Muslim Laws, or
WLUML). Second, I argue that neoliberal capitalism and Islamic fundamental-

ism are among the defining features and consequences of global restructuring and globalization in the late twentieth century; hence it is logical to examine those feminist networks that focus on these issues. It is noteworthy that the Gloria Declaration—issued by the Eighth International Women and Health Meeting in Rio de Janeiro in March 1997—identified two major systemic obstacles to achieving women's health and rights: globalization of the market economy and religious fundamentalism. That declaration emphasized Christian and especially Catholic restrictions on women's sexual autonomy, as well as Islamic fundamentalism, and criticized the role of the Vatican at venues such as the 1994 International Conference on Population and Development and the 1995 Fourth World Conference on Women. Third, I decided to give prominence to the feminist critique of neoliberal economic policy because I felt it important to correct a certain misunderstanding concerning the women's movement, which is that feminists are either concerned exclusively with personal and reproductive rights or oriented primarily around violence-against-women issues. My decision to include three TFNs that engage with economics is meant to show that global feminism is taking on some of the major policies and institutions of our time—including neoliberal capitalism, the World Bank, the International Monetary Fund (IMF), and the World Trade Organization (WTO)—and inserting a distinctly feminist perspective in global discussions about economic justice.

Female Labor and Women's Mobilizations in an Era of Globalization

Why did the transnational feminist networks emerge in the mid-1980s and not earlier? What was the context?

The women's movement of the second wave, which began in North America and Europe in the 1960s, consisted of feminist groups that emerged within national borders and addressed themselves to their own nation-states, governments, employers, and male colleagues and kin. As women's groups expanded internationally, they remained primarily nationally based and nationally oriented. Feminist groups encompassed liberal, radical, Marxist, and socialist ideologies, and these political differences constituted one form of division within feminism. Another division took the form of North-South, or First World–Third World differences in terms of priority feminist issues; many First World feminists saw legal equality and reproductive rights as key feminist demands and goals, while many Third World feminists emphasized underdevelopment, colonialism, and imperialism as obstacles to women's advancement. The Cold War also cast a shadow on feminist solidarity, in the form of the East-West divide. Disagreements over what constituted priority feminist issues came to the fore at the beginning of the United Nations' Decade for Women, and especially at its first and second world conferences on women, which took place in Mexico City in 1975 and in Copenhagen in 1980, respectively. The disagreements at the Mexico City and Copenhagen conferences pitted women activists from the North and from the South, and revolved around prioritizing equality and sexuality issues versus economic and political issues.[8]

A shift in the nature and orientation of international feminism began to take place in the mid-1980s, during preparations for the third UN world conference on women, which was held in Nairobi, Kenya, in 1985. The shift took the form of bridge building and consensus making across regional and ideological divides, and the emergence of a women's organization of a new type. What enabled this important change in the women's movement to take place were three critical economic and political developments within states and regions, and at the level of the world-system: the transition from Keynesian to neoliberal economics, along with a new international division of labor that relied heavily on (cheap) female labor; the decline of the welfarist, developmentalist state; and the emergence of various forms of fundamentalist movements. These developments led to new thinking and new forms of organizing on the part of activist women in both developing and developed countries. Chapter 4 will describe the evolution of the women's movement and organizations in more detail, but here I will provide some introductory comments.

In the latter part of the 1970s, the international political economy began to be slowly transformed from one based on Keynesian economic principles of full employment, large public sectors, and government deficit financing to one led by the neoliberal philosophy of balanced budgets, tight monetary policy, and the contraction of the public sector wage bill. This change was made ostensibly to solve fiscal crises and indebtedness, although various explanations have been offered to explain global economic restructuring.[9] In the 1980s, global restructuring took the form of Reaganism in the United States, Thatcherism in the United Kingdom, and structural adjustment policies and austerity measures in developing countries.[10] In the 1990s, it took the form of the transition from communism to capitalism in the former Soviet Union and Eastern Europe. Among the consequences of the post-Keynesian and post-communist transition to neoliberal capitalism was the feminization of poverty, or the growing female share of the population living under the poverty line.[11] Meanwhile, cross-national research, including studies by those working in the field of women-in-development or women-and-development (WID/WAD), showed that an ever-growing proportion of the world's women were being incorporated as cheap labor into what was variously called the capitalist world-economy, the new international division of labor, or the global assembly line.[12]

Women's access to an increasing share of many kinds of jobs occurred in the context of the post-Keynesian shift, which came to be characterized by growing unemployment, a decline in the social power of labor, and an increase in temporary, part-time, casual, and home-based work. In the 1980s, women began to be disproportionately involved in irregular forms of employment increasingly used to maximize profits; at the same time, they remained responsible for work related to the family. This is to say their growing labor-market participation was not accompanied by a redistribution of domestic, household, and childcare responsibilities, in part due to cutbacks in social services. The changing nature of the state vis-à-vis the public sector meant the withdrawal, deterioration, or privatization of many public services used by working-class and middle-class women and their families. In addition, women remained disadvantaged in the new labor markets, in terms of wages, training, and occupational segregation. In the late 1980s, ILO economist Guy Standing termed this phenomenon the "feminization of labor." He argued that the increasing globalization of production and the pursuit of flexible forms of labor to retain or increase competitiveness, as well as changing job structures in industrial enterprises, favored the "feminization of employment" in the dual sense of an increase in the numbers of women in the labor force and a deterioration of work conditions (labor standards, income, and employment status).[13]

Another important development at the level of states, regions, and the world-system that led to the narrowing of the political and ideological divide between First World and Third World feminists was the rise of Islamic fundamentalism in Muslim countries and Hindu communalism in India. These movements sought to recuperate traditional norms and codes, including patriarchal laws and family roles for women; they put pressure on states to enforce public morality, increase religious observance, and tighten controls over women—ostensibly to protect the nation or culture from alien influences and conspiracies.[14] Such movements alarmed feminists in the peripheral and semiperipheral countries where the movements emerged.

Divergences, therefore, began to narrow in the mid-1980s as a result of the changing environments in both the North and the South, including the rise of neoliberalism and the growth of fundamentalist movements. The new economic and political realities led to a convergence of feminist perspectives across the globe: for many First World feminists, economic issues and development policy became increasingly important, and for many Third World feminists, increased attention was now directed to women's legal status, autonomy, and rights.

As a result, the mid-1980s saw the formation of a number of transnational feminist networks that brought together women from developed and developing countries alike to respond to economic pressures and patriarchal movements: Development Alternatives with Women for a New Era (DAWN), Women in Development Europe (WIDE), Women Living under Muslim Laws (WLUML), and the Sisterhood Is Global Institute (SIGI). The beginning of the 1990s saw the emergence of the Women's Environment and Development Organization (WEDO) and the Association of Women of the Mediterranean Region (AWMR), while other TFNs already had formed around women's health and reproductive rights, and around peace and antimilitarism. Table 1 provides information on some of the key TFNs, grouped by priority issue. Here I will mention just a few: Women Working Worldwide, a coordinating group based in London; the International Association for Feminist Economics, which consists primarily of feminist social scientists who seek to develop an alternative model to neoclassical economics and neoliberal policies; the Asia-Pacific Research and Resource Organization for Women (ARROW), based in Kuala Lumpur, which focuses on reproductive health and rights; and the KARAT Coalition for Regional Action, formed in 1997 and spanning thirteen countries in Central and Eastern Europe, now working collaboratively with WIDE. Two feminist networks that focus on communications are the International Women's Tribune Center, based in New York, and ISIS (International Women's Information and Communication Service), with one center in Quezon City, Philippines, and another in Santiago, Chile. ISIS International produces *Women in Action, Women's World,* and other communications. A 2002 issue of *Women in Action* included articles on media (mis)representations of the Afghan crisis and Israeli-Palestinian conflict, while a 2002 issue of *Women's World* had updates on women in Sierra Leone, the Democratic Republic of Congo, Sudan (as well as Sudanese refugees in Kenya), Burundi, Afghanistan, Pakistan, Albania, India, Kosovo, and Colombia. Communications and information-exchange among

TFNs, as well as alliances and collaborations with other transnational advocacy networks, have been made possible by advances in the information and computer technologies.

TFN activities and partnerships with other advocacy networks resulted in some successes at the UN conferences of the 1990s. For example, TFN lobbying led to the insertion of important items in the final Vienna Declaration of the 1993 Conference on Human Rights, such as the assertion that violence against women was an abuse of human rights, and attention to the harmful effects of certain traditional or customary practices, cultural prejudice, and religious extremism. The declaration also stated that human rights abuses of women in situations of armed conflict—including systematic rape, sexual slavery, and forced pregnancy—were violations of the fundamental principles of international human rights and humanitarian law. As we shall see in subsequent chapters, TFNs were also influential at the 1994 International Conference on Population and Development (ICPD), the March 1995 Social Summit, and the September 1995 Beijing conference.

As TFNs proliferated in the 1990s, they helped to bridge the North-South divide among women activists and transcended the earlier political and ideological differences through the adoption of a broader feminist agenda that included a critique of neoliberalism and structural adjustment policies as well as an insistence on women's reproductive rights, bodily integrity, and autonomy. Eventually, that common agenda took the form of the 1995 Beijing Declaration and Platform for Action. Along the way to Beijing, though, there were other venues where the world's women agreed on issues pertaining to the public/private divide, their roles in production and reproduction, and their visions for justice. These included the UN world conferences of the 1990s—the United Nations Conference on the Environment and Development (UNCED) in Rio de Janeiro in 1992, the Human Rights Conference in Vienna in 1993, the International Conference on Population and Development (ICPD) in Cairo in 1994, and the World Summit for Social Development (the Social Summit) in Copenhagen in 1995. At these conferences, women declared that environmental issues were women's issues, that women's rights were human rights, that governments were expected to guarantee women's reproductive health and rights, and that women's access to productive employment and social protection needed to be expanded.

As noted, the global feminist agenda calling for full citizenship rights for women as well as an end to harmful economic policies and violence against

Table 1. Types of Transnational Feminist Networks

Transnational Feminist Network	Website	Location
ADVOCACY FOR WOMEN'S HUMAN RIGHTS		
Arab Women's Solidarity Association (AWSA)	www.awsa.net/	Egypt, U.S.
Association for Women's Rights in Development (AWID)	www.awid.org/	Canada
Center for Women's Global Leadership (CWGL)	www.cwgl.rutgers.edu/	U.S.
Equality Now	www.equalitynow.org	U.S., Kenya
ISIS Women's International Cross-Cultural Exchange (ISIS-WICCE)	www.isis.or.ug/	Uganda
Madre	www.madre.org/index.html	U.S.
Network of East-West Women (NEWW)	www.neww.org/	Poland, U.S.
Research Action and Information Network for the Bodily Integrity of Women (RAINBO)	www.rainbo.org/	U.S., U.K.
Sisterhood Is Global Institute (SIGI)	www.sigi.org/	Canada
Women Living under Muslim Laws (WLUML)	www.wluml.org/	Nigeria, Pakistan, Malaysia, U.K.
Women, Law, and Development International (WLDI)	www.wld.org/	U.S.
Women's Alliance for Development (WAD)	www.womenbg.org/	Bulgaria
Women's Caucus for Gender Justice	www.iccwomen.org/	U.S.
Women's Human Rights Network (WHRNet)	www.whrnet.org/	N/A
Women's Learning Partnership for Peace, Development, and Rights (WLP)	www.learningpartnership.org/	U.S.
PEACE, ANTI-MILITARISM, CONFLICT-RESOLUTION		
Association of Women of the Mediterranean Region (AWMR)	http://digilander.libero.it/ awmr/int/index.htm	U.S., Cyprus
Women for Women International (WWI)	www.womenforwomen.org/	U.S.
Women in Black	http://balkansnet.org/wib/	various countries
Women's International League for Peace and Freedom (WILPF)	www.wilpf.org/	U.S.

Table 1. Continued

Transnational Feminist Network	Website	Location
Women's Learning Partnership (WLP)	www.learningpartnership.org/	U.S.
World Council of Muslim Women (WCMW)	www.connect.ab.ca/~lfahlman/ wcomwf.htm	Canada
ENDING VIOLENCE AGAINST WOMEN		
Women against Violence Europe (WAVE)	www.wave-network.org/	Austria
Zonta International Strategies to Eradicate Violence against Women (ZISVAW)	http://zontadistrict4.bfn.org/ html/zisvaw.htm	U.S.
REPRODUCTIVE HEALTH AND RIGHTS		
Family Care International (FCI)	www.familycareintl.org/	U.S., Latin America, Africa
Health, Empowerment, Rights, and Accountability (HERA)	N/A	N/A
International Women's Health Coalition (IWHC)	www.iwhc.org/	U.S.
Latin American and Caribbean Women's Health Network (LACWHN)	www.reddesalud.org/ english/sitio/portada.htm	Chile
Research Action and Information Network for the Bodily Integrity of Women (RAINBO)	www.rainbo.org/	U.S., U.K.
Women's Global Network for Reproductive Rights (WGNRR)	www.wgnrr.org	The Netherlands
CRITIQUE OF ECONOMIC POLICY		
Alternative Women in Development (Alt-WID)	N/A	U.S.
Asia-Japan Women's Resource Center	www.jca.ax.apc.org/ajwrc	Japan
Development Alternatives with Women for a New Era (DAWN)	www.dawn.org.fj/	Fiji
International Women's Tribune Center (IWTC)	www.iwtc.org/	U.S.
Network Women in Development Europe (WIDE)	www.wide-network.org	Belgium
Women's Environment and Development Organization (WEDO)	www.wedo.org/	U.S.
Women's International Coalition for Economic Justice (WICEJ)	www.wicej.addr.com/	U.S.

women culminated in the preparation of the Beijing Platform for Action, which was adopted on 15 September 1995 at the close of the UN's Fourth World Conference on Women. It contained language calling for gender-sensitive socioeconomic development, an end to structural adjustment policies, the importance of the North's taking a lead with respect to sustainable consumption, and the goals of women's personal autonomy and their political and economic empowerment. Global feminists frequently refer to both the Cairo Plan of Action and the Beijing Platform for Action, as well as the UN's Convention on the Elimination of All Forms of Discrimination against Women, in their national and international campaigns for women's rights. Inasmuch as most of the world's governments have signed on to these documents, they provide a useful legal and discursive tool, and global feminists frequently invoke their moral authority. Certainly these documents have helped to create an international climate more conducive to feminist aspirations and goals. The mission statement of the Beijing Platform for Action begins thus:

> The Platform for Action is an agenda for women's empowerment. It aims at accelerating the implementation of the Nairobi Forward-looking Strategies for the Advancement of Women and at removing all the obstacles to women's active participation in all spheres of public and private life through a full and equal share in economic, social, cultural and political decision-making. This means that the principle of shared power and responsibility should be established between women and men at home, in the workplace and in the wider national and international communities. Equality between women and men is a matter of human rights and a condition for social justice and is also a necessary and fundamental prerequisite for equality, development, and peace. A transformed partnership based on equality between women and men is a condition for people-centered sustainable development.

Such sentiments, as well as the more organized nature of the transnational women's movement, came into play in September 1996, when the Taliban took control of Afghanistan and instituted a harsh gender regime. The diplomatic isolation of the Taliban and the global importance of Afghan women's human rights during the latter part of the 1990s should be seen as a success story of transnational feminism. In response to pleas for solidarity and support from Afghan women expatriates in Pakistan, feminists throughout the world brought pressure to bear on their governments not to recognize the Taliban, and TFNs such as WLUML and SIGI were especially effective in transmitting information, news, and action alerts, and in working with UN agencies to keep up the pressure on the Taliban. As a result, only three governments—those of Pakistan, Saudi Arabia, and the United Arab Emirates—recognized the Taliban regime.[15]

At the start of the new millennium, the global feminist agenda continued to be expressed in critiques of multinational corporations (MNC)s, the World Bank, the International Monetary Fund (IMF), the ill-fated Multilateral Agreement on Investment (MAI), the World Trade Organization (WTO), and the policy stances of the United States government. Women's groups joined broad coalitions (e.g., Jubilee 2000 for Third World debt cancellation) involving labor, religious groups, environmental groups, and human rights groups to challenge corporate capitalism and global inequalities. Like other groups within the global justice movement, TFNs have criticized the World Bank and International Monetary Fund for their corporate bias and for policies that undermine the well-being of workers and the poor; the WTO is criticized for conducting its deliberations in secret and not subjecting them to rules of transparency and accountability. TFNs and others argue that the new rules of global free trade undermine existing national laws that protect workers, the environment, and animals; and that WTO intellectual property provisions allow large corporations to appropriate (through patents) the knowledge and products of Third World countries and their local communities. Additionally, transnational feminists argue that the employment losses and dislocations brought about by the new international trade agreements have been disproportionately borne by women. What is distinctive about the discourse of TFNs is the call for gender justice as well as economic justice, and for an alternative macroeconomic framework that takes gender relations seriously as a concept and a social fact.

What is it that TFNs do? And what are their specific objectives? Chapters 5, 6, and 7 discuss this in detail, but here I will provide an overview. First, TFNs create, activate, or join global networks to mobilize pressure outside states.[16] Examples are WLUML's action alerts and SIGI's e-petition drives pertaining to violations of women's human rights in Muslim countries. TFNs build or take part in coalitions, such as Jubilee 2000, the Coalition to End the Third World Debt, Women's International Coalition for Economic Justice, the Women and Trade Network, 50 Years Is Enough, and Women's Eyes on the Bank. Since "the Battle of Seattle" in November 1999, WIDE and DAWN have become active players in the global justice movement, taking part in the annual World Social

Forum and working closely with ATTAC, the France-based group that seeks economic justice and redistributive taxation at national and global levels.[17]

Second, TFNs participate in multilateral and intergovernmental political arenas. They observe and address UN departments such as ECOSOC and bodies such as the Commission on the Status of Women (CSW); they consult UN agencies, regional commissions, and the Development Assistance Committee of the Organization for Economic Cooperation and Development (OECD); and they participate in the World Bank's External Gender Consultative Group. They take part in and submit documents to intergovernmental organization (IGO) meetings, such as the UN's Human Rights Conference in Vienna in 1993 and the Financing for Development Conference that took place in Monterrey, Mexico, in 2002; they increase expertise on issues and prepare background papers, briefing papers, and reports; and they lobby delegates and cultivate supporters. The purpose of such interaction with IGOs is to raise new issues, such as gender and trade, gender and macroeconomics, and women's human rights, and to influence policy.

Third, TFNs act and agitate within states to enhance public awareness and participation. TFNs work with labor and progressive religious groups, the media, and human rights groups on social policy and humanitarian, development, and militarization issues. For example, WIDE-Austria has been active in efforts to defend immigrants and liberalize immigration policy. In Pakistan, Shirkat Gah, WLUML's branch office in Lahore, has organized protests against patriarchal laws in Pakistan and for Afghan women's rights, while Baobob, the Nigerian-based group that is also associated with WLUML, has protested the Islamization of laws in Nigeria. The AWMR has long worked with WILPF (Women's International League for Peace and Freedom) on peace and demilitarization of the Mediterranean, tirelessly passing resolutions and sending petitions to parliaments. Such examples show that TFNs link with local partners, take part in local coalitions, and provoke or take part in public protests. The TFNs that focus on economic policy issues promote social democratic policies, such as the Tobin Tax on financial speculation,[18] the 20/20 compact to devote 20 percent of development assistance and 20 percent of national budgets to the social sectors, ILO labor standards, gender budgets, and valorization of women's unpaid work. In terms of economic analysis and economic policy prescriptions, they are sympathetic to the United Nations Development Program's (UNDP) concept of human development.[19] Those that focus on women's human rights monitor governments, offer solidarity, and raise in-

Table 2. *Transnational Feminist Networks: Major Objectives*

TFN	Objectives
DAWN (Development Alternatives with Women for a New Era)	Gender justice and economic justice; transformation of economic policy and decision-making by IFIs; reproductive rights and health for women, especially poor women in the Third World; redistribution of global wealth (e.g., Tobin Tax).
WIDE (Women in Development Europe)	Enhanced European development assistance to ACP countries; feminist alternatives to economic theory and European and U.S. trade and foreign aid policies; transformation of economic policy and decision-making by IFIs and the WTO.
WEDO (Women's Environment and Development Organization)	Make women more visible as equal participants, experts, and leaders in policy-making from the community to the international level, and in formulating alternative, healthy, and peaceful solutions to world problems; implementation of Beijing Platform for Action; democratization of the WTO.
WLUML (Women Living under Muslim Laws)	Promote the human rights of women in Muslim countries and elsewhere; expose fundamentalist and state collusion; extend support and solidarity to women suffering violations; implementation of CEDAW in all Muslim countries.
SIGI Sisterhood Is Global Institute)	Support and promote women's human rights at the local, national, regional, and global levels in all countries. In the 1990s the focus was the rights of women in Middle Eastern countries.
AWMR (Association of Women of the Mediterranean Region)	Enhance the status of women, children, and environment in the eighteen countries of the Mediterranean region; realization of women's equality, social justice, full employment, and demilitarization.

ternational awareness. For example, WLUML submitted a shadow report on Algeria to the UN's Committee on the Elimination of Discrimination against Women (CEDAW) that was critical of both the government and the Islamist groups that terrorized women during the 1990s; others produce reports on countries' implementation of the Beijing Platform for Action. All TFNs stress the importance of the 1994 International Conference on Population and Development and the 1995 Fourth World Conference on Women in realizing the international community's stated goals of eliminating poverty and expanding women's rights. Tables 2 and 3 summarize some of the major objec-

Table 3. *Transnational Feminist Networks: Activities by Arenas*

TFN	National governments	Media	Intergovernmental institutions	Extra-institutional arenas
DAWN	Lobby national policy-makers on economic and reproductive rights issues		UN (esp. UNIFEM, UNDP, UNFPA, UNRISD), 1990s conferences; SID/WID; WB EGCC; OECD/DAC	Demonstrated at the entrance of the Doha ministerial meeting venue, 2002
WIDE	Lobby national policy-makers; pressure governments and EU on trade and economic policy	Press releases	Reviewing international agreements, esp. EU trade and aid; OECD/DAC; Vienna, Cairo, Copenhagen, Beijing conferences	Participation in the Seattle NGO forum of late 1999
WEDO	Monitor governments' implementation of Beijing Platform for Action; lobby congresspersons; disseminate *News & Views*	Press kits	Reviewing international agreements; UNCED, Social Summit, Beijing conferences; now working with WHO on anti-smoking/tobacco issues	Participation in the Seattle and Washington, D.C., protests of 1999 and 2000
WLUML	Legal reform and cultural change; modernization of family laws; implementation of CEDAW	Action alerts	Attended all UN conferences of 1990s, focusing on the NGO fora; Algerian Shadow Report to CEDAW	Women's International War Crimes Tribunal (December 2000, Japan); local protests in South Asia, Nigeria, etc.
SIGI	Lobby national policy-makers; petition-writing	Press releases	Vienna, Cairo, Beijing conferences and prepcoms	Internet petitions and action alerts
AWMR	Resolutions and petitions sent to national parliaments	Press releases	Annual resolutions sent to UN	Local protests in Italy, Malta, Cyprus, etc. Involvement in the World's Women's March 2000

tives and activities of the transnational feminist networks examined in this book.

Whether working at the state, regional, or global levels, TFNs have framed issues and introduced new concepts: "engendering development," "feminization of poverty," "care economy," "women living under Muslim laws," "women's rights are human rights," "gender justice and economic justice." Many of these concepts have been adopted by major international organizations, including UN agencies, the World Bank, and the donor agencies of the core countries. A new concept, "reinventing globalization," was the focus of two TFN conferences in 2002: the Association for Women's Rights in Development (AWID) and the Association of Women of the Mediterranean Region (AWMR).

The new information and computer technologies (ICTs) have allowed transnational feminist networks (and other advocacy networks) to retain flexibility, adaptability, and nonhierarchical features while also ensuring more efficiency in their operations. That is, TFNs are now able to perform optimally without having to become formal or bureaucratic organizations. Avoiding bureaucratization is particularly important to feminists. The network form of feminist organizing, which is exemplified by the TFNs examined in this book and which is discussed at length in chapters 4–7, suggests a form of organization that may be more conductive to the era of globalization, as well as more consistent with feminist goals of democratic, inclusive, participatory, decentralized, and nonhierarchical structures and processes.

Globalization, Gender, and Global Feminism

I have said above—and discuss in more detail in chapter 2—that there is an emerging feminist scholarship on globalization, and at least two perspectives may be identified within it: feminist political economy and feminist postmodernism. The approach that I take in this book may be described as materialist or Marxist-feminist or feminist political economy. The conceptual point of departure is that the nexus of capital, class, and gender determines how women and men are involved in and affected by the economic, political, and cultural dimensions of globalization in various parts of the world. This approach is compatible with theories such as world-systems analysis, dependency theory, and comparative political economy but is a corrective to these largely gender-blind theories, in that the intersection of class and gender in feminist political economy renders the sexual division of labor and especially female labor central to the analysis. That is, pride of place is given to the exploitation of female labor (or its deployment along the commodity chains of the world-system) and its contribution to the accumulation of capital, as well as to the ways in which the sexual division of labor and gender ideologies shape definitions of skill, allocation of resources, occupational distribution, modes of remuneration, and the relative value of male and female labor. Moreover, the importance attached to class and gender consciousness, forms of organization, and resistance to capitalist and patriarchal domination shows that a Marxist-feminist approach is attentive to agency as well as structure, and to "globalization-from-below" as well as "globalization-from-above."

A key difference between the classical Marxist-feminist analyses of the 1970s and the newer analyses of globalization is that we are compelled to examine the operations of capital, class, and gender not only within borders but also across them. The sexual division of labor remains pertinent at the household and labor market levels, but we now study its dynamics globally, for example in terms of the way it informs commodity chains, formal and informal markets, the so-called global assembly line, and labor migration flows, as well as decisions about foreign direct investment (FDI) and structural adjustment policies.

In the past, feminist scholars argued that development studies ignored gender; today, we see a similar sidelining of gender issues in (economic) globalization studies, despite the significance of women's incorporation into the global economy as a source of relatively cheap labor in both the formal and informal sectors, despite the importance of women's paid and unpaid reproductive work, and despite feminist studies of the state and of the highly gendered discourses and images inscribed in economic globalization (for example, "Davos Man"). To take gender seriously in development and in globalization studies means to understand the effects of globalization on gender (such as the feminization of labor, the feminization of poverty, the traffic in women) and the effects of gender on globalization (the sexual division of labor, male bias and masculinist priorities in economic policies, gendered symbolic representations of the globalization project). Surely it cannot be too difficult to observe that globalization, flexibilization, and feminization are related processes.

The other side of the coin, of course, is to study resistance and forms of collective action. I have long argued that the effects of female labor incorporation have not been uniformly negative, for there have been unintended consequences of women's economic participation that include the mobilization of women into feminist organizations, into trade unions, and into transnational feminist networks. In this book in particular, I analyze the gender dynamics of (economic) globalization to show that the worldwide expansion of a female labor force, the important (albeit exploited) role of paid and unpaid female labor in the global economy, and the persistence of social and gender inequalities underpin the rise of a women's movement on a world scale. The global social movement of women is characterized by a set of grievances, claims, and objectives (global feminism), and an effective organizational type (the transnational feminist network). TFNs thus reflect one aspect of the globalization process (opportunities for mobilizing and recruitment through ICTs and ease of travel), while also responding to its dark side (neoliberal capitalism, patriarchal fundamentalism).

The claims and demands of "globalizing women" are addressed to states, to global civil society, and to institutions of global governance. They ensure that women's issues remain on the international agenda, and that local activists receive solidarity and support. In our globalizing world, we have not yet seen the formation of a transnational working class or transnational worker organizations. But we do see a global social movement of women and transnational feminist networks that criticize neoliberal capitalism, call for the return of the welfarist, developmentalist state, and endorse a kind of global Keynesianism with decent work, labor rights, and human rights. This transnational feminist movement feeds into the larger global justice movement and offers concrete proposals for an alternative to capitalist globalization that is grounded in human rights.[20]

As we shall see in the next chapter, globalization is a contested concept and contentious phenomenon, with different dimensions and varied effects on social groups. But we can identify at least one positive aspect of globalization— the proliferation of women's movements at the local level, the emergence of transnational feminist networks working at the global level, and the adoption of international conventions such as the Convention on the Elimination of All Forms of Discrimination against Women (CEDAW) and the Beijing Declaration and Platform for Action. The TFNs that I discuss in this book are comprised of individual activists and women's groups rooted in local communities and national contexts. They determine their own priorities but come together globally (e.g., at annual congresses or regional meetings) to work out a common agenda, including a vocabulary and a set of strategies to accomplish their objectives. The targets of their advocacy and activism are simultaneously local structures, national governments, and global institutions. TFNs reflect the interplay of the local and the global and bridge the divide in an innovative organizational form that eschews nationalist preoccupations and is premised on commonality and solidarity.

To deploy the concepts of transnational feminism or global feminism is not to deny that there are cultural, class, and ideological differences among the women of the world.[21] But the concepts do refer to an observed isomorphism in women's organizing and mobilizing, including a similar vocabulary and form of organization. It is significant that WIDE's manual on economic literacy has been translated into at least six languages, including Arabic; a Lebanese women's group has used the WIDE manual in its own research and advocacy work on globalization, macroeconomics, trade, and gender.[22] However, unlike world-polity theorizing that "puts the institutional character of transnational development front and center" and argues that "culture is increasingly global,"[23] and unlike perspectives that emphasize ideas, discourses, and agency at the expense of structure,[24] I argue that global feminism and transnational feminist networks are the logical result of the existence of a capitalist world-economy in an era of globalization, and the universal fact of gender inequality. In other words, material, social, and economic forces and factors have given rise to new identities, discourses, values, and forms of organization led by women.

CHAPTER TWO

Globalization and Its Discontents

Capitalist Development, Political Movements, and Gender

As in economics, the social sciences have long focused on processes and institutions within single states, societies, and economies. Until very recently, the terms *global* and *transnational* were either alien to or marginal to mainstream social science theories. *International* and *world* were of course understood, but supranational developments could hardly be fathomed. Outside of the mainstream, dependency theory and its more sophisticated variant, world-systems theory, challenged Marxism's emphasis on class conflicts within single societies, drawing attention to the transnational nature of capital and labor flows and the implications thereof for economic and political processes at the societal level, as well as for the reproduction of global inequalities.[1] Back in the mainstream, theories of social movements and "new social movements" also focused on national-level dynamics—and mainly in the West or in "post-industrial society."[2] But no sooner had these theories gained prominence in the 1980s than new developments began to challenge some of their basic assumptions.

The new developments included forms of governance and forms of activism at the global level, as well as transnational shifts in political economy.

New governance structures included the ever-growing power and influence of multinational corporations, the World Bank, the IMF, and the WTO, along with the emergence of regional blocs such as the European Union (EU) and the North American Free Trade Agreement (NAFTA). These institutions of global and regional governance were also behind shifts in international political economy which entailed the move from Keynesian or state-centered economic models to neoliberal or free-market economic strategies. Thus the "structural adjustment and stabilization" policies that were advocated for the Third World during the 1980s and 1990s, the transition from socialism to capitalism in the Second World, and the free-market imprint of Reaganism and Thatcherism in the First World all seemed to be part of a global process of economic restructuring.[3] Parallel to the economic restructuring of the world economy in the 1980s there emerged a transnational Islamic fundamentalist movement—largely in the Middle East, North Africa, and South Asia—that sought to curb Western political and cultural influences and recuperate traditional social and gender norms.[4] The response to these new global developments took the form of transnational collective action, including the emergence of transnational social movements and advocacy networks that focused on human rights, the environment, and economic justice.[5] Women, too, began to organize and mobilize across borders, particularly around the effects of economic restructuring and of Islamic fundamentalism.[6]

Globalization, therefore, has compelled a rethinking of economic, sociological, and political categories, and a reconsideration of the organizational form of contemporary collective action. But this rethinking has not always led to consensus. Globalization has been approached from different disciplinary vantage points, and there remain disagreements within disciplines regarding, for example, the novelty of globalization, the extent to which global structures have weakened national structures, the permanence versus the contingency of globalization, and the negative versus positive entailments of globalization. Among feminist scholars, there is also some disagreement as to the defining features of globalization and their gender dynamics.

Globalization: The Latest Stage of Capitalism

Is globalization—the increasing integration of developing countries in world trade and world finance, along with deregulation and liberalization of markets, asset diversification, and increased activity by multinational corporations—a new historical stage? The sociologist Ankie Hoogvelt believes that it is, and writes that economic globalization has three key features: a global market discipline, flexible accumulation through global webs, and financial deepening. Similarly, British sociologist Leslie Sklair refers to the globalization of capital on a historically unprecedented scale.[7]

But according to others, globalization is not new. Vandana Shiva, Indian physicist, feminist, and environmentalist, argues that colonization of the Third World was the first stage of globalization. To world-system theorists such as Immanuel Wallerstein and Christopher Chase-Dunn, globalization is just another word for the processes that they have always referred to as world-systemic: integration into the economic zones of core, periphery, and semiperiphery, with their attendant hierarchies of states, and forms of resistance known as antisystemic movements. Moreover, the capitalist world-economy has experienced cyclical processes and secular trends for hundreds of years. Marxists such as Ellen Meiksins Wood argue that globalization is a redundant term for the internationalization of capital. Paul Hirst and Grahame Thompson, authors of *Globalization in Question,* regard globalization as a "necessary myth."[8] Many on the left regard globalization, at least its economic dimension, to be an extension of imperialism. Thus globalization would be considered the latest (if not the "highest"—apologies to V. I. Lenin) stage of capitalism.

Among those who accept the term and the process, debate rages over whether globalization is good or bad, and whether it is inevitable or changeable. Neoliberal economists and other advocates of the free market argue that economic globalization will have positive effects on economies' growth rates, their development prospects, and people's welfare.[9] For progressives like Walden Bello, Martin Khor, David Korten, Jerry Mander, and others, globalization means just the opposite; the global economic process reproduces great and growing inequalities of wealth and incomes within and across countries. Furthermore, it is not an inevitable stage but the result of conscious neoliberal policy-making by "globalizers" or the agents of globalization such as multinational corporations and international financial institutions. Globalization, therefore, should be vigorously opposed by organized movements starting at the grassroots, local, and community levels.[10] Many trade unions leaders have decried the social costs of globalization, such as unemployment, job insecurity, and continued poverty, and they have called for the establishment of core labor standards, fair trade, democratization of global economic management, a tax on speculative financial flows (the so-called Tobin Tax), and a shift of focus from markets to people.[11]

For some economists, such as Jay Mandle, the OECD's Jean Bonvin, or those who produced the 1999 UNDP *Human Development Report,* globalization is "janus-faced" but there is some room for maneuver within its confines to reduce inequalities, provided that investment and trade between advanced and less developed countries increases. In a report issued in April 2002, Oxfam-UK argued that trade liberalization could benefit developing countries, but it does not invariably do so; what is more, the multilateral trade system is weighted against the interests of developing countries mainly because core countries practice double standards by urging developing countries to liberalize while keeping their own markets closed to imports such as agricultural products and textiles.[12]

Debates continue on the growth of income inequalities across and within countries, and whether or not inequalities are associated with globalization and especially with the liberalization of prices, labor markets, financial markets, and trade. OECD research by Angus Maddison on inequalities between nations since the nineteenth century shows rising cross-national inequalities since the 1970s. Anthony Atkinson documents rising inequalities in the industrialized countries (except in France). Research by Roberto Patricio Korzeniewicz and Timothy Moran on twentieth-century trends in inequality finds rising cross-national inequalities but a mixed picture within countries. Economist Lance Taylor found that globalization and liberalization have not been uniformly favorable in terms of effects on growth and income distribution. Among the eighteen countries studied, only Chile after 1990 managed to combine high growth with decreasing inequality—in contrast to increasing inequality over the preceding fifteen years. Volker Bornschier has offered several explanations for increasing inequality since the 1970s, including macroeconomic policy shifts, as well as technological and educational changes. His research, as well as that of Atkinson, suggests that public policy and social norms matter, even within a capitalist context. Others maintain that growing inequalities are not the result of globalization, and that trade liberalization in facts benefits economies and populations. According to Ajit Ghose, growing inequality across countries is in fact caused by nonliberalization of trade in agricultural products and lack of basic human and physical capital that has left many developing countries dependent on the export of primary commodities.

Jagdish Bhagwati argues that market imperfections should not be tackled through trade intervention and insists that trade liberalization promotes growth and prosperity.[13]

The terms *globalization, globality, globalism, global,* and *transnational* have been used in a number of ways, and various scholars have sought to distinguish the terms conceptually or to define globalization with more precision. For some, *globalism* should be understood as free market ideology.[14] *Globalization* itself has a weak definition and a strong one. In its weak definition, *globalization* refers merely to the international spread of certain trends; in the strong definition, it refers to a *systemic* process of development and change, or a new process of social system building at the global level. This echoes the main claims of world-system theory (for example, the work of Christopher Chase-Dunn), but other sociologists prefer new concepts, including "compression of the world" and "global consciousness" (Roland Robertson), "transnational practices" through the transnational corporation, the transnational capitalist class, and the culture-ideology of consumerism via the media (Leslie Sklair), the emerging transnational state apparatus (William Robinson), the intensification of worldwide social relations via "time/space distantiation" (Anthony Giddens) or "time/space compression" (David Harvey), and "social structure as interactive information networks" (Manuel Castells).[15]

Another debate pertains to the extent to which globalization has weakened the sovereignty of nation-states and the autonomy of national economies. There are some who believe that inasmuch as globalization entails "deterritorialization" through supranational economic, political, and cultural processes and institutions, the nation-state as a power apparatus has been superseded. The activities of transnational corporations, global cities, and the transnational capitalist class render state-centered analysis outdated, according to this view. Thus Sklair's "theory of the global system" proposes taking "the whole world" as the starting point—that is, viewing the world not as an aggregate of nation-states but as a single unit and object of analysis. Cox, Gray, and others have argued that the options available to states have been greatly diminished by globalization, while Sklair, Robinson, and others have theorized the emergence of a deterritorialized transnational capitalist class, with its attendant institutions.[16] In contrast, Hirst and Thompson argue that the nation-state remains the dominant form of governance by comparison with more global or subnational levels. Similarly, Berger, Dore, and their collaborators show that national governments are still able to pursue different policies and maintain distinctive institutions, and urge caution in generalizing about the extent of economic globalization.[17]

The debate on the state and globalization—which feminists also have taken up, as we shall see shortly—will continue. One should note that in the Middle East, where Islamic fundamentalism and revolutionary Iranian Islam initially saw itself as supranational and railed against "artificial colonialist borders" that divided the *umma,* or the community of Muslim believers, the activities and objectives of political movements have largely remained within national borders. Moreover, territorial state nationalism has deep roots in the region, as the Iran-Iraq war of 1980–88 and the overlong Israeli-Palestinian conflict have demonstrated so vividly. On the other hand, as we saw with the emergence of Osama bin Laden's al-Qaeda network in the late 1990s, globalization does seem to facilitate the formation of loosely organized, deterritorialized transnational groups (with highly objectionable features). *It would appear, therefore, that the capitalist world-system is comprised of a global economy, institutionalized but unequal nation-states, and transnational movements and networks.*

Economists and world-system sociologists view globalization in largely economic terms, but for many observers it is a multifaceted phenomenon. It refers to, inter alia, time-space compression, world culture, the increase in the available modes of organization, the emergence of multiple and overlapping identities, and the emergence of hybrid sites such as world cities, free trade zones, offshore banking facilities, borderzones, and ethnic mélange neighborhoods. Jan Aart Scholte discusses globalization as deterritorialization, producing and diffusing "supraterritorial," "transworld," and "transborder" relations between people. He and Jan Nederveen Pieterse regard "hybridization" to be an important facet of globalization, although both also highlight the unevenness, asymmetry, and inequality that are embedded in the new global mélange.[18]

Feminist Approaches to Globalization and Gender

The literature I have just discussed tends to be inattentive to gender, but an emerging feminist scholarship on globalization puts gender, and often women, at the center of analysis. At present, at least two feminist perspectives on globalization may be identified. In one perspective, feminists analyze the operations of capital via the state, global economy, and international financial institutions (IFIs) through the prisms of gender and class. They are also interested in how consciousness and self-organization offer resistance and alternative frameworks at both national and global levels.[19] Here, the state matters not only conceptually but also politically, for only states can provide adequate social arrangements for which citizens must contribute and from which they may demand accountability. We may refer to this as the Marxist-feminist or feminist political economy approach to globalization. In the second approach, attention is directed to symbolic representations of economic globalization, gendered binaries in the construction of knowledge about globalization, contradictory and decentered organizations, and heterogeneous subjectivities. In this postmodernist or postcolonialist feminist approach, there is a tendency to play down or reject the importance of the state, the global economy, and global feminism in favor of theorizing that emphasizes agency, identities, differences, hierarchies based on race, class, gender, sexual orientation, etc., and multiple forms and sites of power.

In an early version of the postmodernist approach, Inderwal Grewal and Caren Kaplan rejected the center-periphery model associated with world-systems theory or dependency theory in favor of "transnational cultural flows," "the diversity of women's agency," and "scattered hegemonies such as global economic structures, patriarchal nationalisms, 'authentic' forms of tradition, local structures of domination, and legal-juridical oppression on multiple levels."[20] In a more recent contribution, Marianne Marchand took exception with much of the Marxist-feminist or feminist political economy literature that, for example, calls women a "vulnerable group." Her objection was that such an approach "does not allow for any differentiation among women and men in terms of class, race, ethnicity, age, nationality, and education." She criticized approaches that use "dualistic categorizations or dichotomies" such as productive/reproductive work, paid/unpaid labor, and commodity/care economy, and warned that behind such concepts lurks "the danger of a female sphere or maternalist approach." Emphasizing "complexities, contingencies, and contradictions," Marchand endorsed an approach to the emerging world order as one that recognizes "structures of, and practices around, class, gender, ethnicity, race, sexual orientation, and religion."[21] Similarly, Suzanne Bergeron took issue with "globalocentric," "capitalocentric," and state-centered feminist analyses, criticizing much of the feminist political economy literature, including the critiques of structural adjustment, for "emphasizing the role that national policy can play by instituting national restrictions on international capital, social safety nets, fair-play laws, and health and safety regulations." She criticized feminist concepts of globalization that assume the "existence of a power structure in which global capital dominates its others" or that calls for resistance strategies by women based on global identity, such as global feminism. She seemed to prefer "alternative notions of feminist subjectivity" and "scattered hegemonies."[22]

In a number of studies on the gendered nature of globalization, scholars emphasize the ways in which masculinities and femininities are inscribed in its processes and institutions. According to J. K. Gibson-Graham, globalization may be seen as a "rape script" and a masculine project, while L. H. M. Ling refers to globalization as "hypermasculinity"—a line of argumentation also elaborated by Charlotte Hooper and by R.W. Connell, who has argued that the implicit gender politics of neoliberalism includes a "transnational business masculinity." Indeed, the influential magazine *The Economist* coined the term "Davos Man" in reference to the globalized businessmen and politicians who meet in Switzerland for the World Economic Forum.[23] Similarly, Marchand and Runyan wrote:

> In the neoliberal discourse on globalization, the state is typically "feminized" in relation to the more robust market by being represented as a drag on the global economy that must be subordinated and minimized. . . . [However], the state also paradoxically takes on a new role by becoming more akin to the private sector (and thus masculinized) as it is internationalized to assist global capital and as its coercive and surveillance capacities are being enhanced. . . . [M]inistries that focus on domestic health, education, and social welfare are becoming increasingly disadvantaged or "feminized" in relation to ministries of finance and economic affairs that are directly related to the global economy and thus, invested with masculine authority.[24]

Spike Peterson's contribution moves away from the postmodernist focus on difference, specificity, and locality in favor of a feminist metanarrative and an insistence on the "global" as the unit of analysis. Integrating Marxist, feminist, world-systems, and postcolonialist analyses, Peterson offers a new reading of the global political economy that revolves around the productive, reproductive, and virtual economies, all of which draw on and consist of gendered ideologies, identities, and institutions. This new framing, she argues, "provides a way to see informal activities, flexibilization, global production, migration flows, capital movements, and virtual activities as inextricable and interacting dimensions of neoliberal globalization."[25] In a conceptualization that broadens the scope of "the economic" to include cultural processes and gender dynamics, Peterson bridges the Marxist-feminist and postmodernist feminist perspectives, drawing out the strongest arguments in each.

In both feminist approaches that I have discussed, globalization is a gendered process with objectionable features, but in the Marxist-feminist or feminist political economy approach the nexus of capital, class, and gender determines how women and men are involved in and affected by the economic, political, and cultural dimensions of globalization in various parts of the world and at the levels of the global economy, the national economy, and the household. For this reason, Bergeron and other critics of feminist political economy have missed the point. Rather than being strictly "globalocentric," feminist political economy looks at the operations of capital, class, and gender locally, nationally, and globally. Nor is feminist political economy strictly speaking "state centered." Feminists cannot and do not examine the state as a discrete entity, divorced from supranational economic and political forces. For Marxist-feminists in particular, the state remains a salient category and has by no means withered away, but states are weaker or stronger in the global economy, and here the concepts of North and South or, more specifically, core, periphery, and semiperiphery are relevant and useful. Feminist political economists also evince what I call a "critical realist" approach to the state. Highly critical of the patriarchal and neoliberal state, they also recognize it as an institution—or a set of apparatuses—that has direct bearing on women's rights and interests within the society and in the home, largely through public policies and legal frameworks. For example, many women's organizations in Muslim countries are struggling for the reform of Muslim family laws, also known as personal status codes. They appeal to the state to introduce reforms and improve women's legal status, even though it is the state that has instituted and enforced the discriminatory laws. At the same time, feminists in Muslim countries look to CEDAW and the UN's women's rights agenda for legitimacy and support in their struggles with their ruling elites and with the Islamist movements that object to any changes in Muslim family law. Elsewhere, women have appealed to the state to institute equal opportunity policies, or antidiscrimination legislation, or reproductive rights, or family leave policies. And around the world, women have a special interest in the welfare state. Thus in 2002 the network Women in Development Europe (WIDE) expanded its focus on trade to include "a more politically informed power analysis," because of concerns that the rightward shift of many EU governments was resulting in a stronger neoliberal policy agenda "with many human rights violations and an attempt to break down the welfare state."[26] The state matters to women in their daily lives, and of course to Marxist-feminists and feminist political economists in their conceptual approaches.

Feminists have long been concerned with gender and power, but feminist political economists view gender and power differently from postmodernists. Rather than the "scattered hegemonies" posited by postmodernist feminists, we see political and economic power concentrated in multinational corporations based in core countries, in institutions of global governance such as the World Bank, the IMF, and the WTO, and in Washington, D.C.—though we also see these institutions as forms of patriarchal power that work through or around state systems. A Marxist-feminist might agree with Leslie Sklair and with William Robinson concerning the formation of a transnational capitalist class (TCC) that has shaped the global economy and institutions of global governance. But she would also point out that the TCC is an overwhelmingly male capitalist class and largely concentrated in the core countries. And while I for one would agree with Robinson and other globalization theorists that a capitalist transnational state apparatus is emerging, I would point out that this apparatus is stronger and more visible in the core countries—and possibly in the periphery, where World Bank and IMF staff seem to be the main decision-makers—than it is in the semiperiphery. Surely this is why the state still matters to feminist scholars, not to mention women activists in the semiperiphery and activists within transnational feminist networks.[27] For this reason, women's movements work both in and against the state, scrutinize public policies at national and global levels, and make demands on states and international organizations alike.

Globalization and Collective Action

Globalization scholars and activists alike tend to distinguish between "globalization from above" and "globalization from below."[28] The former refers to the neoliberal economic policy environment and the growing power of international financial institutions, trade organizations, and other dominant international forces that have triggered collective responses from labor, environmental, and feminist groups—that is, from the forces of globalization from below. It may be said that these social forces and social movement organizations are the agents or historical subjects of globalization from below.

The global integration of markets and the adoption by governments of harmful economic policies are key aspects of globalization, and they have been challenged in significant ways by the movements and networks that think and act both locally and globally to challenge the hegemony of corporate capital. Much has been written about the proliferation and growing influence of nongovernmental organizations (NGOs), international nongovernmental organizations (INGOs), and transnational social movement organizations (TSMOs) such as Amnesty International and Greenpeace, and about the relative success of the campaigns of these and other human rights and environmental organizations. Michael Cerny argues that because globalization has profoundly altered the way the structure of goods and assets is shaped—for example, divorcing finance capital from the state and privatizing services—transnational forms of collective action have emerged over redistributive public goods such as health and welfare services and employment policies, which were once the province of the state.[29] To be sure, we have witnessed growing calls at the global level for full employment, job security, decent work, increased development assistance on the part of the core countries, the Tobin Tax on speculative financial transactions, and other redistributive measures. What we also have witnessed is the formation of NGOs, INGOs, TSMOs, and TANs that explicitly target economic globalization and its institutions through various forms of collective action, including direct action.

Examples are the worldwide opposition to the Multilateral Agreement on Investment (MAI) in 1998, dramatic protests in Seattle in November 1999—during the WTO Ministerial Conference that was supposed to launch a "Millennial Round" of world trade negotiations—and the protests against the World Bank and the IMF in Washington, D.C., in April 2000, when a coalition of groups formed to demand an end to the Third World debt. A cycle of protests continued through most of 2000 and 2001, and included the anticapitalist protests in London on May Day 2000, the antiglobalization protests in Melbourne and Prague in September 2000 and in Montreal the following month, and protests in Zurich in January 2001. When the World Economic Forum met at Davos in February 2001, protests took place there, too. Moreover, a counterconference was held in Porto Alegre, Brazil (a stronghold of the left-wing Workers Party of Brazil), in what would become the first of a series of alternative globalization gatherings that have come to be known as the World Social Forum.[30] The cycle of protests continued in Quebec City, Canada, in April 2001, in Goteborg, Sweden, in June during the EU summit, and the following month in Genoa, Italy, where the G-8 were meeting. The tragedy of September 11 put a temporary halt to the antiglobalization protests, but they resumed in early 2002. In February 2002 the World Economic Forum met in New York, and about one thousand antiglobalization protesters appeared. The next month, as the European Union summit took place in Spain, about five hundred thousand people held an anticapitalist protest in Barcelona that also denounced Israeli actions in Palestine and U.S. plans to invade Iraq.[31] During the remainder of 2002, the antiglobalization movement joined forces with the growing antiwar movement, culminating in a huge demonstration in Florence, Italy, in November, where over a half million people from all over Europe gathered to protest capitalism and war making. Millions more marched in early 2003 in antiwar protests around the world. And when the leaders of the main core countries, the so-called G8, met in Evian, France, in early June 2003, an alternative summit, along with protests, took place in nearby Geneva, Switzerland.

Scholars refer to these forms of global activism or supranational politics and solidarity as transnational social movements,[32] transnational advocacy networks,[33] or antisystemic and counterhegemonic movements.[34] Others refer to them as part of the making of the transnational public sphere[35] or global civil society.[36] On the left, activists refer to the global economic justice movement or the anticapitalist/alternative globalization movement.

The new scholarship on globalization, social movements, and transnational advocacy networks provides a useful framework for understanding the activities of the women's movement at the global level, even though the literature often overlooks feminist mobilization. The literature shows that TSMOs and TANs engage in research, advocacy, lobbying, and direct action. These are planned and coordinated through the use of information technologies, while the relatively low cost of international travel and relaxed visa regulations facilitate participation in major events or mobilization for protest actions. As such, a global infrastructure has been built by these transnational social movements and transnational advocacy networks. And as this book will show, transnational feminist networks have contributed to this global infrastructure.

In their 1997 book, Smith, Chatfield, and Pagnucco examined social movements and global transformation, the relationship between transnational social movements and global governance, and implications for social movement theory. They were especially interested in the formation and activities of TSMOs. The case studies in the book showed how movements and their organizations increasingly mobilize transnational resources in national conflicts, generate constituencies for multilateral policy, and target international institutions. Among the cases studied were the Peace Brigades International in Sri Lanka, humanitarian organizations during the Ethiopia-Eritrea conflict, human rights organizations in Latin America, and the work of EarthAction International. The case studies revealed that activists at the national level increasingly draw on international conventions, standards, or treaties to legitimize their own campaigns, lobby within intergovernmental organizations to draw attention to problems within their countries, and help form transnational coalitions or alliances around specific issues or objectives.

Keck and Sikkink argued in their 1998 book that "the rapidly changing configuration of world politics" entails the formation of transnational advocacy networks (TANs) such as human rights advocacy networks, environmental advocacy networks, and transnational networks on violence against women, all of which began to proliferate in the late twentieth century. They showed how nonstate actors interact with each other, with states, and with international organizations, and how international nongovernmental organizations promote institutional and policy changes in the international order. Keck and Sikkink referred to organizations and individuals within advocacy networks as "political entrepreneurs who mobilize resources like information and membership and show a sophisticated awareness of the political opportunity structures within which they are operating." TANs, they explained, engage in "information politics, symbolic politics, leverage politics, and accountability politics" with the objective of changing norms and standards. In some cases they succeed, while in other cases they face constraints. Similarly, for Smith and her colleagues, TSMOs transmit information and thus aid the diffusion of ideas and practices and facilitate mobilization for movement goals. According to one contributor, "they also help diffuse norms and values about participation in policymaking and execution and serve as constituencies for other NGOs and for IGOs, thus fostering democratization."[37]

An important contribution of the Keck and Sikkink volume was its attention to the transnational campaign around violence against women, a campaign that has proven to be very effective. One may question, however, the authors' assertion that the issue of violence was more effective in mobilizing women than was the issue of economic inequalities.[38] It is important to recall that the world's women first mobilized around economic development issues during the United Nations' Decade on Women (1976–85). Two TFNs that are now well known mobilized in opposition to the World Bank and IMF's policies of structural adjustment, which they argued adversely affected the welfare and economic rights of working-class and low-income women. These networks— Women in Development Europe (WIDE) and Development Alternatives with Women for a New Era (DAWN)—remain focused on issues of development assistance, trade policy, and neoliberal economic policies. Both networks monitor and criticize the European Union's development assistance and trade policies with African, Caribbean, and Pacific countries, and the policy frameworks of the World Bank, the IMF, and the WTO. Although it is true that the global women's movement has been very effective in raising awareness about violence against women and, at the 1993 UN conference on human rights, helped to establish international norms that criminalize wartime rape as a human rights violation,[39] it is also true that global feminist activism has drawn attention to the harmful effects of structural adjustment policies, leading the World Bank to modify its policy framework and take gender issues more seriously. (See chapter 5.) Transnational feminism has been effective in both arenas of human rights and economic policy.

Terry Boswell and Christopher Chase-Dunn, writing within a world-systems theoretical framework, have examined antisystemic activity in world-historical perspective. They point out that economic globalization has led to much dissatisfaction and unrest, because of growing income inequalities, declining labor standards, continuing economic difficulties, and the emergence of new forms of global governance that appear hegemonic and undemocratic. And what of alternative frameworks proposed by oppositional movements? "Despite globalization," they write, "international political parties and labor unions have not been among those international organizations on the rise."[40] Noting the rise of social movements and advocacy networks centered on human rights, the environment, and women's rights, and the persistence of labor, ethnic, and other revolts in developing countries, they conclude that: "A cluster of revolts in the semi-periphery, when matched with demands from core social movements and peripheral states for changes in international relations, could make debated issues of global standards an obvious solution. This would in retrospect appear to be a world revolution, one that would initiate new movements for global change."[41] Boswell and Chase-Dunn also acknowledge the progressive nature of the women's movement (although they do not elaborate on its character, activities, or demands), and they suggest that an alliance of global movements— labor, environmental, and women's movements—could pose a formidable challenge to the hegemony of global capitalism and its institutions through the building of global democracy.

Globalization: A Multidimensional and Gendered Perspective

Having considered some of the literature and debates on globalization and global activism, we are in a position to define the concept and process in a way that takes into account its varied dimensions and its gender dynamics.

Globalization is a complex economic, political, cultural, and geographic process in which the mobility of capital, organizations, ideas, discourses, and peoples has taken on an increasingly global or transnational form. As a multi-faceted phenomenon, globalization may be elucidated in terms of economic, political, and cultural dimensions. Economic globalization pertains to deeper integration and more rapid interaction of economies through production, trade, and (unregulated) financial transactions by banks and multinational corporations, with an increased role for the World Bank and the International Monetary Fund, as well as the more recent World Trade Organization. "Global-izers" include the IFIs, the WTO, the U.S. Treasury, the major capitalist states, MNCs, and the transnational capitalist class. Although the capitalist world-system has always been globalizing and there have been various waves of global-ization (e.g., the 1870–1914 period, which is well documented), it is probably true that the trade, capital flows, and technological advances and transfers since the 1970s are more intensive and extensive than in earlier periods. In this respect the world-system perspective is especially useful in identifying cycles and secular trends in the internationalization of capital. The cyclical processes include the rise and fall of hegemons, the Kondratieff waves, a cycle of warfare among core states, and cycles of colonization and decolonization. Secular trends include the long-term proletarianization of the world's work force (in-cluding wage work and informal labor by women and men), growing concen-tration of capital in ever-larger firms, and the increasing internationalization of investment and of trade.[42]

Political globalization refers to an increasing trend toward multilateralism (in which the United Nations plays a key role), toward an emerging "transna-tional state apparatus," and toward the emergence of national and interna-tional nongovernmental organizations that act as watchdogs over govern-ments and have increased their activities and influence. The combination of

INGOs, TSMOs, and TANs constitute the making of a global civil society or transnational public sphere that may be seen as countering the neoliberal and nondemocratic practices and institutions of economic globalization.[43] But a consequence of globalization has been the weakening of state capacity and state sovereignty. Political scientists and sociologists, including feminist scholars, have pondered the prospects of the national state, as well as democratic decision-making and citizen participation, in a context of regionalization and globalization in which international financial institutions have increasing power over national economies and state decision-making. Many are hopeful that international laws and norms will result in a more stable and cooperative world. But as we saw with interventions in Afghanistan in 2001 and in Iraq in 2003, international law has little to say about unilateral military action by a powerful core country such as the United States.

It should be noted that economic globalization has been accompanied by a pervasive ideological campaign that heralds "the market" as the sole legitimate institution and its concomitants—including the private sector, the business class, free trade, and minimal government interference—as the only rational path to growth and prosperity. This is especially true in the United States, where the major media have played an important role in legitimizing neoliberal economics, but the ideology of the market also has encompassed much of social-democratic Europe. For the developing world, the main ideologues of neoliberalism have been the World Bank and the IMF.

Cultural globalization refers to worldwide cultural standardization—as in "Coca Colonization" and "McDonaldization"—as well as to postcolonial cultures, cultural pluralism, and "hybridization." The various aspects of globalization have promoted growing contacts between different cultures, leading partly to greater understanding and cooperation and partly to the emergence of transnational communities and hybrid identities. But globalization has also hardened the opposition of different identities. This has taken the form of, inter alia, reactive movements such as fundamentalism and communalism, which seek to recuperate traditional patterns, including patriarchal gender relations, in reaction to the "Westernizing" trends of globalization. Various forms of identity politics are the paradoxical outgrowth of globalization, which Benjamin Barber aptly summarizes as "Jihad vs. McWorld."[44]

Consistent with the contradictory nature of globalization, the impact on women has been mixed. One feature of economic globalization has been the generation of jobs for women in export-processing, free trade zones, and world market factories. This has enabled women in many developing countries to earn and control income and to break away from the hold of patriarchal structures, including traditional household and familial relations. However, much of the work available to women is badly paid, or demeaning, or insecure; moreover, women's unemployment rates are higher than men's almost everywhere, and informal sectors appear to be expanding. The feminization of poverty is another unwelcome feature of economic globalization. Worse still is the apparent growth in trafficking in women, or the migration of prostituted women.[45]

The weakening of the nation-state and the national economy similarly has contradictory effects. On the one hand, the withering away of the welfarist, developmentalist state as a result of the neoliberal economic policy turn is a uniformly negative outcome for women, in core and semiperipheral regions alike. On the other hand, the legitimacy of the global women's rights agenda allows feminists "on the ground" to make additional demands on the state for women's equality, autonomy, and empowerment. The globalization of concepts and discourses of human rights and of women's rights and the activities of INGOs and TSMOs have emboldened women and created space for women's organizations to grow nationally and transnationally. In turn, this represents a countertrend to the particularisms and the identity politics of contemporary globalization.

As we have seen above, globalization is a complex, multidimensional process that is still unfolding. I would argue, however, that it is at heart an economic process, and that changes in economic relations, institutions, and policies constitute the driving force. It is useful, therefore, to examine more closely these economic processes and their concomitant labor force dynamics, pointing out the ways in which they also reflect gender relations and ideologies. I will also show how the post-Keynesian shift to neoliberalism helped bring about Islamic fundamentalist movements.

The Advent of Neoliberalism

The free market policy environment, global trade regime, and technological advances that characterize economic globalization entail new economic policies and production systems with important implications for national economies, such as skill requirements, labor market regulations, education policy, and employment. The 1980s saw the flourishing of "flexible" or "post-Fordist" productions systems that were guided by neoliberal economic orthodoxy—what some have called "market fundamentalism." In addition to calls for cutbacks in the social and economic activities of the state, the neoliberal policy framework included "structural adjustment policies" for peripheral and semiperipheral countries as the only solution to economic crisis and the only path to economic growth.

Structural adjustment policies, which aimed to balance budgets and increase competitiveness through trade and price liberalization, included reduction of the public-sector wage bill and growth of the private sector, privatization of social services, encouragement of foreign investment, and the production of goods and services for export ("tradables") through "flexible" labor processes.[46] The international financial institutions, especially the World Bank and the IMF, were the chief instigators of this free-market policy shift. Structural adjustment policies were first implemented in some African and Latin American countries as a result of the debt crisis of the 1970s and early 1980s. They were extended to other countries in the mid-1980s and were subsequently adopted in a number of Middle East countries, including Morocco, Tunisia, Jordan, and Egypt.[47] Structural adjustment policies were key elements in the decline of welfarist and developmentalist states in the periphery and semiperiphery.

Structural adjustment became a very controversial topic in the development-studies literature; some development economists found that it worked in some places but not in others, while other economists regarded the entire turn to be a disaster for national sovereignty, economic development, and people's well-being. In the early 1980s, critical voices began to argue that adjustment and stabilization programs in developing countries were having particularly adverse effects on women. Da Gama Santos (1985) recognized that the gender division of labor and the differential positions of women and men in the spheres of production and reproduction suggested that the new policy shifts would lead to very different outcomes for women and men, although these gender differences would differ further by social class and by economic sector. The now-classic UNICEF study, *Adjustment with a Human Face,* highlighted the social costs of adjustment and provided empirical evidence of the deterioration of social conditions in ten countries undergoing adjustment.[48] Subsequent studies found that there were differential impacts on the various categories of the poor, including the "chronic" poor, "borderline" poor, and the "new" or "working poor." As one scholar noted, "structural adjustment's most devastating negative impacts were the constricting of public investment as government budgets shrank, and the failure to address directly the problems of unemployment, poverty and stagnant standards of living."[49]

The feminist development literature (WID/GAD) was especially critical, charging structural adjustment with carrying out its objectives on the backs of the poor and especially on poor women. In many ways, the women of the working class and urban poor became the "shock absorbers" of neoliberal economic policies.[50] Rising unemployment and reduced wages for men led to increased economic activity on the part of women and children. This occurred also in households headed by women, an increasing proportion of all households in most regions. Women had to assume extra productive and reproductive activities in order to survive the austerities of adjustment and stabilization policies (such as higher prices), and to compensate for the withdrawal or reduction of government subsidies of food and services. Moreover, structural adjustment policies—with their attendant price increases, elimination of subsidies, social service decreases, and introduction or increase of "user fees" for "cost recovery" in the provision of schooling and health care—heightened the risk and vulnerability of women and children in households where the distribution of consumption and the provision of health care and education favored men or income-earning adults. Women had to bear most of the responsibility of coping with increased prices and shrinking incomes, as women were the ones largely responsible for household budgeting and maintenance. The gender as well as class biases of structural adjustment were clear. By removing subsidies for education and healthcare, the policies increased the labor time and other burdens of non-elite women. Thus the policies contained an implicit and unspoken assumption of the elasticity of women's labor time, or the idea that women would always fill the gap created by public expenditure cuts in health and social services.

Household survival strategies included increases in the unpaid as well as paid labor of women. In the Philippines, as Sylvia Chant showed, mean household size increased, as relatives pooled their resources. Janet Tanski found that the combined effects of economic crisis and structural adjustment in Peru led to a significant increase in poverty, with worse outcomes for households headed by women. Structural adjustment policies and other forms of neoliberalism were said to be major factors behind the "feminization of poverty."[51]

In this way, not only did structural adjustment have adverse class effects, but by ignoring the social relations of gender and gender ideologies, they often exacerbated unequal gender relations. As Diane Elson and others argued, inasmuch as privatization displaces public provisioning and women are compelled to compensate for cutbacks by increasing their productive and reproductive activities, there is a male bias in structural adjustment and similar neoliberal policies.

The structural adjustment policies and austerity measures of the World Bank and IMF in the 1970s and 1980s led to a wave of protests that were known as IMF protests or food riots. (Countries in the Middle East and North Africa, which later produced Islamist movements, also experienced such riots.) This was followed twenty years later by a new cycle of protests. Although both should be regarded as two stages in the cycle of protest against globalization, we can identify some differences between them. The earlier wave of antiausterity protests was spontaneous; it consisted of discrete protests within national borders; protests were often called by unions and groups of (male) workers; and the protests were for the most part nonideological.[52] The more recent wave of antiglobalization protests is organized; it is transnational; it evinces cross-class alliances of labor, environmental groups, and feminist groups; and the discourse is often explicitly anticapitalist, with clear critiques of multinational corporations, the World Bank, the IMF, and the WTO.

Inequalities and Democratization: Two Faces of Globalization

Earlier in this chapter I referred to the "janus-faced" nature of globalization that some scholars have identified as a result of its negative and positive entailments. Certainly one of the negative consequences of its economic dimension has been the growth of inequalities, which has given rise to much criticism as well as to the emergence of the global justice movement. Another aspect of globalization, which is a part of its political dimension, is the spread of the discourse of democracy, of democracy movements, and of political liberalization and democratization in various countries of the semiperiphery. The following section discusses these two faces of globalization and highlights their gender dynamics.

The adverse effects of economic globalization have been felt within all regions, and especially by their respective labor forces. With increased trade, the prices of imported goods often compete with the prices of domestic products, forcing domestic capitalists to attempt to cut labor costs. In the developed countries, as plants relocated to sites elsewhere in search of cheaper costs of labor and production, jobs disappeared and wages eroded in the declining industrial sectors. As the developed countries shifted from manufacturing to high-tech services, blue-collar unemployment grew, along with the expansion of part-time and temporary jobs. This came at the expense of the kind of stable employment that men came to expect during "the golden age of capitalism," or the A-phase of the postwar capitalist expansion, from about 1950 to 1973. Indeed, World Real GDP grew by 4.6 percent during 1964–73.[53] In the Middle East and North Africa (MENA), growth continued to the mid-1980s, due to high oil prices. But for developing countries as a whole, the B-phase downturn of the 1980s saw a shift from internally oriented to externally oriented growth strategies and the shrinkage of large public sectors and nationalized industries. The result was an expansion of informal sectors, self-employment, and temporary employment. In most of the former socialist world, restructuring led to loss of output, the creation of unemployment, and increased poverty. In both developing and developed regions, the stable, organized, and mostly male labor force became increasingly "flexible" and "feminized." Keeping the cost of labor low encouraged the growth of demand for female labor, while declining household budgets led to an increase in the supply of job-seeking women.

As we saw earlier in the chapter, a debate continues among economists regarding the relationship between growing inequalities and neoliberal economic policies. Critics of globalization, including feminist critics, point out that neoliberal economic policies of liberalization and privatization are behind the observed growth in social inequalities around the world.[54] In the 1990s, the fifth of the world's people living in the highest income countries had 86 percent of world GDP, 82 percent of world export markets, 68 percent of foreign direct investment, and 74 percent of telephone lines. The bottom fifth, in the poorest countries, had about 1 percent in each category. Of foreign direct investment in developing countries and the countries of Central and Eastern Europe in the 1990s, more than 80 percent went to twenty countries, and mainly to China.[55] Goesling argues that the 1980s and 1990s were characterized by the "diminishing significance of between-nation income differences," but even so, he concedes that "between-nation inequality still accounts for more than two-thirds of inequality in the world distribution of income; the world's most staggering inequalities are observed across nations, not within them." According to the UNDP, "the level of inequality worldwide is grotesque."[56]

Within-country income inequalities likewise have grown. World Bank data show that the average per capita income of the poorest third of all countries fell from 3.1 percent of the richest third to 1.9 percent between 1970 and

1995—that is, during the period of globalization. Meanwhile, the middle third suffered a decline from 12.5 percent to 11.4 percent. The total population living on less than $1 a day rose from 1.2 billion in 1987 to around 1.5 billion in the late 1990s.[57] People in some eighty-five countries were worse off in many respects than they were a decade earlier. In the 1990s reverses were recorded in sixteen countries, largely because of the impact of HIV-AIDS in southern and East Africa, and economic stagnation in Sub-Saharan Africa, Eastern Europe, and the countries of the former Soviet Union. In MENA, levels of poverty do not approximate those of South Asia or Sub-Saharan Africa, in part due to subsidies financed by oil wealth and in part due to longstanding religious practices of charity, but the region has seen declining standards of living, the emergence of "the working poor," and rising inequalities.[58] This is because, as in other regions, MENA governments reduced the public sector wage bill, cut subsidies, introduced user fees for schooling and health, and allowed wages to stagnate. Consequently, unemployment grew and household incomes fell. This led to a rise in the supply of job-seeking women from working-class and middle-class families, but gainful employment has eluded them. Double-digit unemployment has plagued the Middle East and North Africa, and unemployment rates have been especially high for women. The economist Lance Taylor has noted that in most of the countries he has studied, the share of the economically active population (or the "participation rate") increased under liberalization, and that the unemployed as a proportion of the economically active went up as well. His conclusion is that "liberalization and deteriorating growth and equity performances can easily go hand-in-hand."[59]

Globalization has coincided with the so-called third wave of democratization. According to Samuel Huntington, the first wave began in 1828 and ended in 1922; the second wave began in 1926 and ended in 1964. The third wave began in 1974, with the collapse of the Salazar/Caetano and Franco dictatorships in Portugal and Spain, followed by democratization in Latin America and some East and Southeast Asian countries in the 1980s and African countries in the 1990s.[60] There has been some political liberalization in countries of the Middle East and North Africa, although full-fledged democratization has not yet occurred, and there remain severe restrictions on political parties, NGOs, free speech, freedom of the press, and the civil and political rights of citizens.[61] But even where democratization has taken place, such as in Brazil, South Africa, and Russia, it has not necessarily brought about economic prosperity or social equity.[62] As we have discussed above (see also chapter 3), the era of globalization has been characterized by growing income and social inequalities across countries and within societies. Such inequalities—which have been the basis for class conflicts and revolutions in the past—may be triggering the cycle of anticapitalist globalization protests mentioned above.[63] For example, American unions were well represented in the anti-WTO protests in Seattle in late 1999; they continue to raise objections to the new rules of the WTO, and in 2003 they began to call for the adoption of a national health plan in the United States. In May and June 2000 there were six general strikes involving millions of workers against the effects of globalization and neoliberalism—in India, Argentina, Nigeria, South Korea, South Africa, and Uruguay.[64] Workers went on strike in Turkey for more pay and for a voice in decision-making, and the same occurred in Iran. In Greece, the federation of Greek telecommunications workers, representing 18,500 of the 19,700 workers in the Hellenic Telecommunications Organization (OTE), mounted a seven-day strike in autumn 2000 when the government announced it would cut its stake in the OTE and support privatization.[65] Argentines rioted in 2001 and 2002, demonstrating their lack of confidence in the governments that had been responsible for the corruption and austerity measures that led to a drastic decline in the standard of living.[66] In 2002–3, about two hundred factories—employing more than ten thousand nationwide and producing everything from tractors to ice cream—were taken over and run by workers.[67] In addition to triggering worker protests at the national level, the existence of inequalities—between classes, the sexes, and countries—forms the basis of antiglobalization protests and informs the activities and objectives of the major transnational social movements, including the women's movement.

Real democracy is of course a major demand of the global justice movement, which seeks greater democratic decision-making on economic policy as well as international security (war and peace) issues. And around the world, feminists have largely welcomed democratization, as it has allowed their organizations to flourish. However, just as democracy has not necessarily brought about economic prosperity or social justice (e.g., in Brazil, South Africa, Russia, or Nigeria), neither has it necessarily brought about political forces and civil society groups that hold values of pluralism, tolerance, and gender equality. In some cases, especially in MENA, "democratic" elections have brought to power Islamist forces—and their patriarchal agendas have alarmed many women in Muslim societies. Indeed, in Jordan, Egypt, and especially Algeria, Islamists sought to institute orthodox forms of religious and moral behavior and patriarchal forms of family relations. Thus we have seen "democracy without democrats," as the scholar Ghassan Salamé has noted.[68] An exception, however, may be Turkey, where seventy years of Kemalism and a decade of democratization produced in 2002 a ruling Islamic party that adhered to the constitutional framework of secular republicanism while also pushing for greater human rights and individual freedoms.[69]

The Emergence of Fundamentalist Movements

I have said above that globalization entails in part an attempt to impose a certain homogenization of economic policies, political practices, cultural symbols, and ideology. This has been met with the resistance of local peoples and social movements, though not all of the resistance has been progressive. Benjamin Barber uses the term *jihad* as shorthand to describe religious fundamentalism, disintegrative tribalism, ethnic nationalisms, and similar kinds of identity politics carried out by local peoples "to sustain solidarity and tradition against the nation-state's legalistic and pluralistic abstractions as well as against the new commercial imperialism of McWorld."[70] Jihad is in struggle against modernity and cultural imperialism alike, and "answers the complaints of those mired in poverty and despair as a result of unregulated global markets and of capitalism uprooted from the humanizing constraints of the democratic nation-state."[71] This is an apt way of contextualizing Islamic fundamentalism.

In the Middle East and North Africa, Islamic fundamentalist movements emerged in the 1970s, expanded during the 1980s, and peaked in the early 1990s. To a certain extent, they reflected the contradictions of modernization, the difficult transition to modernity under way in the region, and the conflict between traditional and modern norms, relations, and institutions. But Islamic fundamentalist movements also emerged as world communism went into decline, as the global economic policy environment shifted from Keynesian to neoliberal, and as talks on a new international economic order (NIEO) collapsed. At the same time, important cultural changes were taking place globally and within countries, including the internationalization of Western popular culture and changes in gender relations and the position of women. The Iranian Revolution of 1978–79, which led to the formation of the Islamic Republic of Iran, had a demonstration effect throughout the MENA region, and indeed the Muslim world. It appeared to many dissidents that a project for the Islamization of state and society could prevail, and that this would be the solution to economic and political crises. It would be a mistake, however, to view Islamist movements as pristine and spontaneous social movements. During the 1970s and 1980s, many were encouraged and financed by external forces—such as Saudi Arabia, Israel, the United States, and various MENA governments—in order to undermine and supplant left-wing or communist movements.[72]

More specifically, we may identify the following factors in the emergence of Islamist movements:

- Economic factors, including the unrealized promises of national development, the persistence of inequalities domestically and internationally, and the implementation of IMF-mandated austerity measures. Some fundamentalist movements targeted both their own nation states and the world capitalist order as sources of injustice— and claimed that the solution would be an Islamic order. The disparities and inequalities within countries had to do with declining oil revenues or corruption or misguided resource allocation priorities (e.g., huge military purchases). Later, they had to do with the austerities associated with structural adjustments.

- Political factors, including authoritarian rule and the absence of democratic or participatory political institutions. As mentioned above, some governments had a hand in the emergence of Islamism. This was true of Iran, Egypt, and Turkey, where strategies to undermine left-wing movements led to the financing of Islamic groups. Even Israel encouraged Hamas as a way of subverting the exclusive authority of the PLO among the Palestinian population. The United States encouraged an Islamist rebellion against a left-wing and modernizing government in Afghanistan, and spent the 1980s militarily and financially supporting the Afghan Mujahideen. A related political factor in the rise of Islamic fundamentalist movements was the non-resolution of the Palestinian problem, which many fundamentalist movements identified as a key reason for their emergence. The Islamization of the Palestinian liberation movement itself is the result of Israeli intransigence toward the state-building project of the PLO and the Palestine National Authority.

- Gender and social change. The role, status, comportment, and attire of women have constituted a major preoccupation of fundamentalist movements. Fundamentalist movements called for veiling because Muslim women had been taking off their veils; the movements called for a return to traditional family values, to female domesticity and the like because women had been entering public spaces and the public sphere, which for so long had been the province of men. Some of this preoccupation of fundamentalist movements is theologically rooted; much of it can be explained in terms of the inevitable emergence of gender conflict at a time of tension between the old patriarchal order and the emerging feminist movement. There is both an ideological and a material basis for this gender conflict.[73]

Islamic fundamentalist movements are responses to internal contradictions and to external threats. They reflect the tensions and contradictions of the transition to modernity and the conflict between traditional and modern values, norms, and social relations. And they are a reaction to the threat of "Western" cultural domination. Women's rights—and the conflict over the roles, rights, and privileges of men and women, and the structure and status of the family—are at the center of this transition, conflict, and reaction. In the MENA region, governments have dealt with the fundamentalist threat in various ways, sometimes by accommodating fundamentalist demands, sometimes by allowing them into the political process, and sometimes by confronting them head-on. Early on, the Tunisian government banned the an-Nahda movement outright; the Syrian government put down its growing Islamist movement violently and effectively. Accommodation was initially the response of the governments of Egypt and Algeria, who adopted measures restricting women's rights as a way of placating Islamist movements; these measures included the reinforcement of the most patriarchal principles of Muslim family law. When Jordan, Egypt, Turkey, and Algeria opened up the political process, Islamists formed political parties and found their way into legislative bodies and ministerial positions. But when Islamists took up arms against governments, sought to overthrow them, or used violence and terror in a way that threatened the power and authority of the state (as in Egypt and especially in Algeria in the 1990s), governments and militaries turned on the Islamist movements, their leaders, and members. In the late 1990s, Morocco witnessed a conflict—albeit a nonviolent one—between feminists and the new socialist government on one side and the fundamentalist movement on the other. The point of contention was a proposed national development plan for the advancement of women that included measures to revise the (patriarchal) family law, which Moroccan feminists had been calling for since 1993. Islamists mobilized against the plan, denouncing it as un-Islamic and (rather cleverly) as a conspiracy of the World Bank, much hated in Morocco.[74]

What do Islamist movements want? Although they arose in the midst of economic and political crises and sometimes even refer to unemployment and deteriorating standards of living as social problems, they are in fact less concerned with economic, military, or foreign policy matters than they are with politics, culture, family, and morality. Reacting to social changes brought about by modernization and secularization, fundamentalist movements are concerned with identity, morality, and the family. This preoccupation places a heavy burden on women, who are seen as the bearers of tradition, religiosity, and morality, and as the reproducers of the faithful. Such views have profound effects on women's legal status and social positions, especially when fundamentalist views are successfully inscribed in constitutions, family laws, penal codes, and other public policies.

In most cases Islamic fundamentalists do not offer an economic plan, or an alternative program on security, or perspectives on international relations. Nor do social justice issues, tied as they are to economic planning and development, appear to interest them. In the absence of a welfare state, Islamist groups do provide social services and run charities, but they offer no perspectives on socioeconomic development. Thus Islamist movements in opposition have had almost no effect on labor law, economic policy, military expenditures, or even foreign policy. By contrast, their influence has been greatest in public policies pertaining to women and the family. This is of course not entirely true of the Islamic Republic of Iran, where an Islamist movement took power. But even there, an "Islamic development plan" never took shape, various ad hoc economic policies have been tried since 1979, and some of the most profound changes came about in the areas of culture, morality, and gender, as well as in the political system (clerical rule) and the legal frameworks (which came to be based on Islamic law), rather than in the economic realm. No Islamist movement or government in power has produced a theory or practice of democratic governance, of the rights of citizens, or of socioeconomic equality. In 1997, when the reformist candidate Mohammad Khatami was elected to the presidency, there was some hope that Iran might develop into a novel Islamic democracy. Years later, however, the democratization of state structures remained incipient and stalled.

By the turn of the new century, scholars were arguing that Islamic fundamentalist movements were on the wane, and that political Islam had lost its attraction and allure, at least in the Middle East and North Africa. This was based on the observation that fundamentalist movements in power had been unable to create economic growth and prosperity (for example, in the Islamic Republic of Iran, in Pakistan, and in Sudan), and that the publics were exhibiting revulsion over the level of violence associated with Islamists (for example, in Algeria, Egypt, and Afghanistan). By that time, too, feminists in Muslim countries had developed various strategies to combat fundamentalism and offer alternatives. Early on, an important strategy was to form a transnational network of antifundamentalist feminists, called Women Living under Muslim Laws (see chapter 5). At around the same time, Iranian women living in exile in Europe and the United States formed feminist groups that were opposed to fundamentalism and the Islamization project in Iran. In Britain, Women against Fundamentalism and Southall Black Sisters took public positions against growing fundamentalism among immigrant communities and what they saw as misguided multicultural policies that conceded too much to (often patriarchal) male leaders of immigrant communities. In Algeria, new feminist organizations formed in the late 1980s in response to the growing power of the Islamist movement. In the refugee camps of Pakistan in the 1990s, the Revolutionary Association of Women of Afghanistan (RAWA) railed against the jehadis and the Taliban. And the Sisterhood Is Global Institute, under the direction of an expatriate Iranian feminist, advanced the cause of Muslim women's human rights, and helped to establish a regional branch in Amman, Jordan. Another innovative strategy has come to be known as Islamic feminism—an intellectual movement of believing women whose interpretation of the Koran serves to challenge political Islam and orthodoxy.

As we shall see in subsequent chapters, women in Muslim countries—including the Middle East and North Africa—have been affected by globalization in its various dimensions. In some countries, women have come to enjoy the benefits of economic growth, foreign direct investment, and NGO activity, finding jobs in factories and the service sector or building careers in public services or the NGO sector. Others eke out a living in the informal sector or join the ranks of the unemployed. Yet others have become victims of Islamist reactions to globalization. Fearing Western influence on their own cultures, traditions, and religion, conservative Islamic thinkers dispute notions of gender equality, glorify the family and women's domestic roles, emphasize public morality, defend veiling, and excoriate Western cultural norms.[75] As Noha El-Mikawy has noted, "The counter-reaction to globalization in Egypt has been conservative and populist, idealizing women, reifying their private role as mothers and undermining their public role as civic partners. Most Islamic activists focus on the family as the highest civil unit and intrude on that unit with authoritarian utterances which reduce women to their biological function and the social role to that of pedagogical agents perpetuating the conservative agenda."[76] In the chapter that follows, I elaborate on those global economic processes that have affected women in distinctive ways and have engendered transnational feminist responses.

CHAPTER THREE

Female Labor, Regional Crises, and Feminist Responses

In an essay that critically evaluated the Keck and Sikkink book on transnational advocacy networks, sociologist Peter Evans emphasized what he called "transnational consumer/labor networks" that target transnational corporations. And in an essay on the disappearance of discussions of inequalities since the 1995 Social Summit, development economist Jacques Baudot argued that only gender inequality was being addressed in international policy circles, "in part because it may be seen as compatible with the basic tenets of the neoliberal creed."[1] Both Evans and Baudot were apparently unaware of the existence of transnational feminist networks and of their decidedly vigorous critique of gender and social inequalities in the global economy.

In this chapter I examine the relationship between the globalization process and the emergence of transnational feminist networks. I argue that the worldwide expansion of a female labor force, the important (albeit exploited) role of female labor in the global economy, and the persistence of social and gender inequalities underpin the rise of a women's movement on a world scale. The global social movement of women is characterized by a set of grievances, claims, and objectives (global feminism), and an effective organizational type (the transnational feminist network). TFNs thus reflect one aspect of the globalization process, while also responding to its dark side.

If female labor incorporation, persistent inequalities, and the hierarchies and crises of the global economy have formed the structural basis of women's mobilizations, the United Nations and its world conferences have played an important role in providing organizational resources. And of course, women's own experiences in the economy, the polity, and the household have provided the impetus for analysis and action. As I demonstrate in this chapter, women's mobilization and collective action have taken the form of increasing participation in trade unions and in transnational feminist networks.

The Feminization of Labor and the Global Economy

Through institutions such as the nation-state and the transnational corporation, the world economy generates capital largely through the exploitation of labor, but it is not indifferent to the gender and ethnicity of that labor. Gender and racial ideologies have been deployed to favor white male workers and exclude others, but they also have been used to integrate and exploit the labor power of women and of members of disadvantaged racial and ethnic groups in the interest of profit making. In the current global environment of open economies, new trade regimes, and competitive export industries, global accumulation relies heavily on the work of women, both waged and unwaged, in formal sectors and in the home, in manufacturing, and in public and private services. Generally speaking, the situation is better or worse for women depending on the type of state and the strength of the economy. Women workers in the welfare states of northern Europe fare best, followed by women in other core economies. In Eastern Europe and the former Soviet Union, the economic status of working women changed dramatically for the worse following the collapse of communism. In much of the developing world, a class of women professionals and workers employed in the public sector and in the private sector has certainly emerged due to rising educational attainment, changing aspirations, economic need, and the demand for relatively cheap labor. However, vast numbers of economically active women in the developing world lack formal training, work in the informal sector, have no access to social security, and live in poverty.

Proletarianization and Professionalization: Industry and Services

Let me begin with a definitional note. In my usage, *proletarianization* refers to the formation of a female working class. I distinguish this from the entry of middle-class women into the professions, which I refer to here as *professionalization*.[2] Proletarianization and professionalization coincide with the involvement of working women in trade unions and feminist organizations, including transnational feminist networks that promote women's human rights or that critique neoliberal economic policies for their adverse impact on low-income women.

As world markets expanded in the 1970s, a process of female proletarianization began to take place. In developing countries—and especially in Southeast and East Asia, parts of Latin America and the Caribbean, and Tunisia and Morocco—growing numbers of women were drawn into the labor-intensive and low-wage industries of textiles, garments, sportswear, electronics, and pharmaceuticals that produced for export as well as for the home market. The surge in women's waged employment in developing countries began in the 1970s, following an earlier period of capitalist development and economic growth that was characterized by the displacement of labor and craft work, commercialization of agriculture, and rural-urban migration.[3] Some called the marginalization of women "housewife-ization";[4] others have described it as the initial part of the "U pattern" of female labor-force participation in early modernization.[5]

During the 1970s, it was observed that export-processing zones (EPZs) along the U.S.-Mexico border and in Southeast Asia, established by transnational corporations to take advantage of low labor costs in developing countries, were hiring mainly women. By the early 1980s, it was clear that the new industrialization in what was then called the Third World was drawing heavily on women workers. Many studies by WID specialists and socialist-feminists centered on the role played by the available pool of relatively cheap female labor.[6] Gender ideologies emphasizing the "nimble fingers" of young women workers and their capacity for hard work, especially in the Southeast Asian economies, justified the recruitment of women for unskilled and semi-skilled work in labor-intensive industries at wages lower than men would accept, and in conditions that unions would not permit. In Latin America, women entered the labor force at a time when average wages were falling dramatically. Around the world, women's share of total industrial labor rarely exceeds 30 to 40 percent, but as Ruth Pearson pointed out, the proportion of women workers in export processing factories producing textiles, electronics components, and garments was much higher, "with figures as high as 90% in some cases."[7] An INSTRAW (Institute for Research and Training on Women) study found that exports of manufactures from developing countries were largely comprised of the kinds of products typically produced by female labor, leading Susan Joekes to conclude that industrialization had been "as much *female* led as *export* led."[8]

The process of the feminization of labor continued throughout the recessionary 1980s and into the 1990s, encompassing countries like Bangladesh, which had one of the largest increases in the share of women participating in the labor force—from 5 percent in 1965 to 42 percent in 1995. In 1978 the country had four garment factories; by 1995 it had 2,400. These factories employed 1.2 million workers, 90 percent of whom were women under the age of twenty-five.[9] Female proletarianization continues apace in China's highly globalized and integrated economy, where huge plants producing for the world market employ thousands of women each.[10] In 2000 it was reported that 90 percent of the workers in the 850 EPZs around the world were women—and "in the majority of cases workers' rights and social protection are non-existent in EPZs. Although they work in factories, what EPZ workers have in common with informal sector workers is that they are unprotected, largely unorganized, female labour."[11]

Feminization occurred also in public services, where throughout the world women's share grew to 30–50 percent—at a time when public-sector wages, like industrial wages, were declining. In Iran, Egypt, and Turkey, women's share of public-service employment (including jobs as teachers and university professors in public schools and state universities, nurses and doctors in state hospitals, and workers and administrators across government agencies) increased during the 1990s. This occurred at a time when salaries had eroded tremendously and more men were gravitating toward the more lucrative and expanding private sector.[12]

As world trade in services has increased and global firms continue to engage in out-sourcing, the involvement of women in various occupations and professions of the service sector has grown. Women around the world have made impressive inroads into professional services such as law, banking, accounting, computing, and architecture; in tourism-related occupations; and in the information services, including offshore airline booking, mail order, credit cards, word-processing for publishers, telephone operators, and all manner of data entry and teleservices. In Barbados, according to one source, some three thousand people, or one in fifty of the country's labor force, were working in informatics in 1997, largely processing airline tickets and insurance forms. Low-cost typesetting is done in China, even by workers who do not understand what they are typing.[13] In India, Bangalore has become a technology hub, where thousands of young women work in offshore customer service centers for such firms as General Electric, British Airways, Amazon.com, and American Express.[14] Women in India represented 30 percent of employees in the computer industry in 2001, and 250,000 jobs were opened for women in the country's mobile phone industry. On the other hand, "many of these jobs are casual or part-time, and of much lower quality than men's."[15] The new technologies have enabled the reorganization of work based on the concept of flexibility.

The world trade in services favors women's labor migration, in contrast to the demand for male manufacturing workers during the earlier periods of industrialization in Europe and the United States.[16] Mexican, Central American, and Caribbean women have migrated to the United States to work as nurses, nannies, or domestics; Argentine women, to Italy to work as nurses; Filipinas and Sri Lankans, to the Middle East to work as waitresses, nurses, nannies, or domestics. Labor shortages in Europe and the growing demand for nurses has led to an out-migration of nurses from Ghana, South Africa, Jamaica, and Trinidad and Tobago.[17] In at least two countries—the Philippines and Sri Lanka—the majority of emigrants have been women.[18] There is also considerable intra-regional female labor migration, such as within Europe (e.g., East and Central Europeans to Western Europe) and Southeast and East Asia (e.g., women from the Philippines to Hong Kong).[19]

During the oil-boom years of the 1970s and afterwards, labor migration in the MENA region involved Palestinians, Egyptians, Jordanians, and Yemenis working in the oil-rich Gulf kingdoms. The remittances sent back by the predominantly male labor migrants allowed households in the capital-poor and labor-sending countries to maintain a relatively good standard of living. For both economic and political reasons, intra-Arab labor migration declined in the 1990s.[20] But this period also saw an increasing number of Moroccan, Tunisian, and Algerian women migrating alone to work in various occupations in France, Italy, and Spain, among other European countries.

The proletarianization and professionalization of women have cultural repercussions and sometimes entail backlashes and gender conflicts. In some advanced capitalist countries, working women often have encountered serious forms of sexual harassment. In the semiperipheral countries of the Middle East, the increasing participation of women in the labor force was accompanied in the 1980s by subtle or overt pressures on them to conform to religious dictates concerning dress. Hence in Egypt, many professional women came to don modest dress and to cover their heads. In the earlier stage of the Islamist movement, the influx of women in the work force raised fears of competition with men, leading to calls for the redomestication of women, as occurred in Iran immediately after the Islamic revolution. Later, although Islamists in Turkey, Iran, Egypt, Jordan, and Morocco did not call on women to withdraw from the labor force—indeed, among their female adherents are educated and employed women from the lower middle class—they did insist on veiling and on spatial and functional segregation. On the other hand, Islamists in Algeria and Palestine have continued to emphasize female domesticity, for reasons of both ideology/theology and male material interests.

The surge in women's employment is characteristic not only of semiperipheral countries. In sixteen European countries, the increase in the number of women in the labor force over the period 1983–91 was quite dramatic, whereas it was relatively modest for men. In six countries the number of employed men actually fell over the period, most significantly by 3.4 percent in Belgium. During the 1990s, the Nordic countries, including Finland, had the highest rate of employment among women, with North America following close behind.[21] The feminization of labor, it should be noted, refers to the influx of women into relatively low-paying jobs, but also to the growth of part-time and temporary work among *men.* This trend was especially noticeable in New Zealand, the United Kingdom, and the Netherlands, mainly in retail trade, hotels and catering, banking, and insurance.[22] Indeed, in the Netherlands, men's part-time work in 1992 was as high as 13.4 percent of total male employment, up from 5.5 percent in 1979. These employment trends for European women and men continued through the end of the 1990s.[23] Unemployment rates vary across the European Union, where some countries show very high rates of unemployment among the young. At the start of the new millennium, Spain had the highest unemployment rate for both women and men (15.4 percent), followed by France (10.8 percent). Spain and France also had the highest female unemployment rates (22.7 percent and 12.8 percent respectively) and highest unemployment rates for young women (36.3 percent and 26.3 percent respectively). Other European countries with two-digit unemployment rates were Finland, Ireland, Slovakia, and Poland. Female unemployment rates exceeded men's in the following countries: Belgium, the United States, Iceland, the Netherlands, Finland, Switzerland, France, Denmark, Luxembourg, Germany, Italy, Spain, Greece, Portugal, Czech Republic, Slovakia, Poland, Mexico. Even in Turkey, with a much lower female participation rate, women's unemployment rate was 99 percent of men's. Clearly women have experienced a disadvantaged position in labor markets in the industrial countries.[24]

The Informal Sector, the Income Gap, and Unemployment

At the same time that women entered the formal labor force in record numbers in the core countries, much of the observed increase in female labor-force participation in semiperipheral countries occurred in the informal sectors of the economy. The extent of the urban informal sector and its links to the formal sector are matters of dispute, and women's involvement in it is rarely captured in the official statistics, but some studies have suggested significant increases in the size of the informal sector and in women's informal economic activities.[25] In Sub-Saharan Africa in the late 1990s, more than one-third of women in non-agricultural activities worked in the urban informal sector. Rates were as high as 65 to 80 percent in Senegal, Benin, Zambia, and Gambia.[26] Rates of urban informal activity among women have become high in parts of Peru, Indonesia, and Iran. Unregistered and small-scale urban enterprises, home-based work, and some self-employment fall into this category, and they include an array of commercial and productive activities. In the urban areas of developing countries, many formal jobs became informalized as employers sought to increase flexibility and lower labor and production costs through subcontracting, as Beneria and Roldan showed in their study of Mexico City and as Cinar revealed for Istanbul and Bursa.[27] Drawing on existing gender ideologies regarding women's roles, their attachment to family, and the perceived lower value of their work, subcontracting arrangements encourage the persistence of home-based work.[28] There is some debate concerning the reasons for women's concentration in such types of work, but some studies suggest that many women accept home-based employment—with its insecurity, low wages, and absence of benefits—as a convenient form of income generation that allows them to carry out domestic responsibilities and care for their children.[29]

The social relations of gender account for the pervasive income gap between men and women workers, a gap that is detrimental to women but lucrative to employers. On average women earn 75 percent of men's wages, with a narrower wage gap in the public sector than in the private sector.[30] Explanations for the gender gap are varied. Some point out that the gender difference in the income gap is based on lower education and intermittent employment among women workers. Others emphasize the role of gender bias. For example, in Ecuador, Jamaica, and the Philippines, women earn less than men despite higher qualifications, a problem that is especially acute in the private sector.[31] Labor-market segmentation along gender lines perpetuates the income gap. Pearson and Mitter found that in the computing and information processing sectors, the majority of high-skilled jobs went to male workers, while women were concentrated in the low-skilled ones.[32] In fact, all of the above factors are true and are consistent. For if "the uneven distribution of rewards has been the necessary pendant of capital accumulation," as Hopkins and Wallerstein argued,[33] then it is the deployment of female labor along the commodity chains of the global economy that guarantees a supply of relatively cheap labor, along with the desired higher profit margins.

Considering the social relations of gender and the function of gender ideologies, it should come as no surprise that despite women's key role in the global economy, the unemployment rates of women in the semiperiphery are very high, as we saw in the previous section in connection with the industrial countries. Global unemployment is partly a function of the nature of neoliberal economic policies, which have entailed massive retrenchment of labor in many semiperipheral countries, in the former socialist countries that underwent marketization, and in the core countries. In many developing countries unemployed women are new entrants to the labor force, who are seeking but not finding jobs. In certain countries where restructuring occurred in enterprises employing large numbers of women, or in export sectors that lost markets, the unemployment rates of women may also reflect job losses by previously employed women. This was the case in Malaysia in the mid-1980s, Viet Nam in the late 1980s, Poland, Bulgaria, and Russia in the early 1990s, and Morocco, Tunisia, and Turkey in the latter part of the 1990s. The Asian financial crisis of the late 1990s entailed further job and income losses for women workers, especially in South Korea, Thailand, and Indonesia. In South Korea, women lost jobs at twice the rate of men, despite the fact that before the crisis, they had been the preferred labor supply with an unemployment rate half that of men.[34]

In some cases, women have experienced job loss as a result of technological advances in the workplace. As has been noted above, many enterprises producing textiles and electronics for export have relied heavily on women workers. And yet as more sophisticated technology is used to produce these goods, women workers have tended to be replaced by men or recruited at a slower pace, as appears to have occurred in the Mexican *maquiladoras*,[35] and in the textiles industries of Spain and Italy. In all regions, high unemployment represents the downside of economic globalization, especially for women workers, who must contend with not only the class biases but also the gender biases of neoliberal economics. The feminization of unemployment, therefore, is as much a characteristic of the global economy as is the feminization of labor.

The analysis thus far may raise questions about the contingency versus permanence of the female labor force, and the possibility that female labor remains a reserve army of labor. Because the mass incorporation of women as proletarians and professionals is a relatively recent phenomenon, it is perhaps too soon to tell definitively.[36] However, I would argue that the incorporation of female labor is indeed a secular trend, due to the structural requirements of the capitalist world-system in the era of globalization, and also due to women's own aspirations. In turn, the contradictions of female labor incorporation have led women workers to join unions and women's organizations.

Women and Unionization

As part of the employment trends described above, more women have been joining trade unions, and have indeed been more likely than men to join unions, at a time when overall union membership has been in decline. In a number of advanced industrialized countries, such as the United States, Australia, and the Nordic countries, women have been the largest growing union constituency. Many unions, in response, are actively recruiting women workers, establishing women's departments, and appointing women trade unionists to decision-making positions. The growth of women's involvement in paid employment and in national-level unions has resulted in greater interest in women workers by the international trade unions.[37]

The International Confederation of Free Trade Unions (ICFTU) and the Public Services International (PSI) have active women's departments as do many national unions. In March 2002 the ICFTU—where women were 35 percent of members, compared with barely 7 percent when the union was formed about fifty years earlier—launched a three-year campaign called "Unions for

Women, Women for Unions." The main theme for 2002 was "women's right to decent work." At the same time, the Executive Board and Women's Committee of the PSI identified pay equity as a priority issue, and launched a two-year campaign around it. For the major unions, the key issues identified by their women members are maternity protection, sexual harassment, balancing work and family life, job security, and decent wages. In addition, the International Labor Organization has determined that organizing women workers, especially in the informal sector, will strengthen unions as well as provide women workers with security and improved working conditions.[38]

Women trade unionists worked with other women's groups during the March 1995 Social Summit and the September 1995 Beijing conference. At the latter, and in recognition of women's growing importance in the global economy, as well as their growing union membership, Objective F of the 1995 Beijing Platform for Action affirmed the unions' important role in regulating and protecting women workers' rights, particularly where women constitute a very vulnerable group, as in export processing zones. Women trade unionists were also involved in the five-year reviews of the Social Summit and the Beijing conference, in 2000.

Both the PSI and the ICFTU attend the annual meetings of the UN's Commission on the Status of Women. Their statements usually describe the exploitative employment conditions that many women workers face, the dangers of "free trade," and the need for implementation of ILO labor standards and other conventions on worker rights, human rights, and women's rights. The PSI has a comprehensive website called WomeNet, which contains news and data about working women around the world. The theme of the ICFTU's Seventh Conference, held in May 1999 in Rio de Janeiro, was "Working Women in the 21st Century: Demanding Our Space, Taking Our Place." As mentioned above, the ICFTU took part in the Beijing + 5 meetings and produced a number of policy briefs. According to one report published during the meetings:

> At Beijing + 5, women trade unionists are concentrating on Strategic Objective F: Women and the Economy. Unions believe that government progress in this area has been poor for a number of reasons—the weakness of democratic political institutions and the absence of a vigorous civil society, defense spending and the devastation caused by armed conflicts. Globalization has had a negative impact with more exploitation in the export processing zones, where the majority of workers are women and the growth of low-paid 3D (dirty, dangerous and degrad-

ing) jobs. Cuts in public services have also hit women disproportionately. Job losses have forced women to emigrate to find work and so migrant women's needs are increasingly important.[39]

The report noted that although women workers have found traditional union structures unwelcoming, they now constituted "the future of the trade union movement" and were much more likely than men to account for the increases in union membership. As a result, "one of the important lessons of the Women's Summit is that unions must change to incorporate women's enthusiasm and ideas to fight globalization. Women need unions and unions need women."[40]

In many developing countries, women workers face difficulties in unionization, including employer harassment, state repression, and the masculine character of the existing trade unions. Still, increasing female labor force participation in Latin American, Asian, and African countries has placed issues pertaining to women workers on the agendas of trade unions and of women's organizations in those regions. In Guatemala, women workers at an export shirt-making factory won a union contract, the first in a Guatemala *maquiladora*.[41] In Japan, the Asia-Japan Women's Resource Center studies and promotes the rights of women workers throughout East and Southeast Asia and publishes a newsletter called *Resource Materials on Women's Labor in Japan*.[42] In Taiwan the Grassroots Women Workers Centre, established in 1988, engages in various activities, including defense of the rights of immigrant women workers, and publishes a newsletter called *Female Workers in Taiwan*. According to its spring 1994 newsletter, "the Centre intends to provide opportunities for factory women and family subcontractors to reform the male-dominated workers' union, and to develop women workers' unions and workers' movements through the promotion of feminism." Similar activities and goals are shared by the Committee for Asian Women in Hong Kong. One important development came about in 2001, when the Hong Kong Domestic Workers Union was formed as an affiliate of the Hong Kong Confederation of Trade Unions. India's famous Self-Employed Women's Association (SEWA) operates as a trade union and a consciousness-raising feminist organization. A similar organization was formed in Durban, South Africa, in 1994 and is called the Self-employed Women's Union.

In the Middle East and North Africa, the involvement of women in paid employment has resulted in the politicization of women and of gender issues, but women have also responded by joining unions (though their proportions remain small), forming their own organizations, and engaging in collective action. In Tunisia, the National Commission on Working Women was created in July 1991 within the Tunisian General Federation of Workers. The commission has twenty-seven branches throughout Tunisia, and carries out surveys and studies pertaining to women and the workplace. Israeli Arab women workers ignored by the Histadrut formed the Arab Women Workers Project, and Palestinian women activists in the West Bank and Gaza formed the Palestine Working Women Society. Morocco's Democratic League of Women's Rights organized a Roundtable on the Rights of Workers in 1995; subsequently a committee structure consisting of twelve participating organizations was formed. The group sought to revise the labor code to take into account women's conditions, to include domestic workers in the definition of wage workers and the delineation of their rights and benefits, to set the minimum work age at fifteen, and to provide workers on maternity leave with full salary and a job-back guarantee. In November 1995, some five hundred women textile workers employed by the Manufacture du Maroc factory outside Rabat went on strike for two weeks to protest "repeated violence" against several women employees. This included the arbitrary dismissal of the general secretary of the factory's union of women workers, her subsequent rape by a foreman, and the firing of seventeen women workers who protested the union leader's dismissal and rape. Morocco's Association of Democratic Women, a feminist organization, then set out to "mobilize human rights organizations and all the women's organizations" in defense of the women workers. The incident shows not only the vulnerability of women at the workplace, but the capacity of women workers to fight in defense of their rights, and the ability of the feminist organizations to mobilize support for women workers.

There are other examples of bold action by women trade unionists in the MENA region, some of which have been followed by state repression. In September 2000, thirty-five women affiliated to the Turkish union KESK who wanted to send letters of support to the UN concerning the Women's Global March 2000 were "detained and ill-treated." The following month, some women who wanted to begin a march to Ankara were confronted by police and arrested in Duzce.[43] And since 1998, Iranian working-class and professional women have formed unions of journalists, publishers, lawyers, teachers, and nurses, despite a political climate that is hostile to independent organizing.

Various transnational advocacy networks have emerged to support women workers. Women Working Worldwide, based in Manchester, England, has links with women worker groups in Central America and in South and Southeast Asia. IRENE (International Restructuring Education Network Europe), based in Tilburg, Holland, organizes educational seminars for unions from around the world, and disseminates a newsletter. Mujer a Mujer coordinates women workers' activities across the U.S.-Mexico border.[44] STITCH is a Chicago-based network of U.S. women that supports Central American women organizing in the maquila apparel-for-export industries. Some of its activists are associated with the International Textile, Garment, and Leather Workers Federation, which has a maquila project.[45]

As Gallin has pointed out, trade unions have championed women's rights since their beginnings and have included many charismatic women among their leaders, including Flora Tristan, Louise Michel, Clara Zetkin, Mary "Mother" Jones, Federica Montseny, Marie Nielsen, and Margarethe Faas.[46] However, the labor movement has been dominated by the culture of the male industrial workers, and the culture of unions has been rather masculine and often unfriendly to women workers. Thus in some cases women created their own unions. In Canada, the Federation of Women Teachers' Associations of Ontario is a women-only organization.[47] Denmark produced the Danish Women Workers' Union, KAD.[48] In more recent years, however, and particularly in northern Europe, Italy, Australia, and North America, union membership is taking on a female face.[49] In 2001, Germany's Trade Union Confederation had a female membership of 2.5 million women, or 31 percent of total members. According to the AFL-CIO, whereas U.S. women accounted for 19 percent of union members in 1962, by 1997 fully 39 percent of all union members were women, and they numbered 5.5 million. In 2002, two out of three new members were women, which is no doubt why the AFL-CIO launched its own "Unions for Women, Women for Unions" campaign.[50] U.S. labor organizations such as UNITE (a textile and garment workers' union) and the Hotel and Restaurant Employees "now understand that feminist issues like sweatshops, comparable worth for women, sexual harassment and education provide the vital pathway toward the expansion and revitalization of their movement."[51]

Since the mid-1980s, women have made their way into positions of power in Australian trade unions at a time when overall union membership began to decline. The numbers of women on the foremost national council, the Australian Council of Trade Unions, rose from zero to one-third; in the mid-1990s in the State of South Australia the three major white-collar unions (teachers, nurses, public servants) were all led by women.[52] In Canada, where 31 percent of women workers (and 38 percent of men workers) were unionized in 1992,[53] women's committees succeeded not only in bringing benefits to women workers but also in bringing "increased energy" to unions such as the Ontario Public Service Employees Union.[54] According to Linda Briskin, "Canada has a strong movement of union women, and a vibrant autonomous women's movement," and these movements have "successfully pressured the unions to take up the issues of childcare, abortion, sexual harassment, pay equity, affirmative action and employment equity, etc.—as women's issues and as union issues."[55] According to Rosemary Warskett, Canadian "union feminism" effectively challenged the narrow vision of industrial unionism. "It is now well established in Canada that collective bargaining demands should address the needs of women and other discriminated groups."[56]

In global terms, the highest union density is found in northern Europe—Denmark, Finland, Norway, and Sweden—where women's participation as workers and as union officials is the greatest. In those countries, union density is very high in community, social, and personal services (68–87 percent), in trade, restaurants, and hotels (47–49 percent), and in manufacturing (80–100 percent), in both the public and private sectors. Women are making up an increasing share of union membership, especially in services, with the most impressive figures found in Denmark. In the 1990s Danish women represented 42 and 62 percent of the two main union federations; they were 30 and 39 percent of the delegates to the union Congress and 13 and 41 percent of members of leading committees, as well as 10 and 30 percent of leaders of individual unions.[57] On at least one occasion that I know of, during the 1990s the Danish labor movement sent an all-woman delegation to the annual Congress of the International Labor Organization in Geneva. In Finland during the 1990s women comprised 45 percent of the membership of one of the two labor confederations (SAK); they also constituted about 37.5 percent of delegates to the SAK Congress, and 40 percent of the union council. The proportions of women in union leadership positions also increased in other European countries, as well as in some of the large international unions.

According to an ICFTU report released in June 2000, many unions have organized campaigns against violence and sexual harassment at work. These include Argentina's CGTA, the CDT in the Democratic Republic of Congo, and

Malaysia's MTUC. Spanish unions concluded agreements with the government on job security and part-time work. Poland's NSZZ campaigned for better maternity protection within the ILO Convention. India's HMS drew up a detailed Charter of Demands for women workers, while Japan's RENGO campaigned for the strict implementation of the Equal Employment Opportunity Law. The ICFTU maintains that "unions have strengthened relations with NGOs and women's organizations and together they have been effective in putting forward women's views and demands to the government."[58] Gallin reports that "unions have increasingly entered partnerships with women's NGOs, organizing drives and forming alliances to represent informal workers' interests."[59]

Female labor incorporation and trends in women's unionization provide the social basis for women's mobilization on a world scale, but they also have occurred in a context of growing inequalities and economic crises. What follows is a cross-regional review of developments that have adversely affected women, and the ways that TFNs have responded.

Global Inequalities, Regional Crises, and Impacts on Women

As more women were drawn into the processes of economic globalization, they became aware not only of persistent social and gender inequalities but also the emergence of periodic economic crises that threaten the well-being of entire communities. Although many economists, particularly those wedded to neoliberalism or globalism, argue that free markets benefit all, others gather convincing empirical data to show that inequalities have been increasing within and across countries. Feminists use the same data to highlight the adverse impacts on women.

According to the UNDP's 1999 *Human Development Report,* while globalization offers great opportunities for human advancement, enriching people's lives, expanding choices, and creating a community based on shared values, markets have been allowed to dominate the process, at the expense of building these shared values and achieving common goals."[60] Market volatility has been behind a number of regional macroeconomic crises, which affect the poor in various ways. Declining labor earnings, unemployment, and inflation combine to reduce household income. Many poor households react to a crisis by postponing preventive or curative health measures, or by reducing the nutritional intake of children, or by withdrawing their children from school.

Sub-Saharan Africa has been in economic decline since the 1970s, and it has the largest proportion of people living on less than $1 a day. Stagnation set in after governments submitted to structural adjustment policies in hopes of attracting foreign investment and loans. Yet the region accounts for only 2 percent of all international trade, less than it did during the last days of colonialism fifty years ago. Although corrupt governments, excessive military spending, armed conflicts, and natural disasters such as drought can explain part of the problem, it is also true that deteriorating terms of trade in the form of steep declines in prices for African commodities are also salient. In countries where socialist-style economies were replaced by deregulated free-market models, farmers and industrialists lost business, workers lost jobs, and many women turned to prostitution—including export prostitution in Europe.

Latin America went through a severe economic recession in the 1980s, and crises erupted again in the 1990s, most notably in Mexico and Argentina in 1995, and Brazil in 1999. According to studies by the Inter-American Development Bank, at the turn of the new century, the wealthiest 10 percent received 40 percent of national incomes, while the poorest 30 percent received just 7.5 percent. One of the reasons is that the vast majority of the working population, and mostly women, work in poor-quality jobs. The crises in Mexico and Argentina imposed severe hardship on the poor, and contributed to the feminization of poverty. In Argentina poverty rose from 16.9 percent in 1993 to 24.8 percent in 1995. Argentina's economy deteriorated further in 2001 and 2002, leading to public riots, the downfall of several governments, and widespread disillusionment with the U.S.-backed free-market policies that were adopted in the 1990s. The IMF prescribed its usual austerity package.[61]

In the 1980s social funds were implemented to help offset the effects of structural adjustment policies (SAPs), but most neglected to improve the income-generating capacity of the poor. The IFIs focused on assisting stabilization and liberalization efforts and generally neglected to help governments protect pro-poor services from public spending cuts. Fiscal strategies to protect pro-poor spending began to take place only during Brazil's devaluation crisis of 1999. Latin America's basic services remain underfunded.[62] As a result, poverty may have increased in Mexico during the 1990s, despite economic growth and NAFTA. At least forty million (or 40 percent) of Mexico's population of 97 million live in poverty, and of that number, seventeen million live in misery.[63] Between 1994 and 1998, the share of the nation's income earned by the 20 percent of wealthiest Mexicans leaped from 49 to 54 percent while the earning of the poorest 40 percent of families fell from 14 to 12 percent.[64] Small wonder that illegal immigration from Mexico to the United States shows no sign of abatement.

During the decade of economic reform, unemployment rose at a rapid rate, according to a 1999 ILO report on Latin America and the Caribbean. The majority of new jobs were in the informal sector, where wages, productivity and social protection are much lower than in the formal sector. The ILO reports that youth unemployment rates usually have been double the national average (and triple for workers aged 15–19), and that women's unemployment rates are between 10–60 percent higher than the rates for men.[65]

The transition to a market economy in Eastern Europe and the former Soviet Union has been associated with increased inequality and social stratification. In the 1990s, living standards fell for a majority of people, unemployment and poverty grew, the distribution of assets and earnings changed radically, and social benefits fell. In particular, the FSU countries saw inequality climb to levels comparable to Latin America.[66] According to research by UNICEF, mortality rates rose considerably, particularly among men in Russia, leaving behind widows who had to cope with unemployment or low wages as household heads. In Central Asia, women were the targets of dramatic job cuts as state-owned companies were sold to the private sector. In many countries of the former socialist world, according to data from the ILO's *Key Indicators of the Labor Market 1999,* female unemployment rates are very high: 12.5 percent in Slovakia; 14.6 percent in Latvia; 20.1 percent in Croatia; 27.4 percent in Bulgaria; 44.5 percent in Macedonia.

Unemployment rates similarly have been very high in the Middle East and North Africa, especially for women: 24 percent in Algeria, Egypt, and Morocco; 14 percent in Syria; 20 percent in Turkey during most of the 1990s.[67] Morocco and Algeria have seen a high rate of impoverishment, a dangerous curtailment of social protection, and a heightened sense of exclusion among the marginalized and the excluded. In 1994, Algeria became unable to service its $26 billion foreign debt, which was consuming 93.4 percent of export earnings, and it had to resort to an IMF and World Bank SAP in exchange for debt relief. The SAP led to a 40 percent devaluation of the dinar, the lifting of subsidies on basic food, and the liberalization of foreign trade. Between 1994 and 1998, 815 public enterprises were dissolved, and Public Economic Enterprises laid off 60 percent of their workers.[68] Although the retrenchments affected mainly men, women's livelihood was adversely affected. More women sought jobs to augment deteriorating household budgets, but gender biases as well as structural economic problems foreclosed employment opportunities. Meanwhile, poverty increased, and government data showed that the percentage of the population living below the poverty line in 1995 was 8.9 percent in the urban areas and 19.3 percent in the rural areas. The poor and vulnerable population, however, was calculated to be 14.7 percent in urban areas and 30.4 percent in rural areas.[69]

Inequalities are wide and the poverty level high in Morocco, too. In 1999 it was estimated that around 20 percent of the population of 30 million lived in poverty, 10 percent in sheer misery, while 30 percent—mostly the young and the elderly—were classified as vulnerable. Around 56 percent of Moroccans were illiterate, and only 18 percent of women could read and write. Unemployment hovers at around 20 percent, though again much higher for women than for men, and the quality of the educational system has fallen markedly. According to Layachi, the socialist government of Abdelrahman Yousoufi was caught "between the pressing problems of his people, on the one hand, and the demands of international institutions which are likely to result in even more hardship, on the other."[70] Or as a Moroccan feminist rhetorically asked at an AWMR annual meeting in July 2000, "How can the state improve the status of women, children, and the poor when international financial institutions are in control?"[71]

Tunisia has done much better in preventing the spread of poverty and has put into place an extensive social welfare system, which may be the only one of its kind in the MENA region. And yet, its trade with Europe may be endangered when the Free Trade Agreement that it signed with the EU comes into effect in 2007. It is estimated that between fifteen hundred and three thousand firms—many of them textiles and garment firms that employ women—will go out of business. The association agreement, which calls for abolishing tariff barriers in Tunisia, could increase imports and trade deficits, and is likely to diminish state revenue from tariffs.[72] This could have an adverse impact on the social welfare programs administered by the state, as well as retrench thousands of women workers.

The Asian financial crisis that swept across South and Southeast Asia exposed the dangers of the global trade economy. The crisis imposed significant costs in Thailand, Indonesia, the Republic of Korea, and to lesser extents, Malaysia and the Philippines. Economic crisis set in when skittish international investors began dumping their Asian holdings, resulting in financial panic, bankruptcy, massive unemployment, and increases in poverty. National governments were unable to stabilize the economic free-fall or cushion the shocks to workers and families. The countries had few policy tools (e.g., social insurance) available to combat poverty directly. (There were limited benefits provided by "provident funds," which are lump-sum benefits for pensioners or disabled workers.) The Republic of Korea did offer unemployment insurance, but its program covered only 22 percent of the labor force and provided only a few months of benefits at a fraction of workers' earnings.[73] Thus, when the Asian economies nosedived, their own safety nets were insufficient to meet the needs of the five million workers thrown out of their jobs or the countless families thrown into poverty. Meanwhile, the IMF response was the traditional austerity regime. As former World Bank chief economist Joseph Stiglitz put it, the IMF demanded reductions in government spending and elimination of subsidies for basic necessities like food and fuel "at the very time when contractionary policies made those subsidies more desperately needed than ever." Moreover, "not only was the IMF not restoring economic confidence in East Asia, it was undermining the region's social fabric."[74] This aggravated the crisis while preventing the affected governments from spending on antipoverty social services and income supports. The IMF later recognized this mistake and reversed its policy.

There is some evidence that women were the special victims of the Asian crisis. Women in these countries, as elsewhere, continue to confront social barriers that crowd them into some industries and occupations, foreclose entry into others, and generally push them onto the margins of economic life. Women are the last hired, the first fired, and the least likely to qualify for benefits provided by their employers or by their governments. Country papers circulated at the January 2000 consultation of the Bangkok-based Committee for Asian Women found that in Hong Kong, the female unemployment rate was as high as 25.8 percent and that women made up a high proportion of irregular workers; that during the crisis in South Korea many married women were made redundant or asked to resign from their jobs; that two thousand Malaysian women were laid off when a world market factory in Penang closed its operations in January 2000; and that even before the crisis, Indonesian women experienced higher rates of unemployment as well as various forms of employment discrimination.[75]

The Republic of Korea was the most industrialized of the affected countries. Prior to the crisis, labor markets were tight, with unemployment at a low 2 percent in 1995 and 1996. But between April 1997 and April 1998, overall employment shrank by 5.1 percent. Women workers suffered the worst of the crisis-induced job losses; employment fell 3.8 percent for men but fully 7.1 percent for women. As jobs became harder to find, both men and women fell out of the labor force, but again, the effect was more pronounced for women. Between spring 1997 and 1998, the participation rate for men in the labor force fell by 0.5 percent, while for women the decline was 2.8 percent.[76]

Younger workers suffered the greatest share of job losses, and younger women suffered more than younger men. Employment rates in the 15-to-19-year-old age bracket fell 8.7 percent for men, but 20.2 percent for women. Unexpectedly, job losses for the 20-to-29-year-old age group were roughly equal: 13.3 percent for men and 13.7 percent for women. Older women also bore a disproportionate share of the job losses. Men between 50 and 59 saw employment rates fall 5.5 percent; for women the same age, employment shrank by 6.6 percent. Employment of men sixty years and older fell negligibly by 0.8 percent, but employment of older women declined 7.5 percent.[77]

In Thailand, 54,000 workers were laid off between January 1997 and February 1998. Slightly more than half were women. But these figures account for only the minority of the work force covered by employer-provided severance benefits and greatly understate the number of layoffs that actually occurred. According to one survey, 60 percent of the workers who lost jobs in Thailand were women over thirty years of age, one quarter of whom had been textile and garment workers.[78]

In Indonesia, during 1998, the garment and textile sector, a major employer of women, was responsible for retrenching 240,000 from paying jobs. Before the crisis, just over 49 percent of Indonesian women were working. By August 1998, this number had increased to more than 56 percent. But this increase was entirely the result of women working as unpaid labor in family-run enterprises. The fraction of women surveyed working at paid employment increased by a statistically insignificant 1 percent, from 36 percent to 37 percent. Meanwhile, job-creation programs by the government, which focused on infrastructure development, benefited men, because women make up only a small fraction of the construction and forestry work forces.[79]

The regional crises briefly described above became the target of criticism from various quarters. Well-known economists such as Joseph Stiglitz and Jeffrey Sachs pointed to misguided policies imposed by the World Bank, the IMF, and the U.S. Treasury, blaming them in particular for exacerbating the

"Asian flu" that resulted in job loss and impoverishment. Women trade unionists and feminist economists did the same, while also stressing the class and gender inequalities and the North-South asymmetries that underpin these policy prescriptions.

Transnational Feminist Responses

Along with other groups in the global justice movement, transnational feminist networks have pointed out that decision-making in the institutions of global governance is undemocratic, and that many financial arrangements and trade decisions undermine international agreements on human rights, women's rights, labor protection, and environmental protection. They have been critical of exploitative working conditions, of the declining role of the state in the provision of social services, and of the volatility of global financial markets. In a regional meeting on the Asian crisis held in Manila in 1998, a woman trade unionist from the Philippines asserted: "The Asian crisis is fundamentally an offshoot of globalization." She accused Asian governments of "opening up their countries for further capitalist exploitation and plunder" through policy schemes such as deregulation, privatization, and liberalization. She continued:

> The widely liberalized financial system of the Philippines economy as dictated by the GATT-WTO and APEC and acceded to by the Philippine government, has provided the initial shot that triggered the trouble. . . . With the rise in the prices of basic goods and the contracting of the purchasing power of the peso, women of the working class need to stretch their hours even more to find ways and means to augment their income. Because there are no jobs available and even a meager capital for a small business is very hard to come by, anti-social activities have become increasingly palatable. Prostitution has always been the last option for many Filipino women who need to keep their families afloat. . . . As the women and children cope to survive, the government prioritizes to cut down on basic social services among others.[80]

Women activists have long called for a serious consideration of women's labor and of their rights. Research has shown that women's labor is a critical factor in many of the mechanisms that make globalization work, including export manufacturing, trade liberalization, and the promotion of sectors such as tourism and financial services. However, the impact of these mechanisms often has been to undermine or weaken women's social and economic rights. In response, women's groups are insisting that "the economic models that underpin globalization need to be transformed not just to ease women's pain but to give them full respect for the role they can play in a global system of well-being and justice. A global economic system in which women are central must be one in which women enjoy their full human rights."[81] WEDO, for example, is adamant about the need for a major overhaul of economic policy decision-making, and of its democratization: "The accepted view among those in power is that the 'benefits' of globalization need to be more equitably distributed, not that macroeconomic decision-making is in need of transformation."[82] A similar view is shared by DAWN: "The eradication of poverty and unemployment cannot be addressed without a fundamental shift in the thinking and direction of the global political economy and its management."[83] And as WIDE has noted, women worldwide have developed strategies and organized themselves to tackle gender and class oppression, on a local level in finding survival strategies, and on an international level by joining forces to develop strategies to influence policies.[84]

The campaign Fifty Years Is Enough/U.S. Network for Global Economic Justice has issued documents describing how IMF and World Bank policies damage women worldwide. "In over 80 countries around the world, the WB/IMF routinely subjugate the social and economic rights of poor and working people, particularly women, to the pursuit of economic reform. . . . These impacts are overwhelmingly negative. Extensive data from around the world show that IMF-imposed austerity and economic reform programs have stripped many women of what meager health and education benefits were once available to them." The group also has developed a critique of trafficking in women—both prostitution and labor migration. In one policy document they wrote: "Not only do women dominate as workers in export industries, but they themselves have become the exports. In Indonesia, for example, women migrants to the Middle East increased from 8,000 in 1979 to over 100,000 in 1999. In the Philippines, women composed more than 60% of the 675,000 documented overseas workers in 1994." The document pointed out that the majority of women migrants were service workers—domestic helpers, entertainers, and related work—subject to harsh conditions and vulnerable to sexual abuse and violence. It continued: "The IMF's undermining labor rights in the name of economic reform is a choice to support and encourage the exploitation of women workers."[85]

Feminists also have recognized that the market gives almost no rewards for care, whether paid or unpaid. In the industrial countries, wages for teaching, domestic service, and other caring work have stagnated, or even fallen. The search for efficiency in the global economy imposes a "market discipline" that is at variance with quality. Cost-minimizing standards drive down quality in schools, hospitals, and child-care centers. However, feminists are quick to stress that this does not mean sending women back to the traditional role of housewife and mother. Nor does it mean that women should continue to be responsible for most unpaid care work or reproductive labor. Instead it means sharing unpaid care services between men and women, reducing men's paid work, increasing their time on family care, and increasing the supply of state-supported care services. For example, the Nordic countries have a long tradition of such approaches, which give public recognition and payment for care, rewarding family commitment but without reinforcing traditional gender roles. Transnational feminist networks often call for the array of social and reproductive rights that are in place in the Nordic countries. This is consistent with their call for the return of the welfarist, developmentalist state.

Given the transnational feminist critique of women's labor conditions, of the volatility and hierarchies of the global economy, and of the adverse impact of neoliberal trade policies, it is not surprising that women's groups of all types were present in Seattle to protest the WTO in late 1999. One group that attended was Feminists for Animal Rights (FAR); they were in Seattle because "WTO dispute panels interpret an animal protection law as nothing more than an unfair trade barrier." FAR was also critical of what it said was the way that the U.S. used the WTO to sabotage animal protection regulations. "When the EU banned the use of artificial growth hormones in beef, both in local production and imports, the US promptly challenged the ban, claiming it put U.S. beef producers at a disadvantage."[86] Other groups present in Seattle were Women in Development Europe (WIDE), the Women's Environment and Development Organization (WEDO), the Women's Division of the United Methodist Church, and Diverse Women for Diversity. All issued position papers on global trade and women's rights. According to one participant, "Women's international organizations and networks participated in numbers in the NGO preparations before the Third Ministerial Meeting of WTO . . . . During the preparations the issue of Human Rights and Trade came up forcefully in appeals, declarations, papers, and discussions. The point was made that Human Rights, as they are defined in international and regional conventions, should not be violated by trade agreements, policies, and rules. The International Human Rights Covenants are by far superior to all trade agreements."[87]

The Women's Caucus issued a Declaration that called for transparency, access to the WTO and participation by NGOs, a comprehensive gender, social, and environmental assessment before any new round, and gender and regional balance in all WTO decision-making. (See Declaration, Appendix.) Diverse Women for Diversity issued a Declaration that reiterated their goal of biological and cultural diversity as the foundation of life on earth, as well as self-sufficiency, self-reliance, and solidarity, locally and globally. (See Declaration, Appendix.)

A Gender and Trade Network was formed by the women activists in Seattle, including women representing WIDE, WEDO, DAWN-Caribbean, the Center of Concern, and Fifty Years Is Enough. In their policy documents, they called for democratic decision-making and insisted that all WTO agreements be bound by existing human rights agreements, such as the International Covenant on Economic, Social, and Cultural Rights (1966) and the Convention on the Elimination of All Forms of Discrimination against Women (1979). At the Seattle protests and afterwards, WIDE stressed that no trade agreements should be allowed to contradict the agreements set forth at the UN conferences of the 1990s: UNCED 1992, Human Rights 1993, ICPD 1994, Copenhagen 1995, and Beijing 1995. Similarly, the Women's International Coalition for Economic Justice (WICEJ) issued a "Declaration for Economic Justice and Women's Empowerment" calling for an "enabling environment [that would] favor political, economic, and social policies, institutions and values that promote human rights and social justice for all peoples." It called for "macro-policies designed to defend the rights of women and poor people and protect the environment, rather than expand growth, trade and corporate profits exclusively. . . . Redefining economic efficiency to include measuring and valuing women's unpaid as well as paid work. Economic efficiency needs to be reoriented towards the effective realization of human development and human rights rather than growth, trade, and corporate profits."[88]

Feminist networks were similarly present at the protests against the World Bank and the IMF and for debt cancellation in Washington, D.C., in April 2000. It was perhaps not surprising that the Women's International League for Peace and Freedom (WILPF) was present, given its long history in the peace and socialist movements, but the presence of liberal-feminist organizations such as the U.S. Feminist Majority and several U.S. radical-feminist groups confirmed that feminists around the world were making the global economy a priority. For example, in the wake of the Seattle protests, the U.S. radical-feminist news magazine *Off Our Backs* devoted an issue to the critique of global economic policies. The issue included an interview with one of the movement lawyers who defended protesters in Seattle and Washington, D.C., another interview with a leading feminist economist and activist on structural adjustment and other neoliberal economic policies, a report on the abuse of domestic workers, an article on women's union organizing in Honduras, and an article on "neoliberalism at work in Nicaragua." The issue included the following admonition: "As a movement, Western feminism has often been criticized for being less than attentive to poor women's and women of color's lives and concerns. Feminism in the U.S. has received even more criticism for wearing cultural blinders when it comes to global women's issues. . . . The fact is that feminists should be the vocal majority in the protests against the WTO, IMF, and World Bank and of globalization in general. . . . Feminists have a responsibility to make this issue a priority."[89]

Much of the new work on trade has been carried out by feminist social scientists active within transnational feminist networks such as DAWN and WIDE (e.g., Gita Sen, Mariama Williams, Brita Neuhold), as well as within WICEJ and Women Working Worldwide (which set up the women's caucus at the first Ministerial Conference of the WTO in Singapore in 1996). As advocates for women, and concerned about social and gender inequalities, they monitor and examine the gendered effects of trade agreements within the NAFTA region and the EU, as well as the impact of WTO rules and agreements on working women in developing countries. There is increasing criticism of the reliance on the market and on trade liberalization. The criticism is that the employment losses and dislocation that often accompany trade liberalization, as well as the consequences of price liberalization and privatization of social services brought about by recent trade agreements, are disproportionately borne by women. It is argued that current trade agreements undermine national development and women's entrepreneurship. Domestic trade liberalization and WTO rules make under-resourced women compete with subsidized food imports, while access to Northern food markets is still limited. The foreign exchange generated by FDI is often used to pay external debt rather than stimulate local production and growth. Trade agreements also undermine commitments made by governments in the 1990s conferences on human rights, the environment, and women's rights. TFNs advocate for the removal of the agricultural sector and trade-related intellectual property rights from the WTO's purview (to ensure food security, protect women small farmers, and prevent "biopiracy"), and for deprivatization of public services such as health and education. They insist that the WTO take social and gender issues seriously, that a gender perspective be incorporated into macroeconomic policies, and that social clauses be integrated into trade agreements. They call for the participation of women's organizations at regional trade meetings. They endorse the Tobin Tax and support a kind of global Keynesianism.

An example of transnational mobilizing around the issues discussed above is the World March of Women 2000. The initiative, which had been launched two years earlier in Montreal, Canada, by the Fédération des femmes du Québec, culminated in a series of coordinated marches and other actions held around the world to protest poverty and violence against women. Nearly six thousand organizations from 159 countries and territories were represented in the rallies and marches held. It is noteworthy that women activists from countries of the Middle East and North Africa, not usually visible in transnational feminist organizing and mobilizing around economic justice, were involved in the planning and execution of the march. Women trade unionists were also involved; for example, in April 2000, some three thousand trade unionists, including many women workers, marched in Durban, South Africa, in an event organized jointly by the ICFTU and its South African affiliates. The demands included affordable and accessible housing and transportation; protection against all forms of violence; equal rights for women in the workplace and throughout society; an end to structural adjustment programs and cutbacks in social budgets and public services; cancellation of the debt of all Third World countries; making gender issues central to labor policies and programs; and treatment and protection for people with HIV/AIDS.[90]

The initiative's *Advocacy Guide to Women's World Demands* described the world as governed by two forces: neoliberal capitalism and patriarchy, defined as the structural causes of poverty and forms of violence against women.

> We live in a world whose dominant economic system, neoliberal capitalism, is fundamentally inhuman. It is a system governed by unbridled competition that strives for privatization, liberalization, and deregulation. It is a system entirely driven by the dictates of the market and where full employment of basic human rights ranks below the laws of the marketplace. The result: the crushing social

exclusion of large segments of the population, threatening world peace and the future of the planet.

. . .

Neoliberalism and patriarchy feed off each other and reinforce each other in order to maintain the vast majority of women in a situation of cultural inferiority,
social devaluation, economic marginalization, "invisibility" of their existence
and labour, and the marketing and commercialization of their bodies. All these
situations closely resemble apartheid.

The World March of Women proposed concrete measures to combat poverty
and incidents of violence against women:

- Implementation of the Tobin Tax on speculative transactions
- An end to structural adjustment policies and to cutbacks in social
  budgets and public services
- Changes to global governance such as the democratization of the UN
  (including the Security Council), and the establishment of a World
  Council for Economic and Financial Security.

These demands were presented to World Bank president James Wolfensohn
on 15 October 2000.

Conclusions

In this chapter I have tried to show that women have been incorporated
into the global economy as a source of relatively cheap labor, and that the so-
cial-gender effects of economic globalization have been mixed. The simulta-
neous emergence and expansion of formal and informal employment among
women should be understood in terms of the cyclical processes and secular
trends in capitalist development and expansion, and the necessary unevenness of those processes. At a meso level of analysis, we can understand trends
in female employment and unemployment in terms of labor-market stratification, various management strategies to extract surplus-value or increase prof-
itability, and (during the 1980s and 1990s) the depressed status of unions. At
the macro level of analysis, the capitalist world-economy is maintained by
gendered labor, with definitions of skill, allocation of resources, occupational
distribution, and modes of remuneration shaped by asymmetrical gender relations. Moreover, gender ideologies define the roles and rights of men and

women and the relative value of their labor. But the effects of this incorporation have not been uniformly negative, for there have been unintended consequences of women's economic participation.

In separate writings, Susan Tiano and Seung-Kyung Kim provide detailed accounts of how women workers in the Mexican maquilas and in a South Korean free export zone, respectively, accommodate and resist the dominating forces of global capitalism and patriarchy. Others, such as Helen Safa, have shown that the entry of women into the labor force in such large numbers has important implications for changes in gender relations and ideologies within the household and the larger society, and for women's gender consciousness and activism.[91] The emergence of working-class consciousness and the labor movement during the nineteenth and early twentieth centuries is paralleled by the emergence of gender consciousness and the women's movement in the late twentieth century and into the new century.

Thus the era of globalization has produced at least two significant forms of women's mobilization. First, as we have seen, women workers have been joining trade unions, and unions themselves have become more attentive to women workers' issues and to issues identified as feminist. Second, feminists—in particular those organized in transnational feminist networks—have responded to globalization processes in vocal and visible ways. In national unions, international unions, and feminist organizations, women respond to the opportunities and the constraints of the globalization process, making demands on employers, states, and the international financial and trade institutions.

In the next chapter, we turn to an examination of women's movements and women's organizations, with a focus on some of the organizational features of transnational feminist networks.

CHAPTER FOUR

The Women's Movement and Its Organizations

Discourses, Structures, Resources

Contemporary women's movements and organizations constitute one of the most prodigious areas of feminist research in the disciplines of sociology and political science. Research covering Africa, Asia, Eastern and Western Europe, the Americas, the Middle East and North Africa, Russia, India, and elsewhere addresses such issues as organizational dynamics, discursive frames, relationship with the state, engagement with public policies, and the role of gender relations and cultural understandings. Feminist scholars also have analyzed the ways that women's movements and organizations contribute to democratization, to civil society, and to expanded concepts of rights.[1] Whether or not all women's organizations may be labeled "feminist," and what to call women's rights activists who eschew the label "feminist" but nonetheless advocate for women's rights and empowerment, is another area of inquiry.

Researchers have noted that in some countries women activists view feminism with skepticism or suspicion, as Western or bourgeois or excessively anti-male.[2] Nonetheless, the activities and concerns of such women activists appear feminist, at least in terms of the broad definition of feminist principles as described by Myra Marx Ferree and Beth Hess.[3] One scholar has therefore concluded that "de facto feminism" is an appropriate term for such women activists and organizations, while two others have defined feminist action as "that in which the participants explicitly place value on challenging gender hierarchy and changing women's social status, whether they adopt or reject the *feminist* label."[4] Self-identified feminists have various priority concerns, but the wider goals are women's empowerment, as well as legal changes and societal transformation.

Whether women's organizations are explicitly feminist or not, there has been a proliferation of women's organizations since the 1970s, when second-wave feminism was in full swing. Many studies have sought to explain the rise of the women's movement and of women's organizations in terms of sociodemographic changes such as growing female educational attainment and participation in the paid labor force, as well as in terms of the contours of political cultures and the influence of the international environment.[5] Sociologists have studied the women's movement as a type of social movement, and have reflected on those processes or changes that have led to a feminist consciousness, a movement, and established organizations.[6] Some have noted that in certain cases (for example, North America, Latin America, Palestine, Iran), feminism grew out of the tensions that women faced within existing social movements and organizations, such as communist, liberation, or student movements. In turn, participation in left-wing movements has provided feminists in some countries (e.g., United States, Palestine, Algeria, Iran) with organizational and mobilizing experience that has helped them to build and sustain their own movements and organizations.[7]

Disillusionment with male-dominated movements and organizations often has led women to form their own movements and organizations, frequently building on personal ties or political networks. This has been the case also in the labor movement, where, as we saw in chapter 3, women trade unionists have formed women's committees or even their own unions because of dissatisfaction with their position in male-dominated organizations. Feminist research in the sociology of organization has demonstrated that many organizations and bureaucracies exhibit a "gender bias" in that they possess masculine styles of management and authority, a division of labor and occupational hierarchy in which men are dominant, and advantages that accrue to men but not necessarily to women. Organizations are "gendered" in that they reflect and perpetuate asymmetrical power relations between men and women in society as well as notions of masculinity and femininity.[8] Feminist organizations have therefore emerged to challenge masculine bias in organizations as well as in the society at large.

Types of Feminist Organizing

Feminist sociologists have found that the structure and types of contemporary feminist groups vary—some are more formally organized, or bureaucratized, than others.[9] Ferree and Martin point out that most women's movements have a loose organizational framework and are characterized by lack of formalized institutional bases of power. This is true not only of the women's movement but of other social movements as well. Using examples from the environmental movement, Luther Gerlach has argued that social movements are "segmentary, polycentric, and reticulate." Social movements have many, sometimes competing organizations and groups (segmentary); they have multiple and sometimes competing leaders (polycentric); and they are loose networks that link to each other (reticulate). Despite the segmentation, there is a shared opposition and ideology across the movement and its diverse organizations. Gerlach maintained that the SPR nature of social movement organizations (SMOs) is very effective, allowing them to be flexible and adaptive and to resonate with larger constituencies through different tactics (e.g., direct action versus lobbying and legal strategies). It also "promotes striving, innovation, and entrepreneurial experimentation in generating and implementing sociocultural change."[10]

By contrast, Suzanne Staggenborg has argued that structurelessness is a disadvantage, and that professionalization and formalization assist the realization of goals. In her study of thirteen SMOs in the pro-choice movement in the United States, she mapped changes in their leadership and internal structures and the impact of these changes on the movement through three periods. She made a distinction between professional (paid) and nonprofessional (voluntary) leaders and staff. Both can be *entrepreneurs* (that is, initiating and building a movement or organization), but usually the real "risk-takers" are the nonprofessional leaders. Professionals often go from one SMO to another, taking their skills with them and making a career out of service to SMOs. "Entrepreneurs" are usually founders, whose leadership style might offend others at some point.[11] Staggenborg also distinguished between a formalized SMO and an informal one.[12] She found that the consequences of professionalization included fiscal stability and organizational maintenance—but also a decline in militant direct action in favor of engagement with the political arena and more coalition work. Staggenborg called this the "institutionalization of collective action."[13]

Decisions about organizational structure, strategies, tactics, and resources to be mobilized certainly shape or determine the course and outcome of the social movement organization. These decisions may be a matter of politics or principle, but they may also be a function of constraints. For example, some women's organizations may deliberately avoid external funding (e.g., the Indian women's magazine *Manushi*) or paid positions (some feminist groups in North Africa) in order to avoid possible cooptation or bureaucratization. On the other hand, as Jo Freeman has argued, movement organizations are not free to choose any strategy. The factors that affect strategic choices or options are the nature of available resources, constraints on the use of those resources, the type of social movement organization, and expectations about potential targets.[14] Cultural understandings, state controls, or unavailability of resources could themselves shape the decision to avoid external funding or paid positions on the part of some movement organizations or transnational feminist networks.

The types of organizations analyzed in this book are feminist networks. Why are feminists building networks? It should be noted that networks seem to be the preferred form of organizing, as Keck and Sikkink showed in their study of transnational advocacy networks. At the same time, extensive sociological research on social networks over the past two decades has demonstrated the importance of networks in diverse facets of social life, including social support, employment, and power and influence in organizations, communities, and nations. Indeed, network ties frequently have been described as social resources that offer valuable support, acquaintances, and information. As Manuel Castells argues, the advantages of networks are flexibility and adaptability, which are especially conducive to conditions of rapid change, such as the current era of globalization. In the past, networks were weak at "mobilizing resources and focusing those resources on the execution of a given task"—functions that large, centralized apparatuses were able to perform more optimally. This has changed, he continues, with the development of new information/communication technologies, epitomized by the Internet.[15] Networks now create "transnational social spaces," or linkages among political actors across borders.[16]

The network form of feminist organizing, which is exemplified by the TFNs examined in this book, suggests a form of organization that may be more conductive to feminist goals of democratic, inclusive, participatory, decentralized, and nonhierarchical structures and processes. The network form also may be more conducive to transnational feminist organizing and mobilizing, and indeed may reflect the opportunities and challenges feminists face in an increasingly globalized world.

Research on women's movements and organizations, therefore, as well as research on social movements in general, has yielded insights that are relevant to understanding the emergence and features of transnational feminist networks. They include the following observations:

- Women's organizations reflect women's collective consciousness, identity, experiences, and aspirations.
- Some feminist movements and their organizations have grown out of left-wing organizations, national liberation movements, labor movements, and other struggles.
- When women form organizations, they may build on preexisting organizations and networks of women.
- Women's organizations may join coalitions with unions, political parties, religious institutions, and other civil society organizations or advocacy networks.
- Women's organizations face issues of centralization, decentralization, institutionalization, professionalization, and charismatic leadership.
- Women's organizations may face challenges such as state repression and resource constraints.
- Networks may or may not be more effective than formal organizations.

From International to Transnational

International feminism—and feminist internationalism—has existed since at least the early twentieth century, but forms of women's organizing and mobilizing have varied over the past hundred years. The TFNs that emerged in the late twentieth century and engage with intergovernmental organizations and public policy issues have distinctive features, but they are not the first such organizations to have existed. First-wave feminism, for example, brought about international women's organizations around abolition, women's suffrage, trafficking in women, antimilitarism, and labor legislation for working women and mothers. Examples of early international women's organizations are the Women's International League for Peace and Freedom (WILPF), the International Council of Women (ICW), the International Alliance of Women (IAW), the Women's International Democratic Federation (WIDF), and the Young Women's Christian Association (YWCA). In promoting women's rights, they engaged with intergovernmental bodies such as the League of Nations and the International Labor Organization.[17] Some women's organizations worked at the regional level to achieve women's rights. In 1933, the Pan American Conference in Montevideo adopted the Convention on the Nationality of Women and the Treaty on the Equality of Rights between Men and Women. According to Berkovitch, "these were the first two official international conventions that explicitly set sexual equality as a principle to be incorporated into national legislation. These documents indeed remained unique during the whole interwar period."[18]

The early twentieth century also saw the emergence of an international socialist women's movement. Within the Second International, the women's organizations of France, Germany, and Russia mobilized thousands of working-class as well as middle-class women for socialism and women's emancipation.[19] In Asian countries, as Kumari Jayawardena showed, many of the women's movements and organizations that emerged were associated with socialist or nationalist movements.[20]

But nationalisms and nation-state projects compromised the international movements and led to their dissolution. The Second International was split when World War I broke out and the leaderships of many unions and social democratic parties sided with their respective ruling classes and regimes. World War I and red-baiting divided the feminist movement in Great Britain as well as the international workers movement. It should be noted that *international* is not the same as *transnational*, which suggests a conscious crossing of national boundaries and a superseding of nationalist orientations. Of the early international women's organizations, only WILPF was able to sustain a transnational character, though its pacific stance meant political isolation.[21]

And what of the internal structure of women's organizations in the earlier period? Stienstra's description of international women's organizations such as the International Alliance of Women (IAW), the Women's International

Democratic Federation (WIDF), and the International Federation of Business and Professional Women (IFBPW) is instructive:

> Many of the established groups retained a very bureaucratic and hierarchical organizational structure, with local chapters, national bodies and an international federation. The impetus for action at the international level came from international meetings every three, four or five years, which gave policy direction. . . . What this created was an elite of increasingly elderly, married, middle- or upper-class women who represented their organizations at the international level and provided direction to NGO activities around women in the United Nations. When combined with the vague mandates, these organizations remained unable to provide the vitality and feminist direction that was needed at the international level.[22]

As we shall see presently, contemporary TFNs are rather different from the earlier women's groups in terms of their organizational features. TFNs and the earlier international women's organizations also differ in their sources of funding. With respect to funding, Stienstra explains that "the established groups also remained constrained at the international level by the sources of their funding. For most, the funding they received came from their members, who were disproportionately located in the North and especially in North America and Europe. The Women's International Democratic Federation, in contrast, received much of its support from individuals and governments in Eastern Europe as well as from socialist movements in the South."[23]

Transnational feminist networks remain constrained by the sources and levels of their funding, but in different ways. They are not, for the most part, mass organizations with dues-paying members. In some cases it is difficult or costly to collect and convert dues in different currencies. And inasmuch as they receive external funding from individuals, governments, and foundations in Western Europe and North America, these sources have led to questions of legitimacy and sustainability.

As briefly mentioned in chapter 1, second-wave feminism began in the 1960s, and, like many other social movements, it was initially nationally based and nationally oriented. In the previous decades, political and economic developments—such as the Great Depression, World War II, and the rise of Keynesian welfare economics in the postwar period—had led movements and intellectuals to focus more on the problems of their own societies, economies, and states. In Africa and Asia, postcolonial projects were focused on nation-building and state-building, and in Latin America and the Middle East, strategies for national development (such as import-substitution industrialization) were being implemented. The social movements of the 1960s—including the student movements of Europe, the United States, Mexico, and Iran—were similarly focused largely on the contradictions of their own societies. This was also true of second-wave feminism in the 1960s and 1970s.

During the UN Decade for Women (1976–85), and in the context of various UN-sponsored women's conferences, clashes occurred among nationally or regionally framed feminisms, mainly due to disagreements between Western feminists, who emphasized women's need for legal equality and for sexual autonomy, and Third World feminists, who emphasized imperialism and underdevelopment as obstacles to women's advancement. The Cold War and the increasing popularity of the Palestine movement for national liberation influenced the perspectives of women activists around the world and precluded unity. Disagreements were especially noticeable at the 1980 conference in Copenhagen, where a condemnation of Zionism led the United States, Israel, New Zealand, and Canada to vote against the Program of Action.[24] In addition to political and ideological differences among women delegates and participants, a characteristic of the early years of the Decade was that delegations often were made up of men rather than women. These problems were summed up in an analysis of the Decade by the late Arvonne Fraser, who is here describing the 1975 Mexico City conference:

> Some Western feminists thought there was too much focus on women and children and not enough on women's oppression and lack of equality. Developing country women emphasized that in the transition from traditional to modern societies, women and children were often left behind. . . . The bickering and political rhetoric was, at times, intense. Latin American women disrupted several sessions by vehemently insisting that equality for women was attainable only after economic and social changes had been made. A group of critical American women led a charge on the U.S. Embassy and another group interrupted AID director Daniel Parker's speech, claiming men had no right to represent U.S. women at the Tribune [the NGO forum] or the conference."[25]

During preparations for the 1985 Nairobi conference, the third UN world conference on women, women's groups began to bridge the previous regional and ideological divides, and there emerged a women's organization of a new type. What was the new context in which this shift took place? We can identify the following major influences:

- Demographic changes and the growth of a "critical mass" of educated, employed, mobile, and politically conscious women around the world.
- Economic crisis, structural adjustment, Reaganism, Thatcherism, the decline of the welfare state, feminization of poverty, and Islamic fundamentalism.
- The UN Decade for Women (1976–85), the WID/GAD paradigm, and the spread of feminist ideology in the developing world.

In the 1970s, as second-wave feminism was developing and expanding internationally, a new economic, political, and demographic context was also taking shape. As we saw in chapters 2 and 3, this new context included the internationalization of capital and global assembly line production; the growing industrial reliance on female labor; and changes in the social and economic functions of the state. Changes in the characteristics of the world's women included a worldwide increase in the population of educated and employed women with grievances and an emergent sense of collective identity. Female sociodemographics in the 1970s and 1980s are salient to our understanding of the emergence of new and expanded forms of women's mobilization. Fertility control freed women's time for civic engagement; educational attainment heightened their awareness, aspirations, and expectations; and employment opportunities provided both working-class and middle-class women with the ability to network and mobilize in unions and professional associations, as well as in feminist groups. In the Third World, sections of the female population joined political parties and took part in left-wing movements. Some of these women became disillusioned with the largely male leaderships and developed a feminist political consciousness and set of objectives. The women who formed or joined TFNs in the mid-1980s and early 1990s fit this profile; they were middle-class, educated, employed, politically active, and mobile.

Political opportunities helped the women's movement, too. In the 1980s, the perception that women's movements did not threaten the operations of capital or the state provided an environment conducive to the growth of the social movement of women internationally.[26] For example, the 1980 military coup in Turkey prohibited left-wing, union, and Islamist forms of organization and mobilization, but feminist groups formed during this period and later became a public presence with their purple needle campaigns against street harassment, the establishment of women's libraries and battered women's shelters, their calls for the modernization of the civil code, and their public stances against Islamization and for democratization. A similar process occurred in Latin America, again in the context of authoritarianism, where the "Encuentros" were initiated by left-feminists. Seven of these region-wide meetings took place between 1981 and 1996, and were an important part of the process of democratization in the region, as Jaquette and others have noted. Mujer a Mujer, a feminist collective of women from Canada, the United States, the Caribbean, and Mexico, and based in Mexico City, was formed in 1984 as an international solidarity project for women workers. In the 1990s it came to deal with NAFTA, among other issues.

As the global economy shifted from a statist to a free-market model and the welfarist and developmentalist state came under attack by the new ideologues of neoliberal capitalism in the early 1980s, feminists in developing and developed countries alike grew alarmed. Meanwhile, the growth of Islamic fundamentalist movements and the willingness of governments in predominantly Muslim states to acquiesce to Islamist political pressure by revising family codes to make them conform to Islamic law led to growing concern on the part of many women activists in those countries. The parallel processes of Islamic fundamentalism, communalism, and similar forms of identity politics in the South, along with Reaganism and Thatcherism and the post-Keynesian shift in the North, led to a convergence of sorts and a shared vocabulary between women activists in developed and developing countries. For feminists in the South, issues of sexuality and personal autonomy assumed importance, while feminists in the North began to recognize the salience of economic factors and forces in their lives.

At the same time, women researchers in developing countries who had been part of the research paradigms known as women-in-development (WID) or women-and-development (WAD) began to develop a more explicit feminist understanding and critique. Bunch and Carillo have discussed how feminist thought was embraced by a number of key Third World women activists and scholars who were involved in development issues. In 1984, Marie-Angélique Savané of Senegal, a founder of the Association of African Women for Research and Development (AAWORD), wrote that a convergence of views from the North and the South was possible: "In the final analysis, the oppression of women is a universal phenomenon. From this standpoint thus, it is possible not only to introduce feminism into the development process but even more critical to render development more feminist. It is clear that the subordination of women emerges out of a dialectical relationship between culture, the economy, and politics. Because of this fundamental reality we cannot separate feminism from development or vice versa." Peggy Antrobus, a political scientist from Jamaica (who later worked in Barbados) and a founder of DAWN, argued in 1987: "Feminism offers the only politics which can transform our world into a more human place and deal with global issues like equality, development, and peace, because it asks the right questions: about power, about the links between the personal and the political; and because it cuts through race and class. Feminism implies consciousness of all the sources of oppression: race, class, gender, homophobia, and it resists them all. Feminism is a call for action."[27]

Thus the global economic environment gave rise to a new consciousness, influenced the formation of new women's organizations, and inspired a new form of women's organizing and mobilizing. As Lucille Mathurin Mair noted, the "multiple socio-economic crises" of the 1980s led to the emergence of women's networks that opened up "partnerships of elite and grassroots women" and "participatory, non-authoritarian structures in which women worked best."[28] An example is the formation of DAWN. The DAWN manifesto points out that, at its inception, the network adopted feminism and poor women as its political points of departure, and thus analyzed gender and class in the development experience. At meetings, network participants discussed women's potential for solving such structural crises as the food-water-fuel crisis, the balance of payments and debt crises, militarization and violence, and a cultural crisis, and alternative visions and strategies were proposed. Women participants came to realize that all issues were women's issues.

Self-empowerment through Organizations

The result of this feminine standpoint—the vantage point or perspective of activists working within the fields of women and development and encountering global economic forces and conservative political forces—was the emergence of a new collective identity of global feminism. The idea that the world's women could contribute something different—a distinctive critique of states, policies, and international institutions and an alternative vision for the home, the country, and the world—was the guiding light behind the formation of TFNs. To get their message across, influence policy, and empower themselves, women needed new forms of organization and mobilization: "Self-empowerment of women through organizations was regarded as crucial for transforming societies into a world women want. It was argued that women should not depend on government but develop autonomously through self-organization."[29]

In the 1980s, therefore, the economic context of crisis and austerity, the political context of right-wing movements, and the sociodemographic context of a worldwide growth in the population of educated, employed, mobile, and politically aware women led to feminist discourses and networking that took on not only an international but a transnational form. TFNs eschewed nationalisms in favor of solidarity beyond borders, while also demonstrating what I have termed a "critical realist" approach to the state.

In this regard, women's organizations were assisted in important ways by the United Nations, which facilitated interaction and cooperation among feminist organizations. As noted previously, key events were the various world conferences, including the world conferences on women, as well as numerous regional preparatory meetings. The four world conferences on women between 1975 and 1995 were perhaps the most important form of UN-assisted networking, as many authors have noted. Zinsser cites the Senegalese feminist writer Fatou Sow to the effect that the Decade gave them "le droit à la parole"—the right to speak out, as well as the right to be heard.[30] Equally important were the women's caucuses that formed in connection with major UN conferences of the 1990s, especially UNCED, the Human Rights Conference, the ICPD, and the Social Summit.[31] The result of these meetings and caucuses was the expansion of global feminism and of transnational feminist networks.

The convergence of socioeconomic and political processes as they affected women and women's growing collective identity and mobilization is underscored in the 1987 book that became the DAWN manifesto: "We know now from our own research that the subordination of women has a long history and is deeply ingrained in economic, political, and cultural processes. What we have managed to do in the last few years is to forge grassroots women's movements and world-wide networks such as never existed before, to begin to transform that subordination and in the process to break down other oppressive structures as well."[32] Some years later, the feminist network WIDE commented on the growing political power of women and the importance of their perspectives:

> In the decade since 1985, women have moved a long way in terms of the agenda we are taking on. We have recognized that while pursuing women's rights, we must also take on the context: the political, economic, and social structures. Women are taking the lead and making a huge contribution to defining the international agenda in terms of human rights, macroeconomics, conflict/peace, and sustainable development. We have a valuable and unique perspective on these issues as women and as human beings. We recognize that feminism in one country is not sustainable—we need feminism on a global scale.[33]

The shift in feminist thought and collective action is further highlighted by three scholar-activists in the Netherlands: "The women's movement initially focused on the micro level of the family and everyday life. By contrast, the second phase addressed the macro level, focusing on women's participation in the political community and issues of inclusion and exclusion. This shift . . . can be observed more generally in the global feminist movement."[34]

The 1990s saw an increasing numbers of feminist networks engaged in research, advocacy, lobbying, and cross-border solidarity, including the six case-study TFNs examined in the next three chapters. Most were present at the UN conferences on women and they formed the Women's Caucus at the UN conferences of the 1990s. But it was in the process leading up to the 1995 Beijing conference and NGO Forum where they played a substantive and significant role in influencing both the process and the policy documents that emerged from preparatory activities and conferences. The strategies employed by women's organizations had been tested in the earlier UN conferences, including drafting new and alternative language for documents, educating participants about how to influence government positions, and lobbying government delegates directly. The use of electronic communications contributed to the effectiveness of efforts to influence the policy process. Women around the world downloaded the UN documents and circulated their critiques and alternative paragraphs. TFNs were present at both the official, intergovernmental conference and the NGO forum, and their representatives actively lobbied sympathetic delegates (mainly from European countries). The president of WIDE also addressed the delegates during the General Exchange of Views. DAWN, WIDE, and WEDO had a number of briefing papers on display and available to delegates.

The communications revolution facilitated the formation and especially the activities of transnational feminist networks. As one scholar has observed, "Women's organizations worldwide are actively using electronic communications to network, to organize and to influence policy agendas on issues of concern to women and to the world. Each day more women's organizations are joining a growing 'virtual sisterhood' that is breaking barriers, building new networks and shifting power."[35] The IWTC was among the first to extend outreach for its GlobalNet alerts to more than eighty thousand organizations and individuals via electronic mailing lists and the Internet. The Internet has not replaced the telephone, the fax, the post, or the annual conference, but it has become the preferred and certainly most efficient mode of communication and dissemination. Its potential to create new spaces for women working within very different cultural environments to access knowledge and to transform it and to network across political borders has been explored in a number of studies.[36] As Lourdes Arizpe notes, "cyberspace will greatly accelerate our capacity to create and build."[37] TFNs now have websites, ListServs, and e-mail alerts, and this allows rapid communications with members and between networks. The websites are especially sophisticated, with newsletters and policy briefs posted on them, sometimes in PDF format.

Collective Identities and Feminist Alliances

Social movement theory has addressed the issue of the formation of collective identities, and the foregoing discussion suggests that transnational feminist identity emerged from the convergence of economic and political developments in the 1980s, as well as from the opportunities afforded by the UN conferences of the 1990s. Feminists in TFNs certainly see themselves as part of the global women's movement, but they also have national and regional identities, and they often direct their feminist advocacy work to their countries and regions. DAWN feminists stress their identity as spokeswomen from the Third World and make demands on their governments as well as on the IFIs and the WTO. WIDE members see themselves as European feminists with a responsibility to ensure that their governments devise development policies that ensure the well-being of women in Third World countries. The U.S.-based activists associated with WEDO similarly see themselves as part of a global women's movement. According to Nadia Johnson, "We're definitely part of the global movement for economic justice for women. And we are working to identify it as a movement rather than a network. A network focuses mainly on information-sharing around key events. But a movement entails growth in numbers, mobilization and recruitment, with various types of activism, and strategies of coordinating them. It entails common identity and goals, both locally and globally. When women strike in a maquiladora, for example, how does that impact us? We see ourselves as part of the movement. So we work at all levels."[38]

A collective identity ensures alliances and cooperation across networks and organizations within the movement. TFNs frequently cooperate with each other on specific campaigns as well as on longer-term strategies. For example, the 1994 International Conference on Population and Development and the 1995 Beijing conference saw close cooperation among DAWN, WIDE, WEDO, ARROW, HERA (Health, Empowerment, Rights, and Accountability, based in New York), and Catholics for a Free Choice (based in Washington, D.C.) on reproductive rights issues. In addition, DAWN, WIDE, and Alt-WID (Alternative Women in Development) produced a paper on alternative economics for the 1995 Beijing conference. A "women and trade" strategic planning meeting, held in December 1999 in Grenada, was coordinated by DAWN and attended by representatives of the Center of Concern (a Washington, D.C.-based progressive Catholic organization) and ALT-WID. This meeting led to the formation of the Women and Trade Network.

The Women's Alliance for Economic Alternatives was created in order to start a dialogue between women from the North and South about new ideas on alternative economics. Other members were WIDE, Alt-WID, the Center for Women's Global Leadership, Third World Researchers and Activists, NAC (National Action Committee on the Status of Women), WEDO, and SID/WID (the Women in Development program of the Society for International Development).[39] At the March 1995 Social Summit, DAWN and WIDE helped to draft the Copenhagen Alternative Declaration. This document was signed by over six hundred NGOs and "supported for its wide-ranging criticisms of a neo-capitalist system that favors giant corporations and gender inequalities."[40] In another collaborative effort, a WIDE bulletin included several articles written by DAWN members and presenting their ideas about social development. In their article "DAWN's Challenge to the WSSD," the network argued that the eradication of poverty and unemployment could not be addressed without "a fundamental shift in the thinking and direction of the global political economy and its management."[41]

DAWN and the Asian Pacific Development Center's Gender and Development Program (APDC-GAD) conducted a women's roundtable discussion entitled "The Economic, Social, and Political Impacts of the South East Asian Financial Crisis" on April 12–14, 1998, in the Philippines. Thirty women representing nineteen groups participated "to understand the workings of patriarchal and classist economics and politics behind the financial crisis and to gain a general overview of how the crisis . . . is impacting South East Asian women."[42] The deliberations of the roundtable illustrated their nonnationalist and even antinationalist perspective on the 1998 Asian financial crisis:

> The participants of the roundtable discussion see the current financial crisis as the dramatic and devastating result of the convergence of problems and forces associated with the "older" issue of global debt management and those generated by the more recent fast-track liberalization of accounts carried out by South East Asian stators in hope of coming out as "winners" in this period of global economic competition. While it was true that speculative attacks by foreign finance did occur this was not the sole cause of the crisis, as some patriarchal-nationalist Asian leaders and economists allude to . . . . Women in the region are impacted by this approach to the management of the monetary crisis in three significant ways. The first is that women are bearing the burden of the combined effects of inflation, recession and cost-cutting measures in the public sector. Increased prices of basic commodities, high interest credit, loss of jobs for men and women, and privatization of social services and utilities mean that poor families are surviving in difficult conditions. All these impact directly on South East Asian women who are the household managers for food, health and daily survival.[43]

In November 1998, DAWN and HERA organized back-to-back meetings in Mexico. Participants expressed their concern at the lack of progress in a number of key areas to secure women's sexual and reproductive rights and health. They issued a "Call to Action" for those with a mandate from Cairo to fulfill their obligations, commit resources, and make women's empowerment and gender equity and equality the principal agenda for the next millennium.[44]

Organizational Features of TFNs

The DAWN manifesto pointed out that in order for organizations to be strong and effective, they must have "resources (finance, knowledge, technology), skills training, and leadership formation on the one side; and democratic processes, dialogue, participation in policy and decision-making, and techniques for conflict resolution on the other."[45] Women's organizations therefore pushed international development agencies—and UN agencies—to allocate funds to support and promote women's organizations.

The issue of external funding for nongovernmental organizations, including feminist organizations, has been a controversial one. Some have argued that many nongovernmental organizations are donor driven, in that funds from donors and their expectations determine the kinds of activities that NGOs carry out.[46] Issues of transparency, accountability, and representation also have been discussed in the literature on nongovernmental organizations. What is more, women's groups operating in Muslim countries that have accepted external funding for their activities have been accused, mainly by Islamist organizations, of being tools of Western cultural imperialism. (That Islamist organizations have been funded by Saudi Arabia, Iran, or Kuwait—which have their own agendas in supporting such groups—seems not to have dented their self-righteousness.) For this and other reasons, some feminist organizations work on a voluntary basis only. However, many women's organizations in developing countries, including those affiliated with transnational feminist networks, continue to seek funding from the European donors for two simple reasons. One is that domestic sources of funding are not readily available; many developing countries do not have the kinds of foundations, grant-giving bodies, or government allocations that would provide women's organizations with operating budgets. Another reason is that authoritarian governments in the global South tend to be rather controlling of nongovernmental organizations and their activities—as demonstrated by the closing down of Egyptian feminist Nawal Saadawi's Arab Women's Solidarity Association (ASWA) in 1991 and the prosecution in Egypt of Professor Saad eddin Ibrahim in 2001–2.[47] Understandably, many women's organizations prefer to remain independent of government control. The result, as one feminist leader has noted, is that "Most of the funding for women's groups comes from international sources. Otherwise, they become dependent on their governments."[48]

As we saw earlier in this chapter, research on social movement organizations has found that some SMOs have a full-time paid leadership, various types of resources to support their activities, and a small or symbolic membership base. Professionalized SMOs tend to choose more mainstream political tactics such as lobbying and special projects. Other SMOs, however, are more informal, do not tend to work through political institutions, and use noninstitutional forms of protest.[49] Stienstra writes that "since the 1970s, international women's movements have used less formal structures, especially networks, as their primary method of organizing."[50] However, the TFNs examined in this book include both formal and informal networks, and professionalized and fluid types of organizations. WIDE and WEDO, for example, are more professionalized than are DAWN and the AWMR. WIDE was, in fact, veering toward a more centralized type of organization in the mid-1990s. As one staff member in the Brussels office remarked, "I always felt that we were too active, more so than the national platforms. The office was too professionalized, too productive, too centralized. Now, the platforms are reactivated. In the past, the flow was from the coordinating office [in Brussels] to the national platforms [in twelve European countries]. Now there is more input from them."[51]

Women's organizations in general, and transnational feminist networks in particular, conform to many of the conventions regarding formal organizations, but seem to avoid hierarchy and bureaucracy. One reason is size; TFNs tend to be relatively small, with a looser and more fluid constituency. DAWN, for example, "counts on the participation of 4,500 women throughout the Third World," according to one of its publications. WLUML links "over two thousand women in several continents," according to Farida Shaheed, a network leader based in Lahore, Pakistan. These are not mass-based organizations; their constituencies are in fact dispersed and far-flung. Another reason is political; as mentioned above, many feminist organizations formed in protest against what they viewed as male-dominated, centralized, or hierarchical movements and organizations. The desire to avoid excesses of power and relations of domination and subordination therefore led to innovative ways of sharing responsibility. "Feminist process"—participatory, democratic, inclusive, with emphasis placed on standpoint and personal experience as well as on knowledge and credentials—has been characteristic of many women's organizations.

Feminist networks function to a great extent as a result of the emotional and political commitment of their members and especially their leadership, who invariably volunteer a considerable amount of their time. Much of the work carried out within women's organizations has been a "labor of love," with free labor-time and personal resources expended toward various tasks. In some cases, women activists prefer such an arrangement to a more formalized structure, including salaries for themselves.[52] In other cases, the vagaries of external funding force cutbacks in staff size and increased labor by leading members. In separate interviews, Bénédicte Allaert of WIDE and Mahnaz Afkhami of the WLP (Women's Learning Partnership for Peace, Development, and Rights) and formerly of SIGI emphasized the difficulties in securing an adequate fiscal base and noted a trend toward less generosity on the part of external funders. "It's extremely difficult for women's organizations to find institutional and financial support, especially on development issues," according to Allaert. For this reason, the non-paid officers, such as the president and past president, "have devoted a lot of time."[53]

The formation of DAWN and preparation of its classic text *Development, Crises, and Alternative Visions* exemplifies "feminist process." The book was written through "extensive debate and discussion with researchers, activists, and policy makers." It was felt that by adopting an open and flexible process— one that drew on varied experiences—the group would be better able to come to a common perspective and objective. As the book's preamble states, "If we ourselves can evolve new working styles, new forms of co-operative organization and practices, this will contribute to the search for genuine alternatives. To build a social order that is just, equitable, and life-affirming for all people, our methods must correspondingly be open and respectful of differences, and must try to break down hierarchies, power, and distrust."[54] Another example comes from WLUML, which calls itself a network of women's groups "with their own national priorities."[55] There is no formal membership, for involvement is informal. A plan of action guides work for a period of about five years. As Hélie-Lucas said: "The Plan of Action is a political document, and specific projects are drawn from it. We come together for the Plans of Action, where we discuss new developments and new priorities."[56]

A drawback to such nonprofessionalized organizations, however, is a tendency toward overwork on the part of a core of members, sometimes leading to "burn-out" and separation from the group. Another potentially negative outcome is the reproduction of the core group who can then become a kind of political elite, or the emergence of a charismatic leader who may abuse power or encounter resentment. Lack of transparency and accountability in financial matters and in decision-making also could result in problems of legitimacy. Unclear authority demarcation and defined responsibilities, along with work overload on the part of some members, could lead to conflict and dissent. This is true, of course, not only of feminist organizations but also of many voluntary organizations or political groups that have little funding and depend heavily on the commitment of a core group of members.[57]

Most TFNs have avoided these problems. In a sense, they are required to, inasmuch as they receive most of their funding not from members' dues but from external sources such as international development agencies and the large foundations based in Europe and North America. They are required to describe their organizational structure, objectives, methods of decision-making, and the results of past efforts. They must include copies of mission statements, action plans, newsletters, joint declarations, and other products. It is true that during the 1990s international donors—European development agencies such as Sweden's SIDA, the Dutch NOVIB, Denmark's DANIDA, Canada's CIDA and IDRC, as well as the Ford, MacArthur, and Rockefeller Foundations and European foundations such as Heinrich Boll and Friedrich Ebert, both of Germany—tended to favor women's organizations and especially the TFNs as a result of a mandate to promote civil society, global civil society, women's participation, and gender equality. But it is also true that they have required their potential grantees to prepare comprehensive proposals in order to receive funding. Mahnaz Afkhami, who led SIGI in the latter part of the 1990s and subsequently formed the Women's Learning Partnership, has pointed out that neither fundraising nor proposal writing has been easy: "As painful as all this grant-writing is, however, it is useful. It helps you clarify your vision, sharpen what it is you want, defend your mission. It is a rigorous and good exercise. It keeps you open and honest."[58]

Notwithstanding the general similarities, there are differences across the TFNs in terms of organizational structure and dynamics. Some have a formal structure, with offices and paid staff; some also conduct annual meetings and hold regular elections. Others have a formal structure, including officers and a board of directors, but no office space or paid staff. Yet others have some paid positions but no board, and meet periodically to work out an action plan. At least two TFNs examined in this book have rotating secretariats. SIGI moved from New York to Bethesda and then to Montreal, each time with a new executive board and president. DAWN moved from India to Brazil to Barbados and then to Fiji, each time with a new general coordinator. WIDE's central office is in Brussels, where much of the lobbying work is done, but it also has a decentralized structure with a rotating presidency (the first from Ireland, the second from Spain, the third from Austria), and strong grassroots and academic links. As Brigitte Holzner, WIDE president, put it: "I feel that our structure is our strength."[59]

It should be noted that despite their nonhierarchical nature, many feminist organizations have strong and sometimes charismatic leaders. Strong leadership can be especially important in getting an organization started. Almost all the TFNs examined in this book are identified with key leaders or founders, although there is no evidence of any abuse of power or resentment of their highly visible leaders. Gita Sen of DAWN, the late Bella Abzug of WEDO, Marieme Hélie-Lucas of WLUML, and Mahnaz Afkhami of SIGI and now of WLP are long-standing leaders and "entrepreneurs" in the women's movement who founded the transnational networks in which they have been involved. AWMR was founded by the daughter of the former socialist prime minister of Malta; she drew on her personal and political ties with women in left-wing organizations and political parties throughout the Mediterranean region to form a network of women devoted to demilitarization, peace, and social justice.

More than any other TFN, WEDO was heavily invested in its founder/director, the charismatic Bella Abzug, whose vision, personality, and contacts defined the organization. A larger-than-life individual with great international appeal, Bella Abzug may have overshadowed and overdefined the organization. Certainly WEDO's work in the 1990s was very much influenced by her radical-feminist and eco-feminist views. Charismatic leadership has its advantages and its drawbacks. After Abzug's death, WEDO seemed to flounder for a while. It lost direction in its agenda and its newsletters reflected that. Soon, however, WEDO found its way again and resumed its activities in a very structured and determined manner.

Having "friends in high places" or supporters in intergovernmental organizations and foundations can extend the global reach, efficacy, or influence of a TFN. Feminist networks can count on "connections" as well as their own reputations to make interventions on policy issues and thus realize their objectives of providing feminist alternatives. For example, DAWN has a strong supporter in Noeleen Heyzer, a founding member who went on to lead UNIFEM, the largest and best-endowed UN women's agency. For its part, UNIFEM (United Nations Development Fund for Women) may be regarded as a "movement agency," inasmuch as it provides funding and a platform for representatives of DAWN, as well as WEDO, WIDE, and nationally based women's organizations. UNIFEM commissioned many background papers from DAWN, WIDE, and WEDO in connection with preparations for the UN's International Conference on Financing for Development, which took place in Monterrey, Mexico, in March 2002.

Still, despite a degree of professionalization and the presence of well-known leaders, none of the TFNs discussed here displays any bureaucratization or centralization in decision-making. Marilee Karl, one of the founders of ISIS, wrote that the new feminist networks rejected bureaucratic forms of organization "in favor of informal, nonhierarchical and open structures and ways of operating." This alternative structure, she wrote, "gives networks a flexibility" and a capacity to respond and take action quickly.[60] Within the AWMR the preferred method of decision-making is consensus of the members, but sometimes votes are taken and a resolution is passed by a simple majority. WLUML prides itself in having "a fluid structure and rejection of hierarchies."[61] Hélie-Lucas herself emphasizes the decentralized, participatory, nonbureaucratic and nonhierarchical nature of the network: "The funders put pressure on us—get professionalized, become managers. We've had visits from NOVIB people [the Dutch international development agency] telling us to be more management-oriented, professional. We resist it. You need people with good spirit and vision. Good typists and accountants you can always find."[62]

An example of WLUML's decentralized and democratic nature is that despite Hélie-Lucas's prominence, she tried for ten years to secure a project on fundamentalist militarization in the network's plan of action. Her idea was finally approved for the Dhaka 1997 action plan. As she explained, the projects and priorities are determined by different regional groups, though the plan of action is decided upon collectively. "We reinforce local struggles, not divert from local struggles. This is the whole point about our network," said Hélie-Lucas. "The network itself is as fluid as you can imagine, but for each project we have a pyramidic structure." She also emphasized the informality, dedication, and passion that permeate the network. "There is a real solidarity among us," she said. "At the August 1999 meeting in New York we had about forty people. We went around the room describing what we were doing. It was so inspiring."[63]

Since its inception, WLUML has operated as a network rather than as an organization or professional association. It began as a one-woman coordination office in Montpelier, France, and then progressed to a small group assuming responsibility for implementation of the plans of action. In the second half of the 1990s, stimulated by successive collective projects, the network developed a more complex and diversified system for decision-making and implementation of network activities.[64] The "core group" consisted of seven persons in charge of international coordination, bookkeeping, and maintaining the overall direction of the network. Three coordination offices—in Grabels, France, in Lagos, Nigeria, and in Lahore, Pakistan—shared information and analyses, issued action alerts, and carried out collective projects.[65] The "coordination group" is a flexible group of active "networkers" assuming responsibility for specific projects. The coordination group (which includes all members of the core group) developed into the most important body for programming, planning, and implementation for the network as a whole. For example, the regional coordinators planned and directed the project on women in Islamic law. In 2000, a series of committees were formed "to involve a larger number of active networkers in the coordination and implementation of specific activities," such as publications and finance.[66]

DAWN's structure is similarly loose, and the various regions that make up the networks set their own priorities. DAWN's steering committee consists of the past and present general coordinators, as well as four research coordinators and seven regional coordinators. Four DAWN founding members are also listed. The newsletter editorial group, which plays an important part in information dissemination, is part of the secretariat. Regional coordinators are based in the Caribbean, Latin America, Africa (one in Francophone and the other Anglophone Africa), Southeast Asia, and South Asia. In 2002, the four research areas were the political economy of globalization, sexual and reproductive rights, political restructuring and social transformation, and sustainable livelihoods.

DAWN-Caribbean is especially active and in 1999 developed a new agenda, steering committee, and coordinator. It was decided that research activities would be undertaken by "multi-ethnic, multi-lingual research teams coordinated by Research Focal Points" on trade liberalization, women's budgets, privatization of social services, communication strategies, and political restructuring and social transformation. This reactivation "signals the launch of another regional effort to strengthen women's leadership in work on defining alternatives to secure and sustain the livelihoods of Caribbean people in this age of globalization."[67]

Although the research and advocacy themes are shared throughout the network, DAWN regions may have their own priorities. For example, Latin America focuses on social reproduction, including reproductive rights and health, and sexuality. The focus of South Africa seems to be political restructuring and social transformation, while Southeast Asia (SEA) takes up issues such as public financing and tax reform. Members of DAWN-SEA are part of the Freedom from Debt Coalition (FDC) that seeks a tax reform package for the redistribution of wealth toward social and gender opportunities and equity.[68] Such region-directed activities are made possible by the network form of a feminist organization, which seems to be the form most suited to transnational organizing, mobilizing, policy-oriented research, and advocacy in a way that includes nonhierarchical and democratic objectives. Moreover, the technological concomitants of globalization allow women's organizations that prefer a democratic and nonhierarchical setup to interact with each other and to conduct their activities in a more "efficient" manner.

Like many other feminist networks and women's organizations, the members and activists of DAWN, WIDE, WLUML, WEDO, SIGI, and AWMR are largely middle-class, highly educated women. In some ways, this class profile can be a disadvantage, inasmuch as the women may be distanced from the concerns of working-class and poor women, even though in at least one case (DAWN), they claim to speak on behalf of poor women adversely affected by economic policies. But many feminist networks and organizations in fact have extensive connections with women of the popular classes, or include "grassroots" women's groups. For example, WLUML includes locally based activist member groups that work with impoverished women in Pakistan and Bangladesh. AWMR includes trade unionists and other activists who work at the local, grassroots level. WIDE's Brussels office deals almost exclusively with offices of the European Union and with members of the European Parliament, but the network's "national platforms" (member groups) include grassroots-oriented women's groups such as WIDE-Austria, which works with immigrants and refugees. At the same time, given that an important objective of these feminist networks is to challenge the ideas, attitudes, policies, and decisions of large sophisticated organizations—including international financial institutions and state agencies—the presence of highly educated women advocates of alternative economics and of women's human rights is necessary and effective.

In the past, "feminist process" was criticized for eschewing organizational structure and efficiency. What my research suggests is that TFNs conform to neither the bureaucratic form of organization nor the structurelessness of the 1960s-style feminist process. Efficiency and participation seem to be valued equally. In addition, transnational feminist networks seem to have devised an organizational structure that consists of active and autonomous local/national women's groups or individual members based in various countries, while also transcending localisms or nationalisms. Often they take explicit exception to the "patriarchal nationalistic" or the "patriarchal religious" stances of the politicians of their countries. Their discourses and objectives are not particularistic but are universalistic. As such, these transnational feminist networks are situated in the tradition of progressive modernist politics, rather than in any new wave of postmodernist or identity politics. Moreover, the organizational form is not a federative or international one; rather, it is *transnational* and indeed, *supranational*.

Kriesberg has noted that by transmitting information, TSMOs aid the diffusion of ideas and practices and facilitate mobilization for movement goals. "They also help diffuse norms and values about participation in policymaking and execution and serve as constituencies for other NGOs and for IGOs, thus fostering democratization." For Keck and Sikkink, too, TANs engage in "information politics, symbolic politics, leverage politics, and accountability politics" with the objective of changing norms and standards.[69] Like other transnational advocacy networks, TFNs engage in information exchange, mutual support, and a combination of research, lobbying, and advocacy toward the realization of their goals of equality and empowerment for women and societal justice and democratization. They often work with or through international organizations (e.g., the UN, the European Commission, and other intergovernmental organizations) to advocate for women. Founders and other members tend to be highly educated social scientists who are fluent in development economics and in international agreements. Leading figures of the human-rights-oriented TFNs are often invited to international conferences as experts, or hired by intergovernmental organizations to write analyses of women's human rights. And as we shall see in the next chapter, the published critiques of TFNs on the adverse impact of structural adjustment policies on women and the poor led the World Bank to form an external gender consultative group and to modify its stand on cutbacks in social spending in developing countries. Thus TFNs engage with and are seeking to influence public policy at national, regional, and global levels.

Conclusion

In core, peripheral, and semiperipheral countries, women have responded to economic, political, and cultural processes that directly affect them by forming feminist groups and transnational feminist networks. In turn, these organizations reflect a diversity of collective identity or consciousness; thus networks may be formed by women who identify themselves as socialist-feminists, as Third World women, as progressive European women, as progressive women in Muslim societies, as progressive Mediterranean women. But whereas feminist groups and women's organizations remain rooted in local, national, or regional issues, their vocabulary, strategies, and objectives have much in common with each other and have taken on an increasingly supranational form.

Many local feminist groups have linked with transnational feminist networks, formally or informally. Transnational feminist networks focus on economic, political, and foreign policy issues, along with issues such as violence against women, women's reproductive health and rights, and legal equality for women. Many use the language of socialist-feminism, criticizing corporate capitalism and arguing for social rights and gender equality. Others use the language of liberal or cultural feminism in their critique of patriarchal institutions and norms and promotion of women's empowerment. All make demands on states, cooperate regionally, and agitate for global changes.

The growth of transnational feminist networks may be regarded as both a reflection of the multifaceted process of globalization and as a response to and criticism of its (economic) vagaries. What began in the early part of the 1980s as the formation of a handful of small feminist networks comprising individuals in a few neighboring countries has been transformed into large, sometimes professionalized organizations with officers, publications, annual meetings, websites, ties to national and international nongovernmental organizations (such as human rights groups), consultative status with the United Nations, and so on. Moreover, contrary to the assertions of certain analysts of new social movements, women's movements and organizations are not necessarily non-economic and identity-focused.[70] As we saw in the previous chapter, the World

March of Women in the Year 2000 declared itself to be against poverty and for the redistribution of wealth, and opposed to violence against women and for respect of women's physical and mental integrity.

Transnational feminist networks organize around socioeconomic and political issues, as well as around reproductive rights and violence against women. One reason may be the left-wing and socialist-feminist background of some of the leading figures in the networks; another reason may be precisely the fact that these networks link developing and developed countries alike. Economic issues have been at least as important as issues of personal autonomy and human rights to feminists in developing countries. TFNs have arisen in the context of economic, political, and cultural globalization—and they are tackling both the particularistic and the hegemonic trends of globalization. They are advancing criticisms of inequalities and forms of oppression, neoliberal economic policies, unsustainable economic growth and consumption, and patriarchal controls over women. In a word, transnational feminist networks are the organizational expression of the transnational women's movement, or global feminism.

CHAPTER FIVE

From Structural Adjustment to the Global Trade Agenda

DAWN, WIDE, and WEDO

When women's skills become sources of great profit for a few, while these women themselves remain the most prominent members of the dispossessed, the market system cannot be considered "free." [WIDE, 1995]

Human development means supporting the development of people's potential to lead creative, useful and fulfilling lives. Human development for all is or should be the direct goal of economic growth processes and transforming gender relations is central to the human development of both women and men. As class, caste, race and other social relations of power are embedded in inequalities between nations and interwoven with gender relations so as to pose major barriers, their transformation is key to human development. [Gita Sen, of DAWN, 1995]

Women do not want to be mainstreamed into a polluted stream. We want to clean the stream and transform it into a fresh and flowing body. One that moves in a direction—a world at peace, that respects human rights for all, renders economic justice and provides a sound and healthy environment. [Bella Abzug, of WEDO, 1998]

Transnational feminist networks have joined the global economic justice movement that, in place of free markets, unfettered trade, and economic growth at all costs, calls for human development and regulations on trade and markets. Indeed, they were early contributors to it, through their critique of structural adjustment in the 1980s and early 1990s. What they bring to the movement is a distinctly feminist perspective that calls for gender justice *and* economic justice. In this chapter we examine three transnational feminist networks involved in "globalization from below." DAWN, WIDE, and WEDO work together, separately, and in coalition with other women's groups as well as other advocacy networks to critique neoliberal capitalism and to formulate an alternative, feminist economics that takes into account women's productive and reproductive labor, and their economic and reproductive rights. As critics of what they see as the heavy-handedness of the institutions of neoliberal capitalism—multinational corporations, the World Bank, the IMF, and the WTO—they call for democratic economic decision-making and the incorporation of human rights and women's rights considerations into trade agreements. In order to accomplish their goals, they carry out research, attend conferences, publish papers, and take part in UN meetings. They formed women's caucuses at the UN conferences of the 1990s, engaged in line-by-line readings of conference documents, and sought to ensure that gender justice and economic justice issues were not watered down. As can be seen from the above epigraphs, they present a critique and a utopian vision of equality and empowerment, as well as practical recommendations to international bodies on how to achieve more immediate development goals.

Development/Economics for/by Women: An Overview

An expanding network of women researchers and activists from developing countries, with affiliated organizations and individuals from the Caribbean, Latin America, the Pacific, South Asia, Southeast Asia, and Africa, DAWN promotes alternative approaches to economic development and more equitable gender systems. In its own words, DAWN is an "autonomous inter-regional organization of the South which acts as a network and catalyst advocating alternative development processes that emphasize the basic survival needs of the majority of the world's people, particularly Third World women and their children."[1]

DAWN originated in a meeting held in Bangalore, India, in August 1984, when Devaki Jain—"the mother of DAWN"—invited women she knew to discuss structural adjustment, the debt crisis, and poverty, as well as the UN's Decade for Women.[2] An economist and activist, Jain had a vision of Third World women coalescing around a Third World critique of development policies and forming a South-South network. She and others were prominent women from Africa, Asia, Latin America, the Caribbean, and the Pacific who spoke eloquent English, were highly educated, had their own NGOs, and were situated in a socialist-feminist or Marxist-feminist framework. Many of them had lived outside their own countries, were very cosmopolitan, and were known as WID/WAD experts. According to Caren Grown, Jain gathered together "a network of Third World women who could engage in advocacy and activities in Third World areas. Their analyses were reflective of the experiences, critiques, and aspirations of many Third World women."[3] The women met again in 1986 at the World Congress of Sociology in New Delhi, and the network was formally launched under Jain's leadership. After two years, the network moved to Rio de Janeiro, where a secretariat was established and Brazilian sociologist and activist Neuma Aguiar served as coordinator. The secretariat rotated to the Caribbean in 1990 under the leadership of Jamaican political scientist Peggy Antrobus, and then moved to Fiji at the end of 1995, where Claire Slatter, a member of the Fiji Parliament, became the new general coordinator.

Following the initial meeting in Bangalore, the network prepared a platform document which was used as the basis of a series of panels and workshops at the NGO forum at the third UN world conference on women, in Nairobi in 1985. That document was eventually published as *Development, Crises, and Alternative Visions: Third World Women's Perspectives*. It highlighted the impacts of four interconnected and systemic global crises—famine, debt, militarism, and fundamentalism—on poor women of the South, and offered alternative visions. Caren Grown recalls that "DAWN brought together thirty women and a unique analysis of economic policy to Nairobi. It was a very important defining moment for Third World women."[4]

DAWN: Voices of Third World Women

Critical of neoliberal and patriarchal forms of development, DAWN sought to formulate an alternative model of socioeconomic development that would be people centered, holistic, sustainable, empowering of women, and based on an analysis of the issues from the perspective of women in the South. DAWN's analysis incorporated the diversity of regional experiences and related the experiences of women at the micro level of the household and community to an understanding of macroeconomics policy and global trends. From the outset, DAWN adopted feminism and poor women as its political points of departure and analyzed gender and class in the development experience. Discussions revolved around women's potential to solve such structural crises as the food-water-fuel crisis, the balance of payments and debt crises, militarization and violence, and cultural crises, and to formulate alternative visions and strategies. The self-empowerment of women through networks and organizations was regarded as a crucial means by which women could transform societies and international relations. Independence from government control was also stressed: "It was argued that women should not depend on government but develop autonomously through self-organization."[5] The network's utopian vision, now a staple of every publication, was first spelled out in their "manifesto," *Development, Crises, and Alternative Visions:*

> We want a world where inequality based on class, gender and race is absent from every country, and from the relationships among countries. We want a world where basic needs become basic rights and where poverty and all forms of violence are eliminated. Each person will have the opportunity to develop her or his full potential and creativity, and values of nurturance and solidarity will characterize human relationships. In such a world women's reproductive role will be redefined: men will be responsible for their sexual behavior, fertility and the well-being of both partners. Child care will be shared by men, women and society as a whole.
>
> We want a world where the massive resources now used in the production of the means of destruction will be diverted to areas where they will help to relieve oppression both inside and outside the home. This technological revolution will eliminate disease and hunger, and give women means for the safe control of their lives, health, sexuality and fertility.
>
> We want a world where all institutions are open to participatory democratic processes, where women share in determining priorities and making decisions. This political environment will provide enabling social conditions that respect women's and men's physical integrity and the security of their persons in every dimension of their lives.[6]

Research on gender and development issues was an important part of DAWN's work from the start, and the network contributed considerably to overall thinking on the subject. Key figures in DAWN such as Gita Sen, Peggy Antrobus, Neuma Aguiar, and Noeleen Heyzer of Singapore (who later became the executive director of UNIFEM) networked with other feminist social scientists and activists to produce telling critiques of structural adjustment. In the wake of the much-discussed UNICEF publication *Adjustment with a Human Face,* they urged the Commonwealth Secretariat in London to convene a commission on women and structural adjustment. Diane Elson, a well-known British socialist-feminist economist who had co-authored papers with Ruth Pearson on the exploitation of female labor in world market factories, joined the commission, which subsequently produced the influential book *Engen-*

dering Adjustment for the 1990s. Latin American members of DAWN produced *Alternatives, Volume 1: The Food, Energy, and Debt Crises in Relation to Women,* and *Alternatives, Volume 2: Women's Visions and Movements,* both of which were published in 1991. A publication on women and the environment was prepared for the 1992 UNCED conference, while alternative economic frameworks were the foci of publications prepared for the Social Summit in Copenhagen and the Fourth World Conference on Women (FWCW) in Beijing. For the ICPD, at which DAWN actively promoted women's reproductive rights, the network contributed *Population and Reproductive Rights: Feminist Perspectives from the South.* Prominent at the Beijing conference, DAWN's activities took the form of participation in panels and workshops at the NGO forum in Huairo that preceded the conference and, at the official conference, lobbying of government delegates and attendance at working groups formed to remove the brackets from contested paragraphs of the draft Platform of Action.[7]

During the 1990s, DAWN researchers worked separately and in collaboration with WIDE researchers to develop an alternative feminist economic framework. Wendy Harcourt, a founding member of WIDE and a leading officer of the Rome-based Society for International Development (SID), organized seminars and conferences that offered a forum for DAWN presentations on structural adjustment, gender and macroeconomics, reproductive health and rights, and related topics. The forum available to DAWN expanded with the launching of the International Association for Feminist Economics (IAFFE) in 1992, which had its first annual conference in Amsterdam in 1993 and subsequently produced its own journal. In 1995 and 2000, social scientists associated with DAWN (and other feminist networks) contributed to two special issues of the journal *World Development* on gender, economic theory, and macroeconomics.[8] Following its feminist analysis and critique of structural adjustment, DAWN turned its attention to the social and gender effects of globalization, including the new global trade regime. It also developed a website and a newsletter, *DAWN Informs.*

Organizationally, the network emphasized regional activity "in an effort to extend its reach and influence, connect more closely with the priorities of women's and civil society organizations in each region and help strengthen capacity to deal with issues arising from the impacts of globalization."[9] In order to influence debates on global development issues and monitor and mobilize around regional processes, DAWN organized its research and advocacy work around three themes. The theme of the political economy of globalization included collaboration with other advocacy networks toward a critique and transformation of global governance and institutions such as the World Bank, the IMF, and the UN system. The theme of sexual and reproductive rights entailed monitoring the follow-up to the ICPD and the Beijing conference with respect to women's sexual rights, male responsibility, and human and citizen rights. The third theme, on political restructuring and transformation, was meant to analyze "the deepening disorder and crises created by current global economic regimes," produce "a critique of mainstream ideas on governance, accountability, [and] state/civil society," and offer "a political framework for social transformation."[10]

As a network of highly educated and prominent women in developing countries, some of whom have held government or other influential positions, DAWN members and founders have served as resource persons or consultants for UNIFEM, UNFPA, UNDP, ILO, and UNESCO, and are often invited to prepare analyses or position papers for various organizations or publications. One such paper, by Gita Sen and Sonia Correa, was prepared for UNIFEM in preparation for the five-year review of the Beijing Platform for Action, in 2000. Entitled "Gender Justice and Economic Justice: Reflections on the Five Year Reviews of the UN Conferences of the 1990s," the paper concluded that the major challenges remained the wide gap between South and North on economic issues pertaining to trade, investment, and redistribution of wealth, and the difficulty of reaching consensus on gender issues within the global justice movement, in part because of the prominence of Catholic social-justice organizations that did not support sexual rights.[11]

WIDE: Voices of European Women

Like DAWN, the network WIDE was organized in response to concerns about global economic developments. Founded in 1985 immediately after the Nairobi conference, it "took off" in 1990, when it acquired a more stable funding base. Some of the founders and earliest members of WIDE—Helen O'Connell, Wendy Harcourt, and Hilkka Pietila—had been involved in socialist-feminism and the WID/WAD/GAD intellectual movements, where they had come to know the founders of DAWN. Early on, WIDE focused on development cooperation and a feminist critique of foreign aid. Recognition of the links between North and South economic and social processes was heightened by the experience of Thatcherism in Britain, the beginning of cutbacks in social spending in Europe, and the expansion of labor market flexibility. WIDE developed a feminist development agenda that included criticism of neo-liberal capitalism, defense of the welfare state, attention to women's unpaid labor, and the EU's relations with Third World partners. The women of WIDE also were inspired by DAWN's broad definition of development and its vision for an alternative form of development, as spelled out in the DAWN manifesto. Thus WIDE's annual conference in May 1995 focused on "Women and Alternative Economics" from a European perspective. Feminist economist Diane Elson, the keynote speaker, discussed strategies for action on issues of property rights, the transformation of markets, and the reform of financial institutions.[12] Like DAWN, WIDE too became involved in the international conferences of the 1990s. In an important accomplishment, its president, Helen O'Connell, was accredited to the official conference in Beijing and presented a statement during the General Exchange of Views, when official governmental delegations read their prepared statements.[13] WIDE had helped to found the Women's Global Alliance for Alternative Economics, and that group also was present at the Beijing conference.

During the 1990s, WIDE developed into a Brussels-based network of European women involved in feminist organizations working on development issues in twelve European countries. Most of the decade was spent on research, lobbying, and advocacy around gender and development issues, with the objective of educating publics, influencing EU policies, and empowering women. In its lobbying and educational efforts, WIDE identified the contradictions and inconsistencies between the EU's stated objectives of aid and development cooperation on the one hand and the adverse effects of structural adjustment on the other. This activity was part of its project of monitoring the Lomé Convention, which since 1975 had been the main form of development cooperation between the EU and seventy African, Caribbean, and Pacific states. At the same time, WIDE sought to influence the debates on women, gender, development, and trade at EU intergovernmental conferences and to monitor the implementation of the Platform for Action of Beijing by the EU and its member states.[14] It produced a wealth of research publications, technical reports, and policy briefs for EU policymakers as well as for its own members.

Individual members of WIDE, as well as the network itself, produced trenchant analyses of gender, development, and economics. The position paper prepared for the Beijing conference, for example, began with an elaboration of the way that the flawed assumptions of neoclassical economic theory guide the wrongheaded policies of neoliberal economics. The inspiration had been

Diane Elson's 1991 book *Male Bias in the Development Process,* which defined male-biased development outcomes as those that result in more asymmetry and inequality between men and women. Elson identified the proximate causes as male bias in everyday attitudes and decisions, in theoretical analysis, and in the process of defining and implementing public policy. The key structural factor shaping these attitudes and policies, Elson argued, was the social and economic organization of access to resources and to child care. In adopting this analysis, WIDE feminists began to emphasize women's reproductive activities, pointing out that much of it is unpaid (if it is domestic and based in the home) or underpaid (if it is occupational and within the labor market). They objected to the unspoken assumptions about women's unpaid family labor inscribed in structural adjustment policies. The "success" of structural adjustment policies, they noted, depended on the interdependence between the productive economy and the reproductive economy (also called by some "the care economy"), although neoliberal policy and theory did not acknowledge this. There were other criticisms, too. WIDE pointed out that programs of expenditure cuts were frequently designed in a way that jeopardized human development targets and undermined the ability of women to respond to new price incentives in agriculture and job opportunities in export-oriented manufacturing (in that women had to compensate with their labor-time for cuts in social sectors). Their recommendation was that all programs for macroeconomic policy reform should include not only targets for monetary aggregates and policy instruments for achieving them but also targets for human development aggregates and policy instruments for delivering them. Moreover, the relation between the policy instruments and human development targets had to be analyzed in gender-disaggregated terms that recognized the inputs of unpaid labor as well as paid labor.

Many WIDE documents, including its newsletter, exemplified the feminist political economy or socialist-feminist approach. For example, WIDE challenged "the laissez-faire dogma that markets are free, equally open to everyone, democratic, and fair."[15] The network believed that in order to achieve economic parity and stability for most women, cooperative and more socialist avenues of economics had to be explored. And WIDE activists spoke of how women must "reclaim the market in a global system where every part of life— even a person's kidney—is increasingly peddled as a commodity, and which sees people as consumers rather than citizens."[16] With its concerns for poor women, low-wage women workers in export sectors, and unpaid caregivers in the context of social cutbacks, WIDE was critical of the neoliberal macroeconomic policy that "prioritizes the economy over humanity, market rights and freedoms over human rights and freedoms," and adopts "an instrumental approach to women's enormous contribution to the development process," wherein "women are presented as a means or an instrument to be used towards a goal of curbing poverty, rather than full human beings who have rights." They pointed out that the process of economic liberalization has differential implications for women and men; "women are forced into situations where they have to work for exploitative wages in over-crowded and deregulated labour-markets; the cutting back of public expenditure and accompanying privatization of public services has increased demands on women's time, income, and energy while, at the same time reducing women's access to essential social-infrastructure." Their position was that "the EU's policy on development co-operation should start from a commitment to promoting and protecting woman's rights and to combating gender-based inequalities. The EU should prioritize: implementation of the Beijing Declaration and Platform for Action; implementation of the 1995 EU Gender Resolution; coherence in all EU policies; and recognizing the reinforcing relationship between gender equality and sustainable development."[17]

WEDO: Bela Abzug's Vision

The feminist network WEDO was founded about five years after DAWN and WIDE, taking over the activities of the Women's Foreign Policy Council and the Women USA Fund. But under the charismatic leadership of the late Bella Abzug, and with an expert on gender and development as its executive director (Susan Davis), WEDO soon developed into an "international advocacy network that works to achieve a healthy and peaceful planet, with social, political, economic and environmental justice for all through the empowerment of women, in all their diversity, and their equal participation with men in decision-making from grassroots to global arenas."[18]

Like DAWN and WIDE, WEDO was intensely involved in the UN conferences of the 1990s. WEDO came to prominence in 1992 at UNCED in Rio de Janeiro, where it was active in showing the links among the state of the environment, economic policy, and women's well-being. Since then, the network has been involved in campaigns against bioengineering and patents on life forms, and a campaign to show the link between environmental concerns and breast cancer. During much of the 1990s, WEDO's politics combined radical-feminism and eco-feminism, a reflection of the influence of one of its leading members and officers, Vandana Shiva, the well-known Indian physicist and eco-feminist who is also active in the global justice movement, and of course the influence of Bella Abzug herself, as in the following statements:

> The challenges to women's goal of a peaceful, healthy and equitable planet remain formidable, but the progress we have made in WEDO's nine years of existence gives us the confidence and hope that women, working together can transform Mother Earth.[19]

> As we contemplate this, the bloodiest century of human history, which dawned at Sarajevo with an incident that launched a world war . . . and it is ending in Sarajevo with brutal murders of children, women and men, mass rape and violence spurred on by age-old ethnic rivalries, greed, the genocide of the civilian population of Bosnia, Herzegovnia, Somalia, and the wars of Rwandas and Chechnyas of the world, is it not time to admit that the present dominance, style and conduct of male leadership has been a disaster?[20]

> In my heart I believe that women will change the nature of power rather than power change the nature of women.[21]

> For we are the Old Ones, the New Breed, the Natives, who came first but lasted, indigenous to an utterly different dimension. We are the girlchild in Zambia, the grandmother in Burma, the woman in El Salvador and Afghanistan, Finland and Fiji. We are the whale-song and rainforest, the deep wave rising huge to shatter glass power on the shore.[22]

> We are poised on the edge of the millennium—ruin behind us, no map before us, the taste of fear sharp on our tongues. Yet we will leap. The exercise of imagining is an act of creation. The act of creation is an exercise of will. All this is political. And possible. Believe it . . . We are the women who will transform the world.[23]

Bela Abzug attended the 1995 Beijing conference, although at that time she was ailing and wheelchair-bound, and she was honored by the UNDP for her life's work in the women's movement. She was clearly one of the few American feminists admired and loved by Third World feminists, as many women from developing countries would approach her and ask to have their pictures taken with her.[24]

After Abzug died in 1998, WEDO dedicated an issue of their newsletter to recollections, quotes, and memories of Bella. Vandana Shiva, member of the

WEDO board of directors, said: "We will, together, continue to build on Bella's dreams and visions."[25] Building on that vision, WEDO in 1999 took a strong position against the war in Kosovo and the NATO bombing of Yugoslavia. At the seventh session of the UN's Commission on Sustainable Development, the women's caucus organized by WEDO issued a statement that criticized neoliberal economic policies for inducing poverty and environmental degradation and called for a realization of the promises made at the Earth Summit. But it also called for "an end to the production and consumption of the products of the world's most entrenched and destructive industry—the arms industry." Otherwise, the statement continued, "there can be no lasting peace and no healthy planet. It is not sufficient to aim to eradicate poverty; we must eradicate the causes of war."[26] An article in a 1999 issue of its newsletter, *WEDO News & Views,* was entitled "Bombs Are Good for Business, for Some," and asserted that "NATO's war machinery is built on its plunder of the rest of the world, the environment and women."[27]

WEDO continued to critique economic policies and practices for their adverse effects on the environment and on the lives of women, children, and the poor. It worked within and outside the UN system to "challenge . . . the hegemonic and undemocratic IFIs and . . . the fundamentalist dogma of the free market."[28] WEDO led the Women's Caucus at the March 1995 Social Summit in Copenhagen and became known for its vigorous critique of economic policy as well as its stance on environmental issues. One of its Board members described WEDO as having a "holistic strategy . . . which links feminist issues—health, gender violence, reproductive rights, empowerment—to a larger economic and political context."[29] The priority issues were: environmental health and bio-safety—focusing on environmental links to breast cancer, persistent organic pollutants, and the global anti-nuclear campaign; global environmental and economic justice—advocacy at the UN Commission on Sustainable Development, World Trade Organization, and the World Bank, and organizing around the Earth Charter and expanded microcredit for women; and gender justice—monitoring and advocacy at the UN forums around the commitments made to women at the Cairo conference and the Beijing conference, focusing on empowerment.[30]

TFNs actively engage with intergovernmental bodies, such as the UN, the OECD, the European Union, and the World Bank. All three networks considered in this chapter were involved in the myriad activities prior to, during, and following the UN conferences of the 1990s, as well as the five-year reviews of the ICPD, the Social Summit, and the Beijing conference in 1999 and 2000, and the Financing for Development Conference in Mexico in March 2002. They have partnered with each other, with other feminist organizations, and with human rights, labor, environmental, and economic justice groups around a number of campaigns and issues, such as preventing the Multilateral Agreement on Investment, protesting the World Trade Organization's rules, and ending the Third World debt. They supported the World March of Women, the worldwide protest against capitalism and patriarchy in 2000 that began as an initiative of feminists in Quebec, Canada. Their global advocacy work has involved partnerships with other organizations and networks to reform international institutions and to ensure that governments live up to the commitments that they made at the international conferences of the 1990s.

Participation in the UN-sponsored international conferences was a priority for the TFNs during the 1990s, although a debate emerged in 2002 as to the efficacy of such participation. TFNs have participated in other conferences as well, such as those organized by the Association for Women in Development, or AWID (renamed the Association for Women's Rights in Development) and by the Society for International Development. Participation in these conferences is often made possible by support from UNIFEM and European foundations such as Germany's Heinrich Böll Foundation and the Friedrich Ebert Stiftung. Conference participation is regarded as a way to lobby government delegations, take part in the drafting of documents, engage in policy dialogues, influence policy-making, and disseminate the analyses and values of the TFNs. This is also done through their newsletters and websites, which serve as tools to inform women, both North and South, about events, conferences, NGO workshops, politics, and debates. WIDE's newsletter, in addition, contains news about the European "national platforms" (member groups) and developments in Eastern Europe. *DAWN Informs* frequently includes articles addressing political or economic questions. And *WEDO News & Views* provides both information and perspectives on issues.

Global Activities: Influencing the UN Conferences of the 1990s

An examination of aims, activities, and projects of transnational feminist networks shows the ways in which they work simultaneously at local, national, regional, and global levels. Individual members are often local activists who use that experience to conceptualize the links with national and global developments. Much of WIDE's published work, for example, has focused on the local, national, and global economies, analyzed through the lens of gender and class oppression. The TFN organizational structure, moreover, is one that usually mobilizes members on a national or regional basis. Manuals, technical reports, and conceptual publications produced by WIDE and DAWN complement the global analyses with country or community-level examples. While the three TFNs examined here work closely with each other and with other transnational feminist networks, WIDE also has formal links with European-based TANs such as EURODAD (the European Network on Debt and Development) and EUROSTEP (European Solidarity towards Equal Participation of People). Together they have produced studies on gender and structural adjustment and on the institutions of the European Union. All three TFNs examined here were also deeply involved with the UN conferences of the 1990s.

The International Conference on Population and Development (ICPD), Cairo, September 1994

Transnational feminists who participated in the ICPD knew from the preparatory meetings that the draft document's language on women's reproductive rights would be challenged by delegations representing the Vatican and a number of conservative Latin American and Muslim countries. They were thus prepared to do battle, and they went to Cairo with some advantages. WIDE had been accredited to the European Preparatory Committee as an NGO involved with planning the ICPD. Feminists working at the MacArthur Foundation who were sympathetic to TFNs "influenced Cairo" in that during the planning stages they had met with UNFPA Executive Director Nafis Sadik to ask that the process be opened up to the women's NGOs. Another factor that helped influence the process was that Bella Abzug of WEDO and Adrienne Germaine of the International Women's Health Coalition (later with HERA) were part of the U.S. delegation.[31] At the ICPD, WEDO was responsible for facilitating the Women's Caucus, as it had done during the two-year preparatory period, and provided line-by-line amendments to the ICPD proposed program of action. The purpose was to encourage the official delegates to "invest in women's empowerment and social development as an alternative to population 'control' strategies."[32] Women's empowerment would entail educating girls, providing access to user-friendly family planning services, promoting reproductive health and safe motherhood, and preventing child and maternal deaths—which in turn were regarded as essential components of sexual and reproductive rights. Negotiations slowed down due to the controversy surrounding not only abortion "but also the Vatican and Muslim delegations' objections to the draft document's definitions of 'reproductive rights' and their relationship to the family, to sex education, and to family-planning services for teenagers."[33] Eventually, a compromise was struck between governments, international organizations, and NGOs.

The controversy surrounding abortion, sex outside marriage, and the family dominated the news, but the ICPD provided a forum for other issues as well. For example, WEDO launched its cancer prevention campaign and set up a public forum on the need for international action to prevent environmentally induced cancers and other health hazards. Margarita Penón Arias, president of the Arias Foundation for Peace and Human Progress, spoke at the WEDO forum held during the ICPD in Cairo:

> Chlorinated pesticides, though often restricted or not registered in the manufacturing countries, are frequently used in developing countries for cotton and banana production and in the fight against malaria. Annual pesticide use in my region reaches levels equivalent to four kilograms (8.8 pounds) per person. In my own country of Costa Rica pesticide application is six times the average use in the rest of the developing world and more than double that in the industrialized countries.
>
> It is indeed frightening that the use of such pesticides continues in my part of the world, especially when we consider that the incidence of breast cancer in developing countries has been rising for the past two decades. Even more frightening, the effects of these toxins will linger for generations. Decades of use means that residues persist in our soils, thereby allowing for their introduction in the food chain. This has added implications for women. As the traditional handlers and preparers of food, the transmission of these toxic chemicals through the food chain increases women's exposure to these venomous substances, even if they do not live in an area of direct application.[34]

The World Summit for Social Development (the Social Summit), Copenhagen, March 1995

As part of the European regional preparations for the March 1995 Social Summit, WIDE was invited to attend the ECE High Level Conference in Vienna in October 1994, where it helped create the NGO document and draft the conference room paper. WIDE's main lobbying purpose was "to document the responsibility of the ECE region towards the rest of the world, not only through aid relations, but also through trade relations and countries' participation in the International Financial Institutions."[35] DAWN produced a document that criticized liberalization policies and proposed "a threefold strategy of reclaiming the state (for the benefit of the majority), challenging the market (to social responsibility), and building the institutions for strengthening civil society."[36]

WEDO and other TFNs lobbied governments to deal seriously with "growing inequities and poverty that affects women in greater numbers than men," as Bella Abzug asserted. Specifically, WEDO organized and facilitated the women's caucus for the Social Summit, whose agenda criticized "the fundamental structures shaping the global economy" and called for concrete actions by governments and international institutions to reduce poverty at least 50 percent by the year 2005.[37] A workshop entitled "Globalization of the Economy and Economic Justice," which was attended by over one hundred women, was co-sponsored by WEDO, along with NAC CANADA (National Action Committee on the Status of Women) and Alt-WID US. The group circulated a discussion paper entitled "Wealth of Nations, Poverty of Women," which identified a common ground between economic restructuring in the industrial economies, the economies in transition in Eastern and Central Europe, and the structural adjustment programs that the World Bank and International Monetary Fund impose upon the debtor countries of the South. They argued:

> These various forms of economic restructuring are being driven by a corporate agenda and a simplistic view of the merits of free market capitalism. These policies have a cumulative effect on increasing the gap between the rich and poor both within nations and between nations.
>
> When these macro-economic policies are evaluated through their experience of women, their negative impact on the quality of life, of women and children, and on the functioning of local communities becomes clear. A disproportionate amount of the human cost of global economic ideology is being borne by women. Governments and corporations are using women's labour, energy, time and sexuality to sustain this agenda of corporate growth.[38]

The women's caucus produced a comprehensive gender analysis of the summit document to ensure informed dialogue on the women's agenda between activists and delegates, and convened the caucus's opening meeting. Daily caucus sessions at the Social Summit developed strategies and tactics on ways to push the women's action agenda forward. The caucus was very critical of neoliberal economic policies and their impact on women and saw the final summit document as providing some relief from the negative impacts of structural adjustment by calling for debt relief—including debt cancellation—to free funds for social problems. They urged the World Bank and IMF to make social development a primary policy focus and to help slow excessive military spending. They reaffirmed the ICPD principles of women's empowerment for social development, and they endorsed the 20:20 formula by which 20 percent of development aid and 20 percent of national budgets would go to social programs.[39]

Two key documents—"Amendments to the Draft Declaration: Background Note Presented to the Chairman" and "Draft Definition of Core Terms of the Summit"—were produced by the women's caucus. Here they noted that "some of the terms proposed by governments in the Social Summit documents . . . did not reflect previous negotiations and agreements about the interrelationships between poverty, economic equity, environmental conservation, human rights and gender equality."[40] In addition to working with the women's caucus, WIDE, DAWN, and WEDO jointly drafted the Copenhagen Alternative Declaration, with "wide-ranging criticisms of a neo-capitalist system that favours giant corporations and gender inequalities," which was signed by over six hundred NGOs.[41]

Jointly with other NGOs and Danish women's groups, WEDO launched the 180 Days/180 Ways Women's Action Campaign on 8 March 1995. The brainchild of both WEDO and Peggy Teagle, a co-chair of the Canadian NGO organizing committee for the Social Summit, the campaign was a kind of countdown to the September Beijing conference. Over the course of the 180 days, "more than five hundred national and international organizations and countless local groups in over eighty countries actively worked to build support for the empowerment of women," which WEDO termed "a pledge for gender justice."[42] At the same time, WEDO developed a "gopher" on the Internet via the Institute for Global Communication, to open up the UN process to greater public involvement and to make Women's Caucus documents available worldwide almost simultaneously with their distribution at UN meetings.[43] (The UN later developed its own extensive website, WomenWatch.)

The Fourth World Conference on Women, Beijing, September 1995

As part of the preparatory work, the UN's regional commissions convened regional meetings to produce country reports and preliminary regional plans of action indicating how the status of women had changed since 1985 and in comparison to men over the same period of time. WIDE asked to work directly with the NGO committee that helped generate a paper for the European committee, and they helped produce a draft platform of action with other NGOs in New York. Keen to ensure that the Beijing Platform was not weaker than the Cairo declaration, WIDE joined a monitoring group made up of several European NGOs, including EUROSTEP.[44] Concern about the role of the Vatican delegation at the ICPD led TFNs to lobby European and other sympathetic governments to hold fast to an agenda that would promote women's reproductive health and rights. WIDE presented the Spanish contingent with a briefing that outlined the important themes to have emerged from Cairo: the girl child, gender, sustainable development, gender equity and equality, and reproductive health.[45] As a result of this monitoring and lobbying, the EU as a whole, and the Spanish delegation in particular, played a prominent role in Beijing in the defense of these issues.[46]

Some of the activities that WIDE sponsored at the Beijing conference included a workshop, organized with Women's Alliance for Development Alternatives (Alt-WID), entitled "Women in a Global Economic Restructuring: Making Links—Identifying Strategies" and a roundtable on "Women's Alliance for Economic Alternatives." The TFN was accredited to send a delegation of five members to lobby the national delegations.[47] For its part, WEDO was active at both the NGO forum, where it held presentations, and at the official conference, where it lobbied officials, facilitated the Women's Linkage Caucus, and joined the UNIFEM panel on economic restructuring. At the NGO forum, WEDO joined eighty women's organizations to create nine days of programs and workshops on the environment and development issues from a gender perspective. WEDO also celebrated the September 6 International Day of Action for Women's Equality, the culmination of the worldwide 180 days/180 ways Women's Action Campaign. And like WIDE—whose finances at the time were such that it extended grants enabling women's groups from developing countries to attend the Beijing conference[48]—WEDO also helped fund more than one hundred women's organizations from developing countries.[49]

During the Beijing conference, an international network of women (including Gita Sen, Peggy Antrobus, and Caren Grown) formed the "Women's Eyes on the World Bank Campaign" to monitor the World Bank's performance and to place women as essential actors within the World Bank machinery. Objectives were to increase the participation of grassroots women in the Bank's economic policy-making and to institutionalize a gender perspective in Bank policies and programs. A petition signed by nearly a thousand activists was presented to World Bank president Wolfensohn, after which the monitoring group was formalized. Laura Frade of Mexico became the coordinator of the Women's Eyes/Latin America Campaign, and she kept tabs on those World Bank projects in Latin America that dealt with health, education, environment, and social development. DAWN also became actively involved in processes and initiatives aimed at achieving policy changes, such as the World Bank's Structural Adjustment Participatory Review Initiative (SAPRI), and the External Gender Consultative Group.

Post-Beijing Activities

Having been active in all the UN conferences of the 1990s, DAWN, WIDE, and WEDO were ready for the five-year reviews, especially those of the ICPD, the Social Summit, and the Beijing conference.[50] At Cairo + 5 they had the opportunity to voice concerns and suggestions about implementation of the ICPD recommendations, also known as the Cairo agenda, which they felt were being thwarted by uncooperative governments and by the Vatican. WIDE pioneered work on gender and trade, and this became a major preoccupation of transnational feminist research and lobbying. At the WSSD + 5, the women's caucus, of which WEDO was a leading member, clashed with the U.S. and the EU on macroeconomic and global governance issues such as debt cancellation, the currency transaction tax (also known as the Tobin Tax), which had been endorsed by TFNs, and trade-related intellectual property, or TRIPs, in relation to essential medicines.

A major focus of WIDE has been to maintain the integrity of the broad development agenda agreed to in the 1990s and to argue that the new global trade agenda should not undermine the recommendations of the 1990 UN conferences, such as human rights commitments and especially the commitment to women's equality. As WIDE explained in its newsletter, "Economic and social policies and programmes should not decrease women's social and economic security or make women more vulnerable to violence, exploitation, and coercion and less able to escape from it. [They should not] eliminate or diminish women's access to basic services like health care and education, violations of women's human rights. Economic and social policies must promote cooperation, peace and community development in both the North and South, instead of competition, war, and social disintegration."[51]

Working on Women and Trade

WIDE's work on women and trade began with a conference in May 1996, after which it produced a conceptual paper on the European Union trade agreements with Asia and promoted economic literacy among its members and constituents through workshops and primers. The network decided to focus on alternative economics and trade and to continue to lobby the European Union on trade policy and developmental aid. There was consensus on the need for WIDE to work with trade unions, NGOs, academics, activists, fair trade organizations, groups focusing on transnational companies and financial institutions, and groups working on the trafficking of women.[52] WIDE's 1997 annual meeting, held in Finland, was attended by some 130 participants from twenty countries. The focus was on globalization, the role of international financial institutions, and impacts on women. Country reports on Russia, the Nordic welfare states, and India showed how economic globalization had affected women. According to the conference report, entitled *Trade Traps and Gender Gaps: Women Unveiling the Market*, "the globalization of markets has unleashed the forces of deregulation of national financial and labour markets, accelerating the onslaught of inequality, poverty, social disintegration and environmental degradation. These negative effects of the global market will only further be exacerbated by current attempts on the part of transnational corporations and their political supporters to modify and improve rules for the operation of the market on their own terms." The report highlighted "the lack of transparency and accountability in economic life in all levels, . . . the lack of accountability to citizens of global economic structures," contrasting these with "the accountability which is built into the locally based economic and trading initiatives of which examples were presented during the conference."[53]

In its work on gender and global trade, WIDE has insisted on "coherence" or consistency of regional and international policies and agreements. That is, new agreements should not ignore, subvert, or supersede previous agreements, particularly those having to do with women's rights, human rights, and labor rights. WIDE argues that agreements made at UNCED, Vienna, Cairo, Copenhagen, and Beijing are at risk of being undermined by trade agreements and the new power of the WTO; that governments are placing less emphasis on implementing the programs that came out of UN conferences and more on implementing WTO rules; and that the global trade regime harms women workers and entrepreneurs. Its annual conference in May 2003 was devoted to an analysis of the global trade regime from feminist and human rights perspectives, a critique of the "fundamentalism of the market," and an elaboration of an alternative model based on "the absolute priority of human rights instruments."[54]

EU enlargement—to include twelve new countries, most of them part of the former Soviet bloc—has been another focus of WIDE's attention since the late 1990s, and the network has sought to work with East European women's networks to formulate expectations and demands regarding the enlargement process from a women's rights perspective. This came to fruition at the May 2000 general meeting, when a group of women associated with KARAT, the Warsaw-based network of East and Central European feminists, was invited to take part.[55] In a 2002 briefing paper on women's rights and gender equality in the European Union, WIDE called on the EU to fulfill its commitment to gender mainstreaming; to reassess economic policy from a gender perspective; to ensure gender equality in labor markets in transition and implementation and enforcement of equal opportunity legislation; and to "transform the enlarged European Union into a regional and global actor for women's rights and gender equality."[56]

When WEDO turned its attention to global trade in the late 1990s, its gender agenda for the WTO had three objectives: to mandate inclusion of women and gender in economic decision-making and governance; to strengthen women's capacity to attain economic equity; and to prevent TNC exploitation of women's indigenous knowledge and plant genetic resources. Like other TFNs, WEDO used intergovernmental political structures, especially the UN, to promote these concerns. For example, its 1998 publication *Women Transform the Mainstream* was published in collaboration with the United Nations Department of Economic and Social Affairs. It consists of eighteen case studies of women activists challenging industry and government for clean water and gender equality in sustainable development.

The main foci of WEDO's work are environmental health and sustainable development, approached through monitoring implementation of major global agreements and ensuring the integration of gender issues, and "engendering" governance at both national and global levels. In 2000 it began a "50/50 campaign" to achieve parity in women's political representation. Its own research on this subject led it to argue that "the quota system combined with proportional representation creates a critical mass of women previously underrepresented on party lists, government bodies, and parliament."[57] WEDO also produces feminist analyses of the global economy and U.S. economic processes and priorities. In a report prepared in collaboration with about a dozen U.S. women's organizations, WEDO noted that despite the unprecedented period of economic growth in the United States, too many women and children—particularly minority and rural women—continued to live in poverty. What had changed was that more women were working than ever before, but they were working for low pay, in insecure jobs where they did not earn enough to adequately support their families. Government policies had not only failed to address this issue, but some policy decisions had actually exacerbated the situation, according to the 2000 report *Women's Equality: An Unfinished Agenda.* According to Executive Director June Zeitlin, "the failure to apply a gender lens in our own domestic economy is magnified many times over when the U.S. promotes these macroeconomic policies in the World Trade Organization and elsewhere in the world."[58] WEDO participated at the Seattle protests against the WTO in late 1999, and members carried placards reading: "Women Want a Gender Agenda at the WTO." Its March 2000 newsletter, *WEDO News & Views,* contained a number of articles on global trade and on the WTO. The organization also prepared a primer, *A Gender Agenda for the World Trade Organization,* which it posted on its website.

Working on Environmental Health

On environmental health issues, WEDO has specific positions, objectives, and campaigns, regarding cancer and the environment and bioengineering and patenting. These link up with some of the major concerns of the antiglobalization movement, the global environmental movement, and the women's health movement. A key activity in WEDO's bioengineering and patenting project was to prevent patents of life forms for private profit at the cost of sustainability, especially in Europe and the United States, where "corporations push to patent genes, human cells, body parts and organs, and all or parts of plants." The TFN also opposed genetically altered seeds.[59] With respect to women's health, following the 1994 ICPD, WEDO organized a series of nationwide workshops and conferences made up of women's health activists, cancer survivors, scientists, doctors, and ecologists. The conferences explored environmental factors in the breast cancer epidemic, such as pesticides, organo-chlorides, and other toxins; radiation from the military and other sources; and low-level electromagnetic fields.[60] Working with Greenpeace to organize the U.S.-based program, WEDO helped start up similar programs in the Netherlands and Brazil. Later, it helped to sponsor and run the Global Action Plan to Eradicate Breast Cancer, an activist agenda launched in Kingston, Ontario, in July 1997.[61] The campaigns were inspired by Bella Abzug's vision: "[Our job] is to do for breast cancer what happened to AIDS in the 1980's—to put breast cancer on the center stage. We need to internationalize the research agenda and network a movement committed to change, not guided by profit. Like AIDS activists, we need to stand up and take charge. We must take on the nuclear industry, the chemical industry, the makers and users of pesticides and organo-chlorides, and other potential sources of poison in our breasts and bodies. And most particularly we must demand action from our governments to legislate, regulate, and discipline transnational corporations and this out-of-control global economy."[62]

One role that WEDO has assumed is that of monitoring countries' behavior on gender, development, and the environment. In the newsletters, WEDO makes brief reports on various countries' progress and regression in the three areas. News items and articles include critiques of corporate capitalism, the commercialization and industrialization of all agricultural and food production, the genetic manipulation of food, and the privatization of health services.[63] It has published a guide called *Mapping Progress: Assessing Implementation of the Beijing Platform*, which has detailed reports on the gains and losses women have made worldwide. Another monitoring report—*Risks, Rights, and Reforms: A Fifty-Country Survey Assessing Government Actions Five Years after the International Conference on Population and Development*—charted the challenges to progress in the areas of women's reproductive health and rights as a result of conservative backlashes as well as economically driven health sector reforms. The 1999 study concluded that the goals of Cairo and Beijing were "linked to the eradication of poverty and the elimination of unsustainable patterns of production and consumption."[64] A 2002 study analyzed the extent to which international financial institutions had involved women in their decision-making processes, and highlighted the fact that fully 100 percent of the board of directors of the IMF and 92 percent at the World Bank were men. The results of the study were reiterated in the UNDP's *Human Development Report 2002*.[65]

The Financing for Development Conference, Monterrey, Mexico, March 2002

As part of their preparations for participation in the Financing for Development Conference, WEDO, DAWN, and WIDE—along with their partners WICEJ, the International Gender and Trade Network, and other economic justice NGOs—issued reports, policy briefs, and working papers on the FfD process, as well as on substantive issues such as gender and macroeconomics, gender and trade policy, the feminization of poverty, gender budgets, and the impact of economic liberalization on women farmers, entrepreneurs, and wage workers. Their newsletters were devoted to exploration of those issues, and policy papers were posted on their websites.

They attended regional preparatory meetings and deliberated over the draft "consensus document." They joined with other NGOs to endorse the objectives of the September 2000 Millennium Summit, which included the goal to halve the percentage of people living in absolute poverty by the year 2015. They criticized the United States for its lead in having removed references to the Tobin Tax from the draft consensus document and urged governments to reintroduce it. (This did not occur.) Many of the TFN activities in connection with the FfD conference were commissioned or funded by UNIFEM. A WEDO program officer conceded that "preparing for the FfD conference has been very difficult, because the issues are so technical." But she explained why TFNs were involved in the FfD conference:

> Our objective in the process is to make sure that at the country level they engender poverty eradication. Women are the world's poorest; they are poor in resource allocation, in income, in capabilities. The sexual division of labor perpetuates this. We want to raise consciousness. We'll also need to monitor implementation in the follow-up process. This is why the network is so important. For example, we may support a gender budget initiative in a particular country if opposition to it arises. WEDO can act as catalyst and coordinator, but the real work

is done at the country level. So we are helping to build a global women's caucus that can support the local women's initiatives.

The U.S. has been unbelievably horrible throughout the process. We have to do a lot of work here in the U.S. and lobby our government. We'll do this with the Center of Concern, Women's Edge, and Interaction, over issues such as ODA [overseas development assistance].[66]

Following the Monterrey conference, all the TFNs that had participated in the process roundly criticized the final consensus document, arguing that it did not include the necessary commitments from industrialized countries to eradicate poverty. They rejected the document's affirmation of the neoliberal model of globalization as the strategy for reducing poverty, which they argued impeded the ability of states to carry out socioeconomic development objectives. According to the statement by the women's caucus, "the Monterrey Consensus promotes the market as a game in which players are rewarded when they create an environment favorable to the private sector in both North and South. . . . For women, who are 51 percent of the world's population and the majority of the poorest, there can be no such consensus. . . . We demand that our governments hold firm to the commitments they have made in UN conferences and their follow-up processes in Rio, Vienna, Cairo, Copenhagen, Beijing, Istanbul, and Durban, for the realization of an equitable, people-centered and gender-sensitive sustainability."[67] In a post-Monterrey bulletin that also discussed issues relevant to the World Summit on Sustainable Development (held in August 2002 in South Africa), WIDE criticized "the ongoing trends at the government and corporate level to dismantle and combat socially and ecologically oriented regulations against further ruthless exploitation of human beings, in particular women's work and knowledge, and of the earth's wealth."[68]

Working in the UN system has preoccupied TFNs, but some feminists have expressed misgivings about it. Just as some feminists (and socialists) have argued against working within state systems to effect change, some global feminists point out that the UN is an intergovernmental system wherein many international agreements yield minimal results. One problem is that states are free to honor or ignore many of the conventions and declarations they sign, particularly in "soft" areas such as human rights, women's rights, the environment, and labor rights. Another problem is that the UN's international conferences tend to be dominated by the core countries, and thus agreements on "hard" issues such as development, finance, and trade do nothing to undermine the interests of the core or challenge the inequalities of the world-system. Thus, grassroots organizing and mobilizing is a more effective strategy, critics argue.

Others, however, stress the difficulty of organizing and mobilizing in many repressive environments and the importance of the UN as a forum for lobbying and advocacy work. After all, it is at the UN that the issues of ethnic cleansing, child labor, sex tourism, market reforms, and rape at wartime have been raised. Given the increasing importance of problematic institutions and policies at the global level, social movement organizations and advocacy networks have no choice but to engage with multilateral organizations. The UN in particular provides a platform as well as a sympathetic environment for critics of global inequalities and injustices. As WEDO board member Rosalind Petchesky stated, "We need democratic, accountable institutions of global governance in the face of globalization and enfeebled, complicit national governments. In this respect, the UN system *is all we have*. Thus we must work *both* inside and outside the system, and that means being more strategic about how we divide our time and members to make our presence felt in a wider range of international forums."[69] Petchesky also highlighted the need for democratization of global governance and the role of women's organizations in such an endeavor: "Our participation in WSSD+5 and Beijing+5 has pointed the way to a strategic agenda for progressive social movements, including women's movements. Such an agenda for those working transnationally over the next decade involves pressing for democratization of the IFIs to make them fully part of and accountable to the UN system and all its member states, and making civil society, especially women's groups, an integral part of that system."[70]

Criticism of participation in UN international conferences became especially vocal after the disappointments of the Monterrey conference on financing for development. It was at this time, too, that questions were raised about the utility of another world conference on women, and the Association for Women's Rights in Development (AWID) initiated a discussion on the matter. It is likely, however, that global feminists will continue to work within the UN system and participate in its conferences, "as these provide opportunities for wider and more effective feminist lobbying and advocacy," especially on economic issues.[71]

Organizational Structures

As discussed in chapter 4, TFNs are committed to democratic, participatory, and nonhierarchical forms of organizing, mobilizing, and decision-making. Consensus building and equality of representation across geographic regions are also major goals. For these reasons, DAWN has a rotating secretariat and its research programs are distributed across the regions. Similarly, its publications reflect considerable consultation and consensus building. That this is a principled position of the network is clear from the preamble to its manifesto, *Development, Crises, and Alternative Visions,* which was produced in a collaborative and participatory manner. The preamble describes how the book was written through "extensive debate and discussion with researchers, activists, and policy makers." It was felt that by adopting an open and flexible process that also drew on varied experiences, the group would be better able to come to a common perspective and objective. *Development, Crises, and Alternative Visions* was drafted by Gita Sen, then at the New School for Social Research in New York City, and her graduate assistant Caren Grown. Meetings were held in each of the regions represented by DAWN members, where draft chapters were critically analyzed. The book was first self-produced and subsequently published by Monthly Review Press in New York. In keeping with the initial book-writing process, DAWN developed an organizational structure intended to be participatory, democratic, and nonhierarchical. For example, in the late 1990s, Gita Sen headed the research project on globalization; her approach to globalization, however, had been criticized within DAWN, and she had been asked to rewrite it.[72]

DAWN: Participation through Networking

The organizational structure of DAWN includes a rotating secretariat led by a general coordinator. There are regional coordinators for the Caribbean, Latin America, Francophone Africa, Anglophone Africa, Southeast Asia, and South Asia. Research coordinators are chosen for projects on the political economy of globalization (Gita Sen, India), social reproduction (Sonia Correa, Brazil), sustainable livelihoods (Vivienne Wee, Singapore), political restructuring/social transformation (Viviene Taylor, South Africa). Focal points are in East Africa, Central Africa, North Africa, and South Africa. Research focal points are sexual and reproductive rights (in Africa and the Pacific), and globalization (in Africa, Latin America, Pacific). Another part of the organizational structure is the "DAWN Founding Members"—in 1999 these were Neuma Aguiar, Peggy Antrobus, Hameeda Hussain (Bangladesh), and Devaki Jain. Like other TFNs, DAWN has some paid positions, while many assignments are carried out by volunteer labor. Caren Grown was a paid employee of DAWN during 1984–87; the general coordinator also receives a stipend. Members, officers, and researchers are recruited through or from various networks. For example, Sonia Correa was recruited from SOS Mujeres to work on preparations for the ICPD.[73] Members of DAWN can be active in other networks. As such, DAWN is a network of networks.

A controversial position taken by DAWN after the network was officially launched was that only Third World women living in Third World countries could become members. This reflected and reinforced its collective identity as a network of Third World feminists and a South-South organization. The goal was to develop a feminist perspective from the developing world and to cultivate organizational and analytical leadership among women from developing countries. This principled position extends to practical matters such as subscriptions to the newsletter, *DAWN Informs;* the newsletter is free to members based in the South, and in 2002 it cost $20 for members and friends in the North. DAWN is linked to a number of other Third World feminist networks such as CAFRA (Caribbean), AAWORD (Africa), Indian women's organizations, ISIS (Chile and Philippines), Asian-Pacific Resource and Research Center for Women (ARROW), HERA, and women's organizations in Brazil, Mexico, and other Latin American countries. These links take the form of joint research projects, policy statements, and panel presentations.

Like other TFNs as well as many TANs, DAWN is not a mass organization. Its strength lies in its gendered political and economic analysis and its broad network of highly educated and well-connected members rather than in its grassroots ties. On the other hand, individual members may be founders of NGOs working at the local level. According to one of its publications, DAWN "counts on the participation of 4,500 women throughout the Third World."

As we saw in chapter 4, TFNs can count on connections, including friends and supporters in influential positions, to sustain their efforts. For example, UNIFEM's executive director, Noeleen Heyzer, is a founding member of DAWN who supports the work of TFNs. UNIFEM funded many of the activities related to the post-Beijing reviews and the financing for development conference. Catherine McKey of the Ford Foundation approved the first grant to DAWN that launched the organization, allowing them to gather at Nairobi and to

produce the book. The Brazil office of the Ford Foundation was also supportive, as was the MacArthur Foundation later, when DAWN friends Caren Grown
and Leni Silverstein and founding member Carmen Barrosco ran program
areas. DAWN has also counted on funding from bilateral donor organizations,
especially those of the Nordic countries, which are seen as less ideological and
more flexible.

Although DAWN's research and advocacy themes are shared throughout
the network, each region may have its own priorities. For example, Latin
America focuses on social reproduction, including reproductive rights and
health, and sexuality.[74] The focus of South Africa seems to be political restructuring and social transformation, while Southeast Asia takes up issues such as
public financing and tax reform. Members of DAWN-SEA are part of the Freedom from Debt Coalition (FDC), which seeks a tax reform package for the redistribution of wealth toward social and gender opportunities and equity.[75]
DAWN-Caribbean is especially active and in 1999 developed a new agenda, a
new steering committee, and a new coordinator. It was decided that research
activities would be undertaken by "multi-ethnic, multi-lingual research teams
coordinated by Research Focal Points" on trade liberalization, women's budgets, privatization of social services, communication strategies, and political
restructuring and social transformation. This reactivation "signals the launch
of another regional effort to strengthen women's leadership in work on defining alternatives to secure and sustain the livelihoods of Caribbean people in
this age of globalization."[76]

WIDE: Targeting the EU in Brussels

WIDE is a European-based network that currently includes nine national
platforms, each of which is itself a network of women's groups, or "national
platforms." The first national platform established was in Ireland, and a more
recent addition was Austria, which has become among the most active of the
national platforms. The others are Spain, France, Belgium (with two platforms, one French and the other Flemish), Great Britain, Switzerland, Finland,
and Denmark. Each has its own program of work but shares information with
the Brussels office; the latter also schedules the annual conference and the
general assembly. At the May 1995 general assembly in Brussels, for example,
each national platform presented a report on its activities and its plans for the
Beijing conference. The general assembly was chaired by the president, had a
financial report by the treasurer, and a report by the coordinator of the

Brussels office. The same procedure took place at the general assembly in May 2000.[77] The conference—also known as the consultation—that precedes the general assembly is an important part of WIDE activities and outreach; each has a specific theme and guest speakers, and EU officials are invited to attend and to participate in various ways. In May 2002, the conference theme was "Europe Moving to the Right: Where Lie the Alternatives for Transnational Feminism?" Speakers addressed the question in terms of the gendered nature of neoliberalism, militarism, and xenophobia; the impact on development cooperation; and responses by social justice movements. Marianne Ericksson, Swedish member of the European Parliament, noted that women's rights could be diluted in the draft Convention on the Future of Europe, "as even liberal MEPs are not committed to making sure that they are incorporated into the treaty."[78]

In the first few years of existence WIDE was based in Dublin but in 1993 moved its office to Brussels, so that it could carry out more effectively its lobby and advocacy work within the European Union, European Parliament, the Council of Ministers, and delegations of member states. WIDE also cooperates with and coordinates its activities with other networks in Europe, such as Protestant and Catholic agencies, EURODAD, and EUROSTEP. WIDE is part of the Global Alliance for Alternative Development, which also includes DAWN and Alt-WID. The focus of the Global Alliance is alternative economics—an effort to interrogate economic theory from a feminist and gender perspective.

European donor and development agencies were keen to fund women's projects in the 1990s, and WIDE benefited from their largesse. Despite its well-known critiques of neoliberal economic policies, WIDE's funding came principally from the EU, and in the mid-1990s it was invited by the Dutch government to submit an application for a large grant. As its reputation spread, WIDE was invited to take part in and prepare position papers for the EU Committee on Women's Rights, the UNDP Human Development Report 1995, the OECD/DAC/WID group, and the preparatory conferences for the Social Summit and the Beijing conference. WIDE continues to receive funding from the EU, from the foreign affairs or development ministries of European countries (e.g., SIDA of Sweden and FINNIDA of Sweden), from large NGOs operating in the Netherlands, Belgium, and Britain, and from such U.S. foundations as Ford and MacArthur. In 2003, the Brussels office had a staff of four multilingual employees, but much of WIDE's work was done by volunteers, as well as occasionally outsourced for the preparation of technical papers.[79]

WIDE's leadership, the central office, and the national platforms have been attentive to organizational tensions. In her remarks at the general assembly in Brussels in May 1995, then president Helen O'Connell mentioned two tensions in the organization's structure. One was the tension arising from the need to have a good working relationship with EU officials, and being able to express criticism of EU policies. The other tension was that between having a central office and being a network. At the time, the tension was resolved through information exchange among the national platforms and between the national platforms and the WIDE office in Brussels. In 2000, political and financial considerations alike led WIDE to move away from the Brussels-centered direction it had been taking and to rely on a more active role on the part of the national platforms.[80] At the same time, WIDE began to collaborate with women's organizations from those Central and East European countries that were to join the European Union. At the May 2000 annual meeting, WIDE and representatives of KARAT, the coalition of Central and East European women's organizations, agreed on principles of EU enlargement that would include attention to women's rights, while also discussing the possibility of joining WIDE as national platforms in the future.

For most of the 1990s, WIDE grew as a transnational network, but funding shortages after 1998 forced a restructuring. The number of original national platforms dropped from twelve to nine, a sign of the difficulties in maintaining a far-reaching network, as well as the limited life span of many local activist groups without adequate resources. In 2000, WIDE reduced the size of the staff in the Brussels central office, hoped to reactivate some of the national platforms, and introduced a new tier of individual, dues-paying members. Several of the platforms, such as Austria, France, and Spain, took on active roles, but the central office continued to predominate.

An advantage of WIDE's location in Brussels is its access to EU officials and members of the European Parliament; moreover, its organizational structure, scope of representation, and caliber of its research products have conferred a legitimacy and respect that reinforce this access. For example, the 2000 annual meeting was attended by a representative of the European Commission's Development Group on Trade and MEPs from Belgium, Denmark, and Germany (mostly Greens or Social Democrats). Two MEPs participated at WIDE's October 2002 conference on the rightward shift of European political parties. In EU and EP circles, WIDE is well known for its work on gender, development, and trade, and for its extensive links with Southern NGOs. The network is frequently asked to prepare papers ("green, white, and position papers" in EU parlance) and is consulted by MEPs.

WEDO: Lobbying through Networks

Unlike the other TFNs, WEDO is more international than transnational in its organizational structure. It is a U.S.-based feminist advocacy network that includes activist women from developing countries among its board of directors. It is not a membership organization. For most of the 1990s WEDO's executive director was the energetic Susan Davis, who was succeeded by June Zeitlin in 1999. The board of directors has included well-known activists and scholars such as Jocelyn Dow of Guyana, Wangari Maathai of Kenya, and Vandana Shiva of India. At WEDO's comfortable offices in midtown New York, salaried staff members lead programs on environmental health, gender justice, economic and social justice, and gender and governance; WEDO also has a communications director and a coordinator for global networking. Three senior advisors—from Denmark, the Netherlands, and Kenya—are consulted frequently, though they are not on staff. There are also student interns from local universities. Each WEDO program has partners in the global South, as well as a key contact known as a focal point. Weekly staff meetings help the program officers share information, exchange ideas, and coordinate their work.

Nadia Johnson, program officer for economic and social justice, described WEDO's strategies to disseminate views and influence decision-making, and pointed to the crisscrossing nature of networks. She also described the process leading up to the WTO's ministerial meeting in Doha, Qatar, in November 2001 and the UN's conference on financing for development in Monterrey, Mexico, in March 2002.[81] External funding, largely from UNIFEM, enabled women from the global South—"especially women from our own networks in Uganda, Nepal, and Central and Eastern Europe"—to attend the prepcoms for the financing for development conference. "Workshops were convened to bring together women at the grassroots level working on related issues, such as land reform and sustainable development. They included our partners who were involved in Beijing and Beijing + 5, as well as focal points and coordinators in the region." Some of these women were involved in other networks, and Johnson pointed out that a common goal is to "spread the networks, let them trickle up and trickle down." Like other TFNs, WEDO has "friends in high places," including a member of the Danish delegation to the Doha ministerial meeting, Janice Goodson Feorde, who is a WEDO senior adviser. In another example of the intersecting nature of feminist networks, Janice Feorde is also a member of the Danish women's organization KULU, which is an organizational member of WIDE. As Johnson stated, "Having more women in delegations is a good strategy."

WEDO works closely with DAWN and WIDE, with whom the network has produced joint papers. Johnson explained that the groups "share the same goal: economic justice for women. We are part of the economic justice movement." Johnson also maintains contacts with the International Gender and Trade Network and the Center of Concern (Maria Riley, Mariama Williams); the Women's International Coalition for Economic Justice (Carol Barton, New York); and the Association for Women's Rights in Development, or AWID, which had become more of an activist feminist network since Canada's Joanna Kerr had been elected president. "At the February prepcom [for the Financing for Development Conference] we had a women's consultation. Mariama was there, and so were we. Mariama was asked to come up with the women's advocacy paper and recommendations. I moderate the LISTERV. The importance of the latter for information exchange should not be underestimated."[82]

Funding from UNIFEM, the UNDP, the Ford Foundation, Finnish groups, and others—"the Nordic region is very giving"—sustain WEDO's operations, but these resources are limited. WEDO finds that financial constraints affect its ability to reach out to more partners, constituents, and policy-makers:

> We have limited resources, both human and financial. Here at WEDO I'm the only staff person working on economic and social justice. We need more staffing, more capacity. We need quarterly newsletters, economic literacy training, more research, more computers. There's a lot of work to be done.
>
> It's always hard to maintain a network, to keep the information-sharing and the dialogue going. One has to cultivate relationships within a network and work to keep them. Keeping the network coherent and cohesive is equally important. One way I do that is, for example, I might send an e-mail to Helen, our focal point in Uganda, to see if she is interested in pursuing a particular idea or initiative. But we could use more funds to develop joint initiatives.[83]

Achievements and Limitations

Taking on the major institutions of global capitalism is a daunting project for any social movement, but especially for feminist groups, who have less political leverage and relatively fewer resources than other social movement organizations or transnational advocacy networks. For example, although individual DAWN members (e.g., Gita Sen, Peggy Antrobus, Sonia Correa, Gigi Francisco) are well connected and are active in major international initiatives and prominent in international gender-and-development circles, the network is not always as visible. Gita Sen noted that at the Millennial Round of the WTO in Seattle, "there was a huge global mobilization by civil society. Every union, every NGO working on development was there. But women should have been present in larger numbers to press for our concerns. We haven't developed enough organizations that can work at that level. DAWN, for example, is just a network. We don't have a big, dedicated staff or equipment."[84]

Yet TFNs working on economic justice issues have had some successes that need to be acknowledged. WIDE's research on the trade links between Europe and Latin America culminated in a publication on gender and trade indicators that became a lobbying tool and then a teaching tool, used, for example, at the Institute of Social Studies in The Hague. The instrument was subsequently adopted by the European Union.[85] Referring to DAWN, Caren Grown maintained that it "has been an important catalyst in raising economic issues in the global women's movement." The very emergence of the TFN, she continued, was "a great achievement," in that "for the first time, Third World women took an independent stand and said, 'We have our own issues and voices, and we can interpret our own reality.' They [DAWN] were the only ones then, they were the first." As feminists with political experience from developing countries, the women of DAWN offered a unique perspective. Moreover, the timing was right for the emergence and spread of TFNs, for shortly afterwards, the communications revolution helped them expand.

As TFNs expanded, a number of international and multilateral organizations took note, adopted some of their concepts, and responded to some of their critiques. Years of feminist analyses and collective action have led some international institutions to adopt a gender perspective, and in this respect the work of TFNs such as DAWN and WIDE has had a positive impact. The United Nations and many of its specialized agencies, funds, and programs now prioritize women and gender issues in their publications, projects, and policies, and this has helped to legitimize women's activities and demands both nationally and globally. In 1995, the UNDP's Human Development Report Office produced its annual *Human Development Report* with a focus on gender equality and inequality. As a complement to its well-known human development index (HDI), it produced two new indices, the gender empowerment measure (GEM) and the gender development index (GDI). Since then, every global HDR ranks countries according to HDI as well as GDI and GEM. This has served as a model for the national human development reports, which are produced by teams of social scientists within the developing countries.

The World Bank has responded in some measure to women's demands. For example, in 1994, Minh Chau Nguyen of the World Bank embarked on a tour of a number of countries to promote the World Bank's new policies on integrating women into planning and projects, including a policy paper entitled "Enhancing Women's Involvement in Economic Development," and to respond to criticisms by women's groups.[86] Thereafter the World Bank produced a flurry of publications on gender and development.

Following the 1995 Beijing conference, the World Bank responded to worldwide criticism, especially from women's groups, by adopting new policy priorities—at least in principle. The Bank declared that it would assist "member countries in their efforts to bring about the fuller integration of women into all stages of the development process and improvement in their economic situation." There were four major objectives: (1) to enhance women's roles in productive and social activities, (2) to facilitate women's access to productive resources, (3) to reduce women's social, legal, and economic constraints, and (4) to strengthen institutions responsible for promoting women's economic and social participation. The Women in Development Unit of the Social Programs and Sustainable Development Division was given the primary responsibility for ensuring the integration of gender considerations in Bank lending programs. Each regional department was assigned a gender specialist working full time on operations. In addition, the World Bank established the External Gender Consultative Group (EGCG), shortly after the Beijing conference. The EGCG convenes in Washington, and it held its first annual meeting in 1996, with Gita Sen of DAWN as its chairperson and other noted feminist researchers and activists as members. Its work plan and the priorities include commentary on the Policy Research Report on Gender and Development, feedback and monitoring of participatory processes for development of gender sector strategy, and feedback on gender in the World Bank's annual publication, *World Development Report*. The EGCG was also promised a key role in the preparation of a gender-focused *World Development Report*.

Some feminists have raised questions about co-optation while others regard the World Bank's new approach as paying lip service to gender issues.[87] It is not yet clear how effective or influential the World Bank policy shift and the gender specialists are. The newly formed Gender Sector Board was put on an equal footing with health, education, finance, energy, poverty, and civil society, at least formally. But one concern was that the sector boards, which were meant to support the operational programs, had little money themselves, and weaker staffing. A major criticism is that the World Bank's cognitive framework, which is neoclassical economics, leads it to make "the business case for gender equity" rather than pursue gender justice and economic justice.[88]

Nonetheless, the developments described above provide an apposite example of how a transnational social movement—in this case, the transnational women's movement—can compel a powerful international institution to address issues of accountability and participation. According to Zenebeworke Tadesse, a founder of AAWORD (and a board member of the Women's Learning Partnership for Development, Rights, and Peace) who hails from Ethiopia, "transnational women's groups have demystified the idea that women's issues are narrow [e.g., solely reproductive]; they have shown how gender matters in macroeconomic issues, in trade and in finance. It is an accomplishment that the World Bank's president announced that gender justice is a worthy goal."[89]

At the same time, the scholar-activists within TFNs are cognizant of the radical nature of their critique and the lack of will, so to speak, on the part of governments and multilateral organizations to effect the sort of changes that global feminists seek. As Zene Tadesse put it, "Macroeconomic issues are sacrosanct. Governments don't necessarily pay attention [to us], as they have bought into the neoliberal doctrine." She feels that real change could occur as women enter political and policy arenas, although she adds, "Unfortunately, the legislatures lack capacity on issues of economics and public investments." What is needed, then, is "more advocacy and coalition-building; we need to democratize decision-making; and we need to raise questions about how budgets are formed and resources allocated. We need both rights/legal reforms and public expenditures." This "critical realist" approach to the state recognizes limits to the progressive agenda, given the nature of the state, and to state capacity in an era of globalization. As a result, collective action by the women's movement and women's organizations, in tandem with other organizations, could be effective in achieving common social justice goals. "It was important for women to define the issues. But it is important to work with men, too, in broader coalitions. We have transcended the fear of working in mixed groups. We can now work with men without the fear that they will dominate us or without losing the edge that women bring to the table."[90]

There are other challenges. "Women activists have to bridge the gap and transcend the divide" between their formulations about economic justice and gender justice and the understanding and implementation "on the ground." They have to learn how to "translate these formulations in a way that makes sense to the average woman."[91]

Conclusions

Economic globalization has created a more integrated, but still unequal, global economy, along with the growing power of institutions such as the World Bank, the IMF, and the WTO. The state still matters, but economic policies—whether structural adjustment policies or the global trade agenda—increasingly have been adopted for the "international community" as a whole. At the same time, a worldwide consensus on gender equality has emerged, encouraged by the United Nations and some of its specialized agencies, such as UNIFEM, UNFPA, and the UNDP. For that reason, transnational feminist networks dedicated to economic policy issues on behalf of poor and working-class women have focused their energies largely on multilateral organizations, international conferences, and global agreements. In so doing, they have contributed to the making of global civil society or the transnational public sphere—that site of civic engagement and connectedness, and of collective action and solidarity that is outside the state, market, and family, and beyond nationalist constraints. As such, DAWN, WIDE, and WEDO are manifestations of "globalization from below," reacting to the inequalities and injustices of "globalization from above."

The transnational feminist networks examined in this chapter see themselves as part of the global social movement of women, the global justice movement, and global civil society, and they have contributed to the global social movement infrastructure. A key strategy is to work closely with UN and other multilateral bodies, as many transnational advocacy networks do, to influence policy. But their practical engagement with international organizations and the world of policy-making is framed by their more ambitious goals of fundamental social change: reinventing globalization and replacing the current neoliberal model with a model grounded in social justice, human rights, and gender equality; the return of the welfarist, development state that is accountable to its citizens, including women citizens; and the transformation of gender relations from patriarchal to egalitarian.

As we have seen, DAWN, WIDE, and WEDO share many values and goals, and often collaborate on research, advocacy, and lobbying at the regional and global levels. They may differ organizationally—for example, DAWN is less of a professionalized, formal organization than are WIDE and WEDO, and WIDE works at the national and regional levels more than does WEDO—but all three are comprised of politically astute and strategic-minded women with perspectives on the global economy as well as on their national economies. As Caren Grown remarked: "The women in DAWN have very clear ideas about what their governments ought to be doing. They have positions on labor standards, trade, intellectual property rights, and other issues."[92] And they understand the connections between economic justice and other issues pertaining to women. As Nadia Johnson of WEDO noted: "Globalization has become a major issue, and it has galvanized women. That's why there has been a lot of work done around economic justice issues. Economic policies have become important, to feminist researchers and to funders. There is also recognition of how economic issues impact violence against women."[93]

CHAPTER SIX

Feminists versus Fundamentalists

Women Living under Muslim Laws and the Sisterhood Is Global Institute

At the level of national politics, effective lobbying and advocacy strategies must be devised and initiatives pursued. The discourse of politico-religious groups must be consistently and loudly opposed at all levels, local, national, and international. Local initiatives need to be strengthened through linkages at a national and international level, and strategies must be evolved to address, effectively respond to, and modify contextual constraints within which women are obliged to live their lives. No single women's group can adequately assume such diverse roles. However a multitude of autonomous groups effectively networking may achieve the critical mass needed to transform women's struggles into workable strategies for bringing about gender-equitable society. [Farida Shaheed, of WLUML, 1995]

At the center of this concept [global feminism] is the idea that the conditions women have in common outrank and outvalue those that set them apart. As historical victims of patriarchy, they are naturally united across history; they must now transcend political and cultural divides that are contemporary effects of traditional patriarchal politics. . . . Because Muslim countries have not been colonial powers, Muslim women, like other women from the South, are in a better position politically to help with a global movement for women's human rights. Many among them are multicultural, familiar with the West, multilingual, and conversant with international organizations and politics. Their freedom, however, is curtailed by a male-oriented hegemonic social structure at home and by their lack of access to the means of communication domestically and internationally. [Mahnaz Afkhami, of SIGI and WLP, 1995]

We have seen how responses to globalization in its varied dimensions have taken a number of forms. One reaction has emanated from fundamentalist groups. Benjamin Barber counterposes "jihad" and "McWorld" to connote the reaction of tribal, religious, and national groups—various forms of particularisms and identity politics—to the hegemony of corporate capital and Western norms. Such groups also have highly patriarchal agendas. Transnational feminist networks, therefore, have had to "battle" on two fronts: against corporate neoliberal capitalism (McWorld, to use Barber's coinage) and against patriarchal nationalisms and fundamentalist movements (jihad in Barber's sense of the term).[1] This chapter examines two such TFNs—Women Living under Muslim Laws (WLUML) and the Sisterhood Is Global Institute (SIGI), as well as a newer TFN that operates in the Muslim world: the Women's Learning Partnership for Peace, Development, and Rights (WLP). These TFNs call for the advancement, equality, and human rights of women in the Muslim world, and urge governments to implement the UN-sponsored Convention on the Elimination of All Forms of Discrimination against Women, along with the Beijing Platform for Action. As advocates of democratization, civil society, and women's rights, they are fierce opponents of fundamentalism, and have taken positions against those versions of cultural relativism and multiculturalism that undermine women's equality and autonomy in the name of respect for cultural or religious traditions. They also have paid special attention to the violations of women's human rights in the Islamic Republic of Iran, Algeria, Bosnia, Afghanistan, Iraq, and Nigeria.

WLUML and SIGI were both formed in 1984, mainly in response to the growing crisis of fundamentalism but also, in SIGI's case, in response to preparations for the third UN world conference on women. Both networks have been identified with strong leadership—Algeria-born Marieme Hélie-Lucas in the case of WLUML, along with the Pakistani feminists Farida Shaheed and Khawar Mumtaz, and in the case of SIGI, Iran-born Mahnaz Afkhami, along with the American feminist writer Robin Morgan. During the 1980s and 1990s, WLUML's administrative base was in France, and in 2001 moved to London.[2] During most of the 1990s, SIGI was headquartered in Bethesda, Maryland, where Mahnaz Afkhami resided. In 2000, Afkhami, a movement entrepreneur as well as a movement intellectual, completed her term as president of SIGI and moved on to form the Women's Learning Partnership.

Origins, Aims, and Alliances: An Overview

Both WLUML and SIGI may be described as antifundamentalist networks of Muslim feminists and secular feminists who link with other women's networks to advance the human rights of women in the Muslim world. As we shall see, they are similar in organizational structure to the TFNs examined in the previous chapter. WLUML, SIGI (especially during the 1990s), and now the Women's Learning Partnership have been centrally concerned with women's human rights, but they differ from other women's human rights groups in their focus on women in Muslim countries and communities. WLUML in particular was the first such feminist network to emerge.

The international solidarity network WLUML formed in response to concerns about changes in family laws in the countries from which the founding members came. The group came together on the initiative of Marieme Hélie-Lucas, an Algerian citizen who had taught epistemology and social science methodology for twelve years at the University of Algiers. Hélie-Lucas had been a left-wing activist on political and women's issues, and like other dissidents she had faced harassment. She left Algeria in 1982 and settled in Europe. This was a time of transition in Algeria, from the era of Arab socialism under Houari Boumedienne (who had died in December 1979) to a period of economic and political restructuring under Chedli Bendjedid. The new government was also drafting a patriarchal family law, which alarmed many women and led to the formation of an Algerian feminist movement.[3] In July 1984, nine women—from Algeria, Sudan, Morocco, Pakistan, Bangladesh, Iran, Mauritius, and Tanzania—set up an Action Committee of Women Living under Muslim Laws in response to situations arising out of "the application of Muslim laws in India, Algeria, and Abu Dhabi that resulted in the violation of women's human rights."[4] By early 1985, the committee had evolved into an international network of information, solidarity, and support, and Hélie-Lucas became the guiding light behind the network WLUML.

Tasks for the network were established at the first planning meeting, in April 1986, involving ten women from Algeria, Morocco, Tunisia, Egypt, Sudan, Nigeria, India, Pakistan, and Sri Lanka. The tasks were: to create international links between women in Muslim countries and communities; to exchange information on their situations, struggles, and strategies, in order to strengthen and reinforce women's initiatives and struggles through various means (such as through publications and exchanges); and to support each others' struggles through various means, including an Alert for Action system.[5] Since then, WLUML has become a network of women who are active in their local and national movements but who meet periodically to reach consensus on a plan of action. For example, the 1997 plan of action identified the following as priorities: the continuing rise of fundamentalism; militarization/armed conflict situations and their impact on women in Muslim societies; and sexuality. Some thirty-five activists from eighteen countries gathered in Dhaka, Bangladesh, to agree on the plan.

Fiercely antifundamentalist since its inception, WLUML began to issue warnings as early as 1990 about an "Islamist international" with the organizational, human, financial, and military means to threaten secularists, feminists, and democrats.[6] As one activist notes, "the organization also has denounced the presence and in some instances the protection by the West" of Islamists such as Anouar Haddam, who was a member first of the Algerian Front Islamique du Salut (FIS) and then of the Group Armée Islamique (GIA).[7] Because of the FIS and GIA record of terrorism, including harassment, kidnapping, rape, and murder of Algerian women, WLUML has opposed any legalization of these groups without prosecution of those responsible for crimes, and has protested the granting of political asylum in the West to individuals associated with these organizations.

SIGI came into being following the completion of the book *Sisterhood Is Global: The International Women's Movement Anthology,* edited by veteran American feminist and writer Robin Morgan. Many of the book's twenty-five contributors went on to be involved with SIGI. Marilyn Waring—former New Zealand member of parliament and author of an influential study of how the system of national accounts systematically undercounts women's economic contributions—was an early executive director. Gertrude Monghella of Tanzania became a member of the board—and later was appointed the secretary-general of the UN's 1995 Fourth World Conference on Women. And Mahnaz Afkhami—author of the anthology's essay on Iran who had been president of the Women's Organization in Iran but went into exile after the 1979 revolution—became vice-president, executive director, and finally president of SIGI. Initially conceived as a transnational feminist think tank, SIGI went on to be "an international non-government, non-profit organization dedicated to the support and promotion of women's rights at the local, national, regional, and global levels," as stated on its website. By late 1999 it boasted members in seventy countries, with "more than 1,300 individuals and organizations worldwide. SIGI works toward empowering women and developing leadership through human rights education."[8]

During the 1990s the network's primary goals were to:

- Inform women of their basic rights guaranteed to them under international human rights conventions and empower them to attain those rights;
- Increase public awareness and concern about human rights abuses committed against women;
- Facilitate the direct participation of women from the global South in international debates concerning their rights;
- Encourage women from all cultures, religions, races, classes, ages, sexual preferences, and abilities to work together to define and achieve common goals;
- Facilitate research and provide training models for women from the developing world in the areas of human rights education, communication, and leadership.

To realize these goals, SIGI implemented four programs. The Women's Human Rights Education Program worked to inform and empower women; the International Dialogues were a series of meetings, conferences, and symposia on issues of concern to women; the Urgent Action Alert Program issued alerts in response to cases of human rights abuses against women; and the outreach and advocacy initiatives aimed to increase public awareness and concern for women's human rights.[9] A number of human rights manuals and more academic studies resulted from these programs, including two books produced following SIGI conferences that have been cited widely and adopted in women's studies programs internationally. *Faith and Freedom: Women's Human Rights in the Muslim World* promotes the universality of human rights while also examining those existing patriarchal structures and processes in Muslim countries that present women's human rights as contradictory to Islam. In *Muslim Women and the Politics of Participation: Implementing the Beijing Platform for Action,* sixteen activists and scholars from Muslim countries and representatives of international organizations describe ways of promoting women's participation in the affairs of Muslim societies.

SIGI has rotated its headquarters every five years in order that the organization not conform permanently to the culture and environment of any area, and to allow it to focus on women's participation in activities in new regions.[10] After its founding in New York, the headquarters moved to New Zealand in 1989, then on to Bethesda, Maryland, in 1993, where Afkhami worked to make the organization prominent and active. She felt her aim was to "help bring about a more equitable representation of women from the Global South in international debates."[11] In January 2000 SIGI moved to Montreal, Canada, where the new president, Greta Hofmann Nemiroff, shifted the organization's focus from the rights of women in the Middle East to economic issues of women in Canada.

The defense and promotion of women's human rights in the Muslim world are the principal aims of both WLUML and SIGI. As fluid networks rather than membership-based organizations, they give priority to creating strong networks and ties of solidarity among women across countries rather than seeking to influence national or global policy through interaction with governments or intergovernmental bodies. But SIGI also sought to enhance its research capabilities, especially during the 1990s and under the direction of Mahnaz Afkhami. When she took over in 1993, SIGI "had a budget of only $18,000. There was no office, no proposals, nothing but a group of famous names connected to it."[12] She set about to develop its "feminist think tank" role through conferences, symposia, workshops, international dialogues, and publications. These were funded by grant proposals that she wrote for UNIFEM and such foundations as Ford, Rockefeller, and MacArthur. In addition, SIGI had a catalyst role to play, in that it engaged in partnerships with Muslim women to enhance their rights and helped to build capacity for women's organizations. In one particularly successful example of such partnering and capacity building, a request for assistance to form a new organization by Asma Khader—the Palestinian-Jordanian activist lawyer and past president of the Jordanian Women's Union—led to the formation of SIGI-Jordan.[13]

The UN conferences of the 1990s helped TFNs to spread their messages, expand their networks, and raise funds for specific projects. But for WLUML and SIGI, and for similar feminist groups, the 1993 UN conference on human rights was a major turning point, in that it helped them to focus on the concept of *women's human rights* and to refine the argument that women's rights were inseparable from human rights. As Afkhami explained: "We all worked together on that concept. It was our focus from the beginning. We had a presence [in Vienna], and that was a launching pad for us. There we all coalesced and came together—the feminist human rights networks."[14] The feminist networks argued forcefully that violence against women in the home, on the streets, or in wartime should be regarded as human rights violations. And they took part in the Tribunal on Violence against Women, organized by veteran activist Charlotte Bunch.

The Vienna conference was the first UN conference that WLUML officially attended, and it did so largely to raise awareness about Islamist violence against Algerian women at the women's tribunal. Charlotte Bunch had raised funds to enable women to attend the Vienna conference and testify at the women's tribunal, and WLUML had recommended that Khalida Messaoudi, an Algerian feminist leader, be invited.[15] WLUML also participated in the 1994 UN Conference on Population and Development, where it joined other feminist networks in criticizing efforts by the Vatican, conservative states, and Christian and Muslim fundamentalists to remove references to women's reproductive rights in the conference declaration. These conferences helped WLUML to expand its collaborations and alliances with transnational feminist networks such as WIDE and Women, Law, and Development International in Washington, D.C.—in addition to its ongoing links with the Institute for Women's Global Leadership at Rutgers University, with Shirkat Gah in Lahore, Pakistan, and with Baobob in Lagos, Nigeria. Said Hélie-Lucas: "We were always present at the NGO forums. We were less interested in the intergovernmental, official conferences."[16] There were no links with UN agencies, and unlike SIGI and other TFNs, WLUML did not seek accreditation to ECOSOC. Like SIGI and other TFNs, however, the network receives funding from the major U.S. and European foundations, as well as the Dutch, Swedish, and Canadian international development agencies, to finance its activities and projects.

According to its mission statement, "WLUML is a network of women whose lives are shaped, conditioned or governed by laws, both written and unwritten, drawn from interpretations of the Koran and tied up with local traditions. Generally speaking, men and the State use these against women, and they have done so under various political regimes."[17] In order to achieve the network's principal aim of increasing women's autonomy over all aspects of their lives—social and economic, cultural and political, physical and psychological—WLUML undertakes a variety of activities. It collects and disseminates information on formal and customary laws in the Muslim world, as well as on women's lives, struggles, and strategies. It advances shared lived experiences through exchanges, including face-to-face interaction among women in the Muslim world. Common projects are identified by women in the network and reflect their diverse concerns. One project was called the Koranic Interpretation by Women, which was launched in Lahore in 1990 and entailed an independent reading and interpretation of the Koran, Hadith, and existing Islamic laws. The ten-year project culminated in a book and increased awareness of the religious women involved of the misapplication of Islamic law in the Muslim world. Particularly active in this project was the Malaysian women's group Sisters in Islam.[18]

The central activity of the network, however, may be identified as its solidarity and support work. WLUML receives appeals and responds to as well as initiates campaigns pertaining to violations of human rights, including women's human rights.[19] All requests from groups or individuals representing varied opinions and currents from within the movement for reform or defense of women's rights seeking support and urgent actions are forwarded throughout the network. As Hélie-Lucas has explained, these actions range from campaigns concerning the repeal of discriminatory legislation, the end of oppressive gender practices, the enactment and/or enforcement of legislation favorable to women, and cases of systematized or generalized violations of human rights; to individual cases where, for example, harsh sentences have been meted, women have been forcibly married against their will, fathers have abducted their children, and women's lives have been threatened. In November 2002, WLUML expanded its information and solidarity work on fundamentalism and women's human rights through a new website called Fundamentalisms: A Web Resource for Women's Human Rights, a joint initiative with the Association for Women's Rights in Development (AWID).[20]

WLUML Activities: A Closer Look

In keeping with its focus on monitoring the human rights of women in Muslim countries, extending solidarity, and raising international awareness, WLUML has issued numerous action alerts. These have been disseminated by the international coordination office in Europe, the Asia office in Pakistan, or the African office in Nigeria. A sample of action alert efforts between 1990 and 1995 that were either initiated by WLUML or disseminated by them on behalf of other organizations include the following: an alert on the campaign to end the trafficking of Burmese women and girls into Thai brothels; an alert on the campaign to prosecute three war criminals of the Bangladesh War of Liberation, now citizens and residents of the UK; an alert regarding violation of women's human rights in Kurdistan (in this case "committed by the relatives

of women or even by members of the autonomous government of Kurdistan");
an alert regarding the appeal by a Pakistani fanatical group for the murder of
four prominent citizens for alleged blasphemy; an appeal by Amnesty International regarding the torture of a nine-year-old Indonesian boy detained on suspicion of stealing a wallet; an alert regarding the rape of an eleven-year-old
Bangladeshi girl by police in Delhi; an alert regarding the campaign to save the
lives of the thirteen-year-old Christian Pakistani boy and his uncle who had
been sentenced to death under blasphemy charges in Pakistan.

There was also an alert regarding the abduction, torture, and killing of
Marinsah, an Indonesian female factory worker and trade union activist; an
appeal from the group Women for Women's Human Rights in Turkey calling
for the revision of Turkey's Family Code; numerous appeals regarding the situation of Algerian women and fundamentalist terror; a condemnation of female genital mutilation; many appeals regarding Bosnia; an appeal by the Union of Palestinian Working Women Committees regarding ill-treatment of
Palestinian women fighters in Israeli jails; an alert regarding the Egyptian government's closure of the Arab Women's Solidarity Association; the campaign
for the International Day of Protest against the continued presence of U.S.
military bases and facilities in the Philippines; an alert regarding the situation
of women in Iran; an alert regarding the reinstatement in the early 1990s of a
law allowing "honor killings" in Iraq.

Besides the action alerts, the activities of the network entail documenting
and disseminating information in the form of dossiers, which describe the situation of Muslim women and legal codes in various countries and report on
the activities of women's organizations. The Dossier is an occasional journal,
appearing in English and in French and intended as "a networking tool with
the aim of providing information about lives, struggles, and strategies of
women in various Muslim communities and countries the world over."[21] A series on women's movements was launched with a report on Iran. WLUML also
reprints publications, such as one produced in 1995 by North African feminists advocating and describing an egalitarian family code.

The Asia coordination office, and specifically the women's resource center
Shirkat Gah, produces the *News Sheet*. In the late 1990s, many articles were
devoted to describing the plight of women in Algeria and in Afghanistan. Although the *News Sheets* disseminate news about the network as well as problems faced by Muslim women in various countries, they do not focus exclu-

sively on Muslim women, but address themselves to women's human rights situation throughout the developing world. For example, in its May–June 2000 issue, the *News Sheet* included an article on women's contribution to a culture of peace, with an emphasis on meetings between progressive women in Pakistan and India, and reports on Sri Lanka and Fiji. Shirkat Gah also devotes its resources to translating and publishing books, including two on the gender implications of the changing political economy of Uzbekistan and Central Asia.[22] Moreover, it produces many reports on the situation of women in Pakistan. Khawar Mumtaz and Farida Shaheed, who are active with WLUML, are often called upon by UN agencies to serve as consultants and prepare reports on women in Pakistan.

Activist Information Dissemination

The 1998 *News Sheets* and Compilations of Information included articles on the atrocities in Algeria, especially the kidnapping, rapes, and murders of women; an Algerian appeal against the conservative Family Code; a article about the efforts by the Democratic League for Women's Rights to secure universal and compulsory public education in Morocco; activities by the Women's Action Forum in Nigeria against a new law; an article about the El Badeel Coalition against "Family Honor" Crimes in Palestine; and articles about the plight of women under the Taliban in Afghanistan. The situation in Yugoslavia was also addressed, with articles about war mobilization in Serbia and the condition of the refugees. Several articles on Kosovo had titles such as: "War in Kosovo and the Logic of Patriarchy: Violation of Human Rights Is an International Issue"; "We Refuse the War! Open Letter from Women in Black against War"; "Seven Years of Women in Black: We Are Still on the Streets." *News Sheets* contained open letters of appeal from different women's and peace organizations to stop the war and violence in Kosovo.

The tone of many WLUML articles is feminist, antimilitarist, and anticorporate. One article described a campaign by AAWORD (Association of African Women for Research and Development) against a World Bank-supported oil pipeline project in Chad and Cameroon. A letter of appeal by AAWORD described the environmental and development problems that would ensue from the project. Another article reported on the Baja tragedy, a chemical spill in the Punjab that killed twenty people and did considerable environmental damage. The article also suggested ways to prevent future environmental tragedies. Elsewhere, the Declaration of African Women's Anti-War Coalition was reprinted and an article described the Women's Vigil for Peace press conference on the effect of the war on the lives of the Kenyan people. An article on the International Criminal Court discussed its strengths and limitations for women. A press statement from the Philippines feminist network GABRIELA—"Women Condemn Tokyo Court's Rejection of Lila's Claim"—described the class action suit by the sexual victims of Japanese soldiers during World War II. And another article was entitled "East Asia–U.S. Women's Network against U.S. Militarism Redefining Security for Women and Children," describing the group's final statement at their second international meeting. GABRIELA issued a statement about their campaign Purple Rose to oppose the sexual exploitation and trafficking of Filipino women and girls. An action alert protested the assault on women and girls of Chinese descent in Indonesia who had been the recent victims of targeted violence. And there was a "Call for Peace" in the Persian Gulf by Turkish and Greek members of WINPEACE. In 2002 and 2003 the *News Sheets* carried articles on the second Palestinian intifada, Israeli military incursions, and women's peace-building initiatives; criticisms of the U.S. stance on Iraq; and updates on the status of women in various Muslim countries, including the appointment for the first time of a woman judge in Egypt.[23]

Opposing national chauvinism and religious discrimination, the WLUML *News Sheet* has carried articles and open letters in opposition to the nuclearization of Pakistan and India, and reported on the six Indians who were killed from the post-radiation blast from the nuclear testing. The *News Sheet* criticized the Pakistani blasphemy law and covered the Christian who was sentenced to death for blasphemy. Another news item reported on the tragic death of Bishop John Joseph, who took his own life in protest of the Pakistani blasphemy law. A "Press Statement by Indian Citizens" was printed that condemned the attacks on Christian buildings by Hindu fanatics. And the *News Sheet* reported on a new campaign: the Movement for the Trial of War Criminals of 1971. This campaign appealed to then Pakistan Premier Newaz Sharif to seek public apology for war crimes and sexual abuses of Bengali women by Pakistani soldiers during the Bangladesh war of independence in 1971.

One 1998 article described the Banjul Declaration, issued by the participants at the Symposium for Religious Leaders and Medical Personnel on female genital mutilation, which declared female circumcision to be a form of violence. In 1998 and 1999 a series of articles concerned women in Iran, Pakistan, and Afghanistan. Iranian women were described as producing films, defying the dress code, and vying for senior political posts. Several articles described notable Pakistani women and their achievements in harsh circumstances. A message by the Revolutionary Association of Women of Afghanistan (RAWA) called on Afghans and the world community to commemorate March 8 with intensified struggles to end the oppression of women in Afghanistan. Another article described the activities of the Sudanese Women's Association in Nairobi. Two memorial articles appeared, one on Kishwar Abid Hussain, a leader and a founding member of the Pakistani Women's Action Forum (WAF) and another on Bella Abzug, the founder of WEDO.

The work of the network has been guided by plans of action, agreed upon in 1986, 1990, and 1997. Collective projects on topics related to women in the Muslim world also have been initiated. These include an exchange program in 1988 that allowed eighteen women from fifteen countries to meet for the purpose of exchanging information on strategies used in different parts of the Muslim world by women activists. According to Hélie-Lucas: "We realized that many local customs and traditions practiced in the name of Islam in one part of the world were in fact unheard of in others. It also became evident that not only are the varied and contradictory interpretations of the Koran monopolized by men but they are also the only ones who have so far defined the status of Muslim women."[24]

This realization led to the initiation of the project on Koranic interpretation by women, which brought together thirty women activists and resource persons from ten countries to read for themselves the verses of the Koran relating to women. "The meeting allowed participants to see just how differently the same verses of the Koran have been interpreted (both through translations and explanations, or *tafsir*) by Islamic scholars and various schools of thought."[25] This effort led to the initiation of the Women and Law Project, involving women in twenty countries who examined legislation, especially the Muslim family codes that discriminate against women and contradict equality clauses in the countries' constitutions. The stated objective of the Women and Law Program was "to empower women living under Muslim laws through knowledge of their rights in their societies and to strengthen their capacity to understand their situations, to act locally, and work together towards meeting their needs. As well, it aims to enhance the participation of women in the development of their societies."

Universal Rights and the Algeria and Afghanistan Campaigns

Like other TFNs, WLUML evinces a discourse and orientation that are universalistic and modernist rather than postmodernist. For example, one dossier criticized a cultural relativism that "explains" honor crimes and other forms of gender oppression in terms of the function of traditions and the noncommensurability of cultures. It is worth quoting at length:

> The issue under question is the attitude that accepts these crimes as part of today's reality and further justifies them by saying that "these people have chosen their own destiny; it is their culture; we have our own culture and they have their own; we should respect their culture and not interfere in their affairs." In other words they say women in Iran are responsible for not having the right to divorce, the right of custody of their children, having to wear the veil, or laws which punish them with stoning!
>
> Introducing and defending any reactionary and suppressive measure against people, especially under the name of respecting different cultures must be condemned because it is against humanity at large. One cannot regionalize basic human rights. One cannot have thousands of sets of standards for women's human rights.
>
> Human rights and women's rights are international in character and substance. Why is it that technology, business and capital soon find their international role and place even in the most backward region but health education, literacy can wait for many years if introduced at all?
>
> Women migrants in Europe and North America have denounced the dangerous softness with which oppressive laws, customs, and practices against women, imported from other cultures, are tolerated or encouraged in host countries—in the name of respect for the Other, of the right to difference, of putting at par different cultures or religions.
>
> Like our own governments, governments of the countries of immigration are prepared to sell out the well-being, the human rights and the civil rights of women for the sake of giving in to the migrant community, solely represented everywhere in the world, by its male members.
>
> The collusion of patriarchies transcends most of the bones of contention between migrants and hosts. This is why, amongst the many laws and customs that could have been imported from the migrants' culture only those pertaining to women, the family and the private sphere are viewed with such tolerance.[26]

In addition to its stance against cultural relativism and misguided versions of multiculturalism, WLUML is very critical of existing political and economic arrangements, and often attributes fundamentalism and women's inequality to economic inequalities and political corruption. Thus it bemoans "the miserable failure of states in many parts of the Muslim world (as elsewhere) to close or even narrow the yawning gap between rich and poor, to provide jobs for burgeoning numbers of unemployed, to stem the insidious corruption that sows disillusionment throughout society, and to provide basic social services, such as health and education, that are essential to a decent life."[27] A solution promoted by many women's groups that the network once endorsed was that development agencies and donor countries broaden the scope of development "conditionality" to benefit women: "Rather than leaving women to the 'goodwill' of their (male) political leaders, states should be obliged by donors to direct a percentage of their aid money to women's projects."[28]

As a network of women in Muslim countries and communities, WLUML may be expected to be an enthusiastic supporter of democratization, especially in the Middle East and North Africa. However, as was noted in chapter 2, global feminists raise concerns about democratization projects that ignore women's rights. And feminists in Middle Eastern countries have experienced democratization processes that have opened up political space for Islamist parties. In the 1990s, Islamists in Jordan's parliament blocked legislation that would reform the country's family law in women's favor and that would impose strict punishments for honor crimes.

But it was the outcome of the political opening in Algeria after 1989 that confirmed the ambivalence of WLUML feminists regarding a strictly electoral democratization, leading Hélie-Lucas to make the following statement in 1993: "There is no sign that the fate of women will be seen as a valid indicator of democracy by the international community. What we see instead is a narrow interpretation of democracy in the exclusive sense of parliamentary democracy. This never prevented Hitler from being elected!" The reference to "a narrow interpretation of democracy" and to the election of Hitler is indicative of WLUML's concern with an electoralism that in certain circumstances can give rise to extreme right-wing, fascistic, or fundamentalist regimes. Following urban riots in 1988 that targeted the consequences of structural adjustment as well as political authoritarianism, the government of Chedli Bendjedid in 1989 declared political liberalization and drafted a new constitution allowing for a multiparty system and the first open elections. But it was the fundamentalist organization FIS that emerged as the front runner. In the run-up to the elections, FIS supporters and its leadership had threatened and bullied feminists and unveiled women and had stated their intention to "use democracy to destroy democracy" and establish an Islamic government. Algerian feminists and the network WLUML were understandably hostile to the fundamentalist agenda and skeptical of the prospect for real democratic outcomes of the 1991 elections. After the Algerian military and ruling party cancelled the results of the elections and the FIS initiated an armed conflict, Algerian feminist organizations were appalled by the ensuing violence—which included the kidnapping and rapes of many Algerian women and girls—and issued the slogan "no dialogue with the fundamentalists." In this they were supported by WLUML.[29]

Indeed, the Algeria campaign was a major one for WLUML, and the network sought to draw attention to the plight of Algerian women through participation at various UN conferences. They disseminated numerous action alerts and compiled dossiers. They provided funding so that the Algerian feminist leader Zazi Sadou could attend the 1995 Beijing conference and testify at the women's tribunal on violence against women. In January 1999, in concert with the International Women's Human Rights Law Clinic, WLUML submitted a shadow report on Algeria to the Committee on the Elimination of All Forms of Discrimination against Women. A highly detailed report, it documented the violence visited upon women by fundamentalist forces and the continuing discrimination women faced in state policies and in the legal framework.[30] They also put together a dossier on women's human rights violations by the fundamentalists (and by the state).

WLUML has become a strong supporter of the International Criminal Court, which the network sees as important for accountability, compensation, and awareness-raising. In December 2000, WLUML attended the historic Tokyo Tribunal on Japan's military sexual slavery in World War II, and was the initiator of a one-day public hearing on similar contemporary crimes, including the case of sexual slavery by Islamists in Algeria during the 1990s. In 2002 WLUML worked with a New York-based feminist and human rights law professor who helped them file a civil suit against the U.S.-based Algerian fundamentalist Anouar Haddam. The plaintiff in the case was the founder of an Algerian feminist organization and had received death threats from FIS during the civil conflict. The civil suit was regarded as not only a way of seeking recompense and justice but also as a political move to raise awareness about the contention between feminists and fundamentalists.[31]

Another WLUML campaign concerned the plight of Afghan women under the Taliban, and included the preparation in 1998 of a compilation of news reports concerning Taliban atrocities, appeals by Afghan women's organizations, and condemnations by international women's groups and prominent women leaders. WLUML had not actively taken up the case of Afghan women in the pre-Taliban era, when the modernizing and left-wing government of the Democratic Republic of Afghanistan was fighting the Mujahideen, an alliance of Islamists backed by the U.S., Pakistan, and Saudi Arabia, and Soviet troops were in Afghanistan.[32] Still, Hélie-Lucas, Shaheed, Mumtaz, and others in the network had had no illusions about the Mujahideen and their external supporters, and were appalled by their record of incompetence, infighting, and rapes when they came to power in 1992. In 1996, when the Taliban overthrew the Mujahideen and established a particularly repressive gender regime, WLUML went into action to raise international awareness. Shirkat Gah, for example, helped Afghan women refugees in Pakistan disseminate their international appeals. Throughout, WLUML feminists criticized the United States, Pakistan, Saudi Arabia, and other countries for having supported Afghan fundamentalists to the detriment of the human rights of women.

WLUML was also critical of the U.S. bombing raids, which the United States conducted in Afghanistan following the tragedy of 11 September 2001 in order to bring down the perpetrators, the al-Qaeda network, Osama bin Laden, and their Taliban sponsors. They were concerned that the raids brought devastation to ordinary Afghans. And they accused Western countries of having turned a blind eye to—and in the case of the U.S., having actively supported—Islamists. An article in a WLUML newsletter declared:

> Countless documents drawn up by international women's groups bear witness to the denunciations of all of this in recent years. Denunciations that not only fell on deaf ears but also suffered attempts of being silenced through the use of pressure and threats.
>
> Western governments are the prime responsible ones for the creation of these big and small monsters that they are now attempting to fight against. The West never cared when the Taliban attacked Afghan women's rights, when they assaulted them, when they killed them. It has looked in the other direction while in Algeria the radical Islamic groups have kidnapped, raped, killed and ripped to

pieces scores of women—the latest aggression taking place barely two months ago—while in Bangladesh women have to live with their faces scarred by the acid thrown in their faces by fundamentalists.

And now. Is an end to western hypocrisy going to come with the resounding measures being taken against the terrorism of the radical Islamic networks? Will they be compatible with measures of justice? It does not seem just to carpet-bomb a people, the Afghan people, who in the last years have been the prime victim of a regime which has been indirectly tolerated and harboured. There must be another way of achieving justice.[33]

SIGI Activities: A Closer Look

During the 1990s, through conferences, brainstorming sessions, and international dialogues, SIGI developed models to educate women on their human rights. One publication was *Claiming Our Rights: A Manual for Women's Human Rights Education in Muslim Societies,* a guide for leaders of human rights workshops. The workshops were designed to promote human rights awareness among women, and empower them with leadership skills to claim their rights and combat gender-based violence.[34] After its publication in 1998, *Claiming Our Rights* was adopted in twelve countries and translated into Arabic, Azeri, Bengali, Hindi, Malay, Persian, Russian, Urdu, and Uzbek. By late 1999, over two thousand women and men had participated in the test workshops around the world.[35]

Claiming Our Rights was implemented through test workshops in the Middle East, North Africa, South Asia, and Central Asia, led by field coordinators affiliated with SIGI. The philosophy and method behind *Claiming Our Rights* were flexible education, participation, dialogue, consensus building, individual consciousness raising, and respect for different priorities. For example, Malaysian single mothers confronted the issues of alimony negotiations and child custody battles and greatly benefited from discussions on Islamic law. A report explains: "The diverse educational, sectarian, and socioeconomic backgrounds of workshop participants necessitated that coordinators and facilitators respond creatively to the expectations of the different groups. . . . Participants in Seema Kazi's workshop in New Delhi were from extremely poor communities, slums, and shantytowns in and around the city. The Indian participants chose to focus on women's rights within the family over several sessions because the issue held much personal relevance."[36] In other test workshop sites, such as several Palestinian refugee camps, human rights discussion was introduced for the first time. In Syria, the coordinator reported that most of the participants were well educated but had rarely considered the issue of human rights. The workshop enabled the women participants to understand the concept of basic rights and to see violations of these rights in their daily lives.[37] Self-awareness and confidence were points stressed in each group to enable women to recognize these violations and to take a more active role in eradicating them. In turn, the workshops allowed SIGI to learn what improvements needed to be made. *Claiming Our Rights* was subsequently used in Brazil in the form of a radio project. Ten sessions were broadcast over the radio station REDEH.[38]

In another initiative, SIGI developed a manual entitled *Safe and Secure: Eliminating Violence against Women and Girls in Muslim Societies* with aid from the United Nations Development Fund for Women (UNIFEM), the Global Fund for Women, and the International Center for Human Rights and Democratic Development.[39] *Safe and Secure* was a gender violence training manual for those conducting human rights education workshops. Its purpose was to "mobilize and empower women to eliminate gender-based violence." The manual trained advocates and trainers to aid grassroots women in their understanding about universal human rights and the international human rights documents aimed toward ending violence against women and girls. Its goal was to assist women by helping them identify sources of violence in the family, community, and state; helping them to communicate their information about and understanding of violence to other women; and empowering them to influence governments to formulate and implement policies that eliminate violence. As the report on the manual explained: "The model underlying the manual is culture-based, grassroots-oriented, participatory, and non-hierarchical. The framework of the model is used to convey universal concepts of human rights in association with indigenous ideas, traditions, myths, and texts rendered in local idiom. It uses local examples, familiar concepts, and idiomatic language."[40] Discussion groups are formed in which the group leader helps the group to identify the sources and forms of violence against women and girls, understand the themes of violence as defined in international documents and as understood in local contexts, and devise effective strategies to combat violence. Included in the manual are case studies related to thirteen different types of gender-based violence: verbal and psychological abuse; financial and resource coercion; verbal and physical assaults in public spaces; sexual harassment on the job; child labor; spousal abuse; female genital mutilation; rape; trafficking and prostitution; child marriage; honor killings; women in the midst of armed conflict; and state-sanctioned gender apartheid. The manual also includes examples of projects intended to address gender violence in the global South; international legal instruments protecting women's human rights; samples of national legislation on violence against women and girls; a list of organizations that deal with this issue in Muslim communities. Sample questions and interactive learning exercises are intended to stimulate participants to develop ways of ending these violations.

In keeping with its method of bottom-up and systematic human rights education, SIGI developed the manual in a two-part process. In the first part, firsthand reports and data were collected concerning gender-based violence in Muslim communities, and these were adapted to theories and methods of the abolition of violence. Forty activists, advocates, and academicians from universities and international and nongovernmental organizations reviewed the material. They determined the need to place violence against women and girls in local, national, and international contexts to combat the problem effectively. It was also decided to design and implement antiviolence strategies that respected and incorporated local cultural, political, and socioeconomic realities among grassroots populations, and to create an international network of activists seeking to end gender-based violence by sharing information, financial resources, and strategies.[41]

Test workshops were held in Egypt, Jordan, Lebanon, and Zimbabwe. In Egypt, participants were mostly illiterate and discussed such issues as child labor and escaping debt and financial coercion. The workshops in Jordan saw the participation of NGO leaders and supervisors of programs concerning violence against women. Their recommendations included the addition of more case studies and the modification of some of the exercises. Lebanon's test groups included rural women and directors of divisions and teachers in Koranic schools. In a country where violence against women is traditionally a taboo subject, the SIGI program helped to bring the issue to the public's attention. In the second stage of the process of publishing *Safe and Secure,* changes were made to ensure adaptation to a variety of communities and regions based on the information recovered from the test workshops.[42]

A follow-up was the manual *In Our Own Words: A Guide for Human Rights Education,* which begins by describing alternative learning methods through facilitation, and the importance of democratic forms of building knowledge and making decisions. The aim was to provide a structure that would allow women to think for themselves and to plan appropriate action for the promotion of their human rights. The second part of the manual addresses frequently asked human rights questions such as: What are human rights? What is human rights law? How is international human rights law created? What are the NGOs and how to they influence human rights policy? What is CEDAW? The third part guides workshop leaders in their ability to adapt to the different people and issues in their group, and to relate to participants' lived experience. It also suggests strategies for dealing with difficult issues and situations, and explains how cultural relativism can be an impediment to rights.[43]

Like WLUML, SIGI emphasized the universality of rights and rejected notions of cultural relativism in connection to human rights. This was a matter of principle and conviction and the result of observing how governments and religious leaders in Muslim countries (and elsewhere) manipulated cultural relativist arguments to justify practices that discriminated against women. Both feminist networks hold fast to international conventions and norms, such as the UN's Declaration of Human Rights of 1948 and the Convention on the Elimination of All Forms of Discrimination against Women of 1979. At an international conference in San Francisco in October 1998, SIGI President Mahnaz Afkhami led the session "The Universal Declaration of Human Rights at 50: Preface to the Future." Noting that poverty remained widespread, that women were still subservient to men in many cultures, and that basic rights were still denied large sections of humanity, Afkhami underscored the importance of the Universal Declaration and called it "the highest expression of our noblest aspirations as individuals."[44]

These sentiments notwithstanding, Afkhami is aware that not all women's organizations in the global South are comfortable with the conventional discourse of human rights. This is especially true of certain women's organizations in the Middle East and North Africa, which do not necessarily state their aspirations in the human rights framework. As Afkhami explained:

They use a legalistic or developmental approach rather than a human rights approach per se. Also, there is a negative connotation regarding human rights, and it is often seen as an American-defined agenda, as a U.S. political ploy, or as a form of cultural colonialism. That's one of the reasons why women have not picked up the vocabulary. When our training manual was produced, some of our

Middle Eastern partners asked us, "can't you call it something other than 'education for women's human rights'"?

What we've tried to do is to find ways of dealing with the issue of women's human rights in ways with which our partners are comfortable. We don't have a problem with the issue of the universality of rights, or with an international convention such as CEDAW, for example. But we have to be sensitive to local priorities and to respect our partners' self-identified values. And we use local idioms where we can, in order to work toward women's rights. The relativity of rights is not an issue; rather, the priorities and methodologies have to be self-determined.[45]

Organizational Structures and Dynamics

Both WLUML and SIGI may be described as advocacy networks with loose structures. This is also true of a newer Middle-East-based feminist network, the Machreg-Maghreb Gender Link Information Project (GLIP), as well as the Women's Learning Partnership for Rights, Development, and Peace, which Afkhami formed after her term as SIGI president expired in late 1999. Transnational advocacy, information exchange, and solidarity are important goals of such feminist networks, and—as the quotations at the beginning of this chapter indicate—they believe that fluid, nonhierarchical, and democratic organizational forms and methods are more conducive to such goals than is the conventional bureaucratic organization. Nevertheless, there are some differences in their respective organizational structures.

Linking Local and Global: WLUML

WLUML exemplifies the type of transnational activity that does not eschew national issues. Indeed, WLUML leaders frequently emphasize that theirs is "an international solidarity network of women's groups with their own national priorities."[46] At its inception, says Hélie-Lucas, "we deliberately chose to reach out to women who worked on the ground in their countries, in order to enhance their own work by means of international solidarity among us."[47] And yet, she says, "we see ourselves as part of the global women's movement."[48]

Farida Shaheed, a founding leader of WLUML, has written of how the network "creates links amongst women and women's groups (including those prevented from organizing or facing repression if they attempt to do so) within Muslim communities, increase their knowledge about both the common and diverse situations in various contexts, strengthen their struggles and create the means to support them internationally from within and outside the Muslim world." The network "builds a network of information and solidarity; disseminates information through dossiers of information, facilitates interaction and contact between women from Muslim countries and communities, and between them and progressive feminist groups at large, facilitates exchanges of women from one geographical region to another."[49]

Since its inception, WLUML has operated as a network rather than as an organization or professional association. There is no formal membership; involvement is informal; and a plan of action guides the work for a period of four to six years. As Hélie-Lucas said: "The plan of action is a political document, and specific projects are drawn from it. We come together for the plans of action, where we discuss new developments and new priorities."[50]

WLUML began as a one-woman coordination office in France and then progressed to a small group assuming responsibility for implementation of the plans of action. In the second half of the 1990s, stimulated by successive collective projects, the network developed a more complex and diversified system for decision-making and implementation of network activities.[51] In the late 1990s the core group consisted of seven persons who were in charge of international coordination, book-keeping, and maintaining the overall direction of the network. Three coordination offices—an international coordination office in Europe, one in Pakistan (Shirkat Gah) for Asia, and one in Nigeria (Baobob) for Africa—shared information and analyses, issued action alerts, and carried out collective projects.[52] The coordination group was a flexible group of active "networkers" assuming responsibility for specific projects. The coordination group (which includes all members of the core group) had developed into the most important body for programming, planning, and implementation for the network as a whole. For example, the regional coordinators planned and directed the project on women and the law. In 2000, a series of committees were formed to involve a larger number of active networkers in the coordination and implementation of specific activities, such as publications and finance.

As Hélie-Lucas winded down her activities, the main WLUML office moved to London in 2001, but before that, there were eight staff persons in the office in France (including Hélie-Lucas). All were paid positions in administration, accounting, and so on. Shirkat Gah in Pakistan had seventy paid positions.

There was also a WLUML training institute, led by the veteran Bangladeshi human rights lawyer Salma Sobhan.

By 1994 women and women's organizations in some twenty-five countries were associated with WLUML through various projects.[53] According to Shaheed, "over two thousand women in several continents are linked through WLUML. These women have diverse professional and academic backgrounds, organizational frameworks and political perspectives but share a commitment to expanding women's autonomy. Most are actively involved in the women's movement in their own countries or place of residence. In addition, many are engaged in general advocacy initiatives."[54] Elsewhere, Shaheed notes that "an important minority are lawyers and social scientists, but the majority works in development and advocacy programs, often in an integrated manner. . . . WLUML links research groups, media groups and training organizations, grassroots organizations and university academics, Islamic scholars and legal aid and crisis centers. . . . The differences between groups and individuals give WLUML its uniqueness, a channel through which the differences in the lives and strategies of women in the Muslim world can be heard and exchanged."[55]

The differences among women in the WLUML network that Shaheed refers to pertain to different perspectives on Islam, women's rights, and secularism. Women in the network range from atheists (such as Hélie-Lucas) to believers (such as Sisters in Islam, based in Malaysia). All, however, oppose authoritarian Islamization and fundamentalist extremism. For example, Cassandra Balchin, a Pakistani journalist associated with WLUML, was involved in the women's campaigns against Zia ul-Haq's Islamization project. Ayesha Imam, a Nigerian feminist sociologist and human rights activist, formed the women's group Baobob, and in 2002–3 helped raise international awareness about the trials and sentences meted to two Nigerian women who were charged with illicit sexual relations. Asma'u Joda founded a center for women's empowerment in northeastern Nigeria and in the spring of 2002 was working with the WLUML office in London. Both Nigerian women participated in a workshop on "Islam, Women's Rights, and Islamic Feminism: Making Connections between Different Perspectives," which took place in Amsterdam in November 2001, organized by the International Institute for the Study of Islam in the Modern World (ISIM).[56]

Hélie-Lucas has emphasized the decentralized, participatory, nonbureaucratic, and nonhierarchical nature of the network, and its resistance to professionalization. An example of its decentralized and democratic nature is that despite Hélie-Lucas's prominence, she tried for ten years to have a project on fundamentalist militarization included in the plan of action. It was finally approved for the Dhaka 1997 action plan. The projects and priorities are determined by different regional groups, though the plan of action is decided upon collectively. "We reinforce local struggles, not divert from local struggles. This is the whole point about our network," said Hélie-Lucas. "The network itself is as fluid as you can imagine, but for each project we have a pyramidic structure."[57] She also emphasizes the informality, dedication, and passion that permeate the network.

Like other transnational feminist networks, WLUML stresses information exchange, mutual support, and international solidarity toward the realization of its essential goal of advancing women's rights in the Muslim world. Through its projects and its documentation and dissemination activities, WLUML has expanded the creative use of scarce resources and helped individuals and groups to form contacts and exchange knowledge, thereby increasing their effectiveness. Such a strategy "strengthens our local struggles by providing support at the regional and international levels, at the same time as our local struggles strengthen the regional and international women's movement in a mutually supportive process."[58]

Linking Local and Global: SIGI

During the 1990s, SIGI's membership included founding members, individuals within its network, and affiliated institutions and organizations (e.g., a Dalit women's organization in Nepal, several centers in the U.S.), which collaborated on projects. Like WLUML, SIGI's membership was "quite loose," as Afkhami has stated, and there was no active recruitment of members.[59] Members and officers have been a mix of activists, academics, and NGO workers from numerous countries. In addition to those mentioned at the beginning of this chapter, other leading figures in SIGI have been Maria Lourdes de Pinta Silgo of Portugal, Hilkka Pietila of Finland, Zenebeworke Tadesse of Ethiopia, Letitia Shahani of the Philippines, Jacqueline Pitanguy of Brazil, and Asma Khader of Jordan.

Unlike WLUML, SIGI had a more formal organizational structure: president, vice-president, treasurer, secretary, steering committee, advisory board, executive director. The steering committee was regionally representative, and included such women as Marjorie Agosin of Chile, Bouthaina Shaaban of Syria, Patricia Giles of Australia (a former senator), and Vanessa Griffen of Fiji, who was also affiliated with the Asia-Pacific Research Center in Kuala Lumpur, Malaysia. When Afkhami became president of SIGI in 1993, "the first two years were a real struggle." Still, "When I began we had a lot of great ideas and projects." These were funded in part by the membership, but largely by major foundations and international organizations, such as the MacArthur Foundation, UNIFEM, the Vaughan Foundation, the Global Fund for Women, and the International Center for Human Rights and Democratic Development. During most of the 1990s, funding for transnational feminist activity was plentiful, and Afkhami said in 1999, "I've done very little fund-raising. I've been so immersed in the content of the material we're producing. So it's just as well that people come to invite us to write proposals."[60] The generous funding served SIGI well, and allowed the network to maintain office space and a staff of five, organize conferences, attend international conferences, publish books, prepare human rights manuals, issue alerts, prepare briefings, and assist in the establishment of SIGI-Jordan led by Asma Khader, and SIGI-Uzbekistan led by Marfua Tokhtakhadjaeva.

Khader is the well-known human rights lawyer who has taken on honor crimes and discriminatory family laws in Jordan and among Palestinians, and Afkhami has described her as "a giant" among the leading figures of SIGI and Middle East women activists alike.[61] Afkhami also considers the opening of the center in Amman to be a major achievement, for both SIGI and the women's rights movement in the Middle East. The Amman center has worked on draft legislation for the creation of women's shelters throughout Jordan and for the criminalization of honor killings, and Khader works on women's legal cases in other countries in the region, often in collaboration with local women's organizations.[62] Afkhami went on to explain that SIGI sought to facilitate women's rights activities, not to expand its own organization. "Although we opened the center in Jordan, our idea was not to build branches, or 'an empire,' but to encourage the establishment of autonomous, affiliated groups."[63]

Another accomplishment is the way that SIGI was able to bridge the divide between local and global levels of activism as well as carry out its work in a collaborative and democratic fashion. According to Afkhami, "The whole process of creating the two women's manuals in the Middle East [on women's human rights and on violence against women] bridged the local and global. We worked with people from different countries in the Middle East, and we encouraged them to work together as well as with us. They decided on their own priorities, and these were decided on in a series of brainstorming sessions.

Then we all worked together on the manuals."[64] SIGI saw part of its mandate as working with other feminist organizations to promote women's human rights. In an interview in 1999, Afkhami said: "We work closely with various groups, for example, Charlotte Bunch's Center for Women's Global Leadership, Women Living under Muslim Laws, WEDO, and UNIFEM, one of our funders." SIGI participated in the UN's 1993 Human Rights Conference, but was more actively involved in the preparations for the 1995 Beijing conference. It organized a post-Beijing conference in 1996, which resulted in the publication of *Muslim Women and the Politics of Participation: Implementing the Beijing Platform*. In terms of involvement with the UN, says Afkhami, "we are not as immersed as others are, but we come in when there is a useful dialogue." In this respect, SIGI came closer to WLUML than to such transnational feminist networks as DAWN, WIDE, and WEDO.

The relationship between women's human rights organizations such as SIGI, WLUML, the Washington-based network Women, Law, and Development International, and the Center for Women's Global Leadership at Rutgers University exemplifies the explicit collaborations and implicit "divisions of labor" that emerge. As Afkhami said with respect to SIGI's relationship with WLUML: "We exchange alerts, attend each other's conferences, and share some members. For example, Sima Kazi [of India] works with both SIGI and WLUML." Another activist who works with both networks is Marfua Tokhtakhadjaeva of Uzbekistan. When I suggested to Afkhami that relations among transnational feminist networks seemed more collaborative than competitive, she replied: "These interconnections, you're right, may be unique to women's organizations. There is lots of positive energy, not negativism. We stay out of each other's turf. For example, Women, Law, and Development International covers Eastern Europe, and we don't."[65] The same understanding was brought over to the Women's Learning Partnership, which Afkhami formed after SIGI's headquarters rotated to Montreal. "After I left SIGI and formed WLP, I waited for about a year to make sure that I would not encroach on SIGI's work with the Middle Eastern partners. So I developed partnerships with Morocco, Palestine, and Nigeria, where SIGI was not active."[66]

Building a New Network: WLP

When it was time to rotate SIGI headquarters Afkhami hoped that the network would move to the global South, preferably the Philippines or a country in Africa. There were candidates there, but "they were not ready to assume the responsibility for the organization, and backed out. We need to build an international presence coming from the South. Hopefully in the next rotation the headquarters will be in the South."[67] In the meantime, Afkhami set up the Women's Learning Partnership for Rights, Development, and Peace, which allows her to continue the work that interests her the most—institution building and capacity building of women's organizations, including the development of technology use among women. The focus areas were initially Central Asia and North Africa, but by 2002 Afkhami resumed her work with the SIGI partners in Jordan, Lebanon, and Uzbekistan. She also established ties with the Beirut-based Maghreb-Mashrek Link, also known as the Gender Link Information Project (GLIP). WLP established a board of directors that meets twice a year to review projects and priorities.

WLP is a network that carries out both consciousness raising and practical work. In an interview in April 2002, Afkhami explained the role and strengths of a transnational feminist network such as WLP:

> We're useful because when you're immersed in local work, you don't want to know what's going on next door. We facilitate dialogue, and we function as a liaison. We have so much experience with religion, and we can share experiences. We promote South-South and South-North dialogue.
>
> What we are also good at is helping to build capacity in women's organizations. They need support and knowledge about innovative things done elsewhere. So we have provided leadership training sessions for women. Of course we do it differently, and in a feminist way. I remember Bella Abzug saying, "Let's not mainstream into a polluted stream." We want leadership to be participatory, horizontal, consensus-building—the essence of democracy.

WLP staff also help the partners in Muslim countries to expand their resources, build their organizations, and network with other women's groups by writing proposals, obtaining grants, doing evaluations, arranging for translations, setting up LISTSERVs and websites, and distributing CD-ROMs. Afkhami sees the function of the WLP as one of "connecting, facilitating, bringing new ideas." As she has explained: "We share a lot of information about women's issues with our partners, but we also try to sort out what's important, so our partners don't have to spend money and long periods on the Internet. If there is a legal campaign under way, we might forward some relevant legislation to help the legal activists. We also have a comparative table on our website with useful comparative data."

Of the TFNs studied in this book, the WLP works most extensively with the media, and is also technically sophisticated in relation to ICTs. For example, after September 11 it organized a live webcast in which various WLP partners discussed the tragedy. In the United States, WLP has developed close relationships with certain public radio stations and key journalists in the print media. The network provides briefs, profiles of Muslim women leaders, and arranges for interviews. As Afkhami explained: "This relationship is very important to us, and enables us to get our ideas across. It's how we get our issues on the table. It gives visibility to our themes and priorities. We put a huge emphasis on the media."[68]

Another important function is fund-raising for women's organizations, especially in countries where governments are authoritarian and controlling of civil society organizations. This is true of almost all the countries in the Middle East, North Africa, and Central Asia where the WLP has partners. In addition, in those countries "there is not a culture of philanthropy apart from donations to religious institutions and charitable contributions to the poor. So they depend on external sources of funding, and here we can help. Of course, it is not easy for us to raise funds, either."[69]

Women's organizations in the Middle East, North Africa, and Central Asia face other issues as well, including some that echo the concerns about professionalization discussed in chapter 4. One of WLP's partner organizations is the Association Democratique des Femmes Marocaines, which is a volunteer organization. Afkhami says that it is difficult to carry out projects with organizations that are purely voluntary. "You need people whose job it is to run things, advocate, lobby, etc. Professionalization is necessary, although you need a combination of volunteerism, too." She explains that some women activists in the Middle East and North Africa are reluctant to get paid, "because they feel that it might diminish the value of what they are doing. This is something that is working itself out. If you are doing developmental work and advocacy and lobbying, you need paid positions. You need an office, secretaries, etc. Voluntarism takes a certain level of affluence."[70] Afkhami's advice was obviously taken by SIGI-Jordan, which is run as a professional office with fifteen paid staff positions, occupied mainly by women but also a few men. The director, lawyer Asma Khader, is, however, unpaid. Her income is from her private legal practice.[71]

Conclusions

The economic, political, and cultural dimensions of globalization—such as the expansion of neoliberal capitalism, the decline of the welfarist and developmentalist state, persistent inequalities, the power of core countries along with the IFIs and the WTO in global governance, and the growth of transnational fundamentalist movements—have been met by collective action on the part of women around the world. In this chapter we have examined feminist networks that formed in response to fundamentalist movements and complicit states in the Muslim world, and that have focused their energies on research, lobbying, and advocacy for the human rights of women in Muslim countries and communities. The growth in the population of educated, employed, and mobile women in the Muslim world also has favored their political mobilization as transnational feminists.

Like other TFNs, transnational advocacy networks and global social movement organizations, WLUML, SIGI, and the more recent WLP have made good use of informal non-movement mobilizing structures such as friendship networks and professional networks, and built alliances with movement structures such as other activist networks. And like the other TFNs examined in this book, they have been funded by major foundations and European governments. Unlike DAWN, WIDE, WEDO, however, they have relied less on individuals in intergovernmental bureaucracies or national delegations and have steered clear of formal ties with UN agencies. This is especially the case with WLUML. Although it circulates petitions that are forwarded to the UN, it does not engage in some of the other activities that are undertaken by other TFNs, such as lobbying at the national level. This is mainly because the network views most of the national governments within its purview as patriarchal, authoritarian, or corrupt. Its emphasis, therefore, is on solidarity and support for women who live under Muslim laws. Still, WLUML, like the other TFNs examined in this book, has contributed to the global social movement infrastructure and the transnational public sphere.

This chapter also has illustrated the ambivalence of some global feminists toward state systems, the UN, and democracy. WLUML in particular eschews the kind of focused work with intergovernmental organizations in which other TFNs engage, as it sees itself primarily as an international solidarity network. And although democracy—like globalization—is the buzzword of our times, WLUML is rightly suspicious of democratic projects that are imposed by force (as in Iraq in 2003–4) or that ignore the human rights of women (as in Algeria in 1990–91). Real democracy comes from below, and it should be seen as the basis for the expansion of citizen rights, not merely as the opportunity for a political group to seize power.

What do the feminist networks dealing with women's rights in the Muslim world consider to be their major accomplishments? For Hélie-Lucas of WLUML, it is "networking—no doubt about it. Knowing what the others are doing. This is our main achievement and success. We have no real disappointments or frustrations."[72] Despite persistent funding constraints and some difficulties within the broad human rights movement, the main accomplishments appear to be the building of formal networks of information exchange and solidarity, and the contribution to global discourses on women's human rights, universalism, and difference. According to Afkhami: "One of the things we wanted was a more equitable representation of women in the international dialogue on human rights. We've been successful in that. We've helped to raise important issues, such as universal rights and feminist ideas." Referring to the global women's human rights movement, Afkhami said, "We have been able to place women's rights on the human rights agenda, when we struggled at the UN conference in Vienna in 1993 to get accepted the notion that women's rights are human rights and are universal." She stresses the importance of the UN record on promoting women's rights, especially in Muslim countries: "International pressures, international conventions—these provide a great tool for mobilizing locally. The conferences have been enormously helpful for networking, and for funding."[73]

But challenges remain, according to Afkhami: "I'm not sure we have succeeded in fully sensitizing the human rights community with respect to women's rights. There tends to be a disconnect between the two, even in the West, even in major human rights organizations." This is especially true in the Muslim world, she added, where human rights organizations and women's organizations have different agendas and discourses, although they would appear to converge on many issues. Coalition building across women's groups but also between women's groups and human rights organizations will be especially important in building democratization and civil society and in challenging both the authoritarianism of the state and the powerful influence of fundamentalism. Although fundamentalism is less powerful than before, "a lot of problems that women face have to do with clerical and religious interventions. We have to take a strong position on these matters." And although

Afkhami identifies herself as a Muslim, she is against theoretical or political positions that oppose universalism in human rights: "I'm surprised by the relativist approach taken by some scholars. In the U.S., for example, there is pressure to accept diversity, different cultures, etc. But at least there is a legal infrastructure here that prevents religious interventions in the legal sphere. The feminist movement has no choice but to take a strong position against fundamentalism and extremism."[74] As we have seen, this is a sentiment that is shared by the network Women Living under Muslim Laws.

CHAPTER SEVEN

The Travails of Transnational Feminist Organizing

The Association of Women of the Mediterranean Region (AWMR)

In addition to organizational—and political—choices, transnational feminist networks must also make decisions on what Jo Freeman has called "strategic options." Decisions made concerning strategies, tactics, and resources to be mobilized can shape or determine the outcome of the movement or organization. At the same time, the options pursued may themselves be the result of constraints. Suzanne Staggenborg has shown how decisions made by feminist groups as to how they would conduct their reproductive rights campaigns affected their outcomes, as did decisions regarding their organizational structure.[1]

Many feminist organizations have resisted professionalization and interaction with governmental or intergovernmental organizations out of principle, or the desire to resist any co-optation or loss of "political purity." *Manushi,* the independent Indian woman's magazine, does not seek funding from sources outside of India. *Manushi* has, however, found it possible to maintain an operating budget that has allowed it to function since the 1980s, because of its success with subscriptions, book sales, and funds from Indian sources.[2] Some transnational feminist networks, however, are faced with the difficult fact that their constituencies are unable to generate sufficient funds to create a sound fiscal base for the operation of the organization. Such financial difficulties may have to do with political principles, but they may be linked also to organizational issues. Previous chapters have shown that transnational feminist networks generally eschew nationalist tendencies in favor of transnational solidarities as well as a transnational organizational form, in which individual or group members pay into a common fund or take part in various fundraising strategies. In some cases, however, a transnational feminist network may consist of national women's groups or individual members with only loose ties and affiliations to the transnational body and a greater concentration on national issues and forms of organizing.

An examination of the evolution and travails of the Association of Women of the Mediterranean Region illustrates such dilemmas. It shows how choices regarding external funding or professionalization can result in a more radical politics but also fewer resources and less consistent activity. It shows, too, how nationalist politics may bedevil the efforts of a TFN to organize women across conflict zones.

The AWMR: Background and Overview

The Association of Women of the Mediterranean Region (AWMR) unites women of Albania, Algeria, Cyprus, Egypt, France, Gibraltar, Greece, Israel, Lebanon, Libya, Malta, Morocco, Palestine, Spain, Syria, Tunisia, Turkey, and former Yugoslavia, now Serbia. It was founded in Malta in 1992 "after seven years of meeting, networking, and joint work."[3] AWMR is centrally interested in "justice, equality, and peace," but it is also concerned with reproductive health, pay equity, environmental issues, family violence, and class, racial, and ethnic inequality. The AWMR is an anticapitalist, antimilitarist transnational feminist network with clear goals regarding its regional mission, the global context, and local actions. It is in many ways a unique organization of women, inasmuch as it unites women from various conflict areas around the Mediterranean, such as Israelis and Palestinians, Serbs, Bosnians, and Albanians, Greeks and Turks, and Greek and Turkish Cypriots. Of all the TFNs studied in this book, the AWMR has the largest participation of Arab women, and is the most explicitly political. Despite its internationalism, however, the AWMR has not always been able to transcend the nationalisms within its region, as will be evident from the description of its 2002 annual conference.

Moreover, the association has been hampered by lack of financial resources. Throughout the years, the AWMR has operated entirely on volunteer labor and a shoestring budget, although for some years it was the beneficiary of a generous grant from a private source. It has no offices, paid staff, organizational facilities, or stable financial resources. The newsletter and other communications have been produced entirely on personal time and personal facilities. Each year, the officers and members of the local organizing committee scramble to assemble funds so that women from soft currency or low-income Mediterranean countries can be subsidized to attend the annual meeting. Over and above membership fees, a considerable amount of personal funds from core members and officers have been expended toward the annual meetings and other activities. Because so few members of the association are academics, all expenses are borne by the association and/or individual members. By 2001, the private source of funding that had been relied upon had dried up, and the AWMR was unable to convene its annual conference of members or to prepare and distribute its newsletter. That July, as the AWMR faced a fiscal crisis, only the members of the board were able to meet in Malta.

The AWMR is, in the words of both its president and its general secretary, "a political organization."[4] Thus its mission statement is as follows:

> We, the women of the Mediterranean Region, conscious of our common cultural heritage and of the strategic importance of our region, seek to transcend economic, gender, cultural, social, racial, national, ethnic, religious, political, and all other barriers to peaceful cooperation.
>
> United in our common aspirations for justice, equality and peace, we pledge to work for a better life for our people and for future generations in a region free of conflict, armaments, pollution, exploitation and all forms of domination and exploitation.
>
> Conscious that the world is calling for greater cooperation between peoples, we, the women of the Mediterranean Region, united in a grassroots movement, working with other national, regional and international women's organizations, will strive to create a new regional and global awareness of the need for greater respect, understanding, cooperation and collaboration in order to achieve a better and peaceful future for humankind.[5]

The AWMR's stated aims are to work toward the following:

- just and peaceful resolution of regional conflicts;
- regional demilitarization and global disarmament;
- elimination of discrimination, poverty, and violence against women;
- human rights, real democracy, and sustainable development;
- the welfare and rights of children;
- education for peace through the family, schools, and media;
- common action to end environmental degradation of the Mediterranean Region.

To achieve these ends, the AWMR networks on Mediterranean regional issues and it creates public awareness though educational and information campaigns, conferences, and occasional demonstrations. It promotes women's ventures and encourages women's participation in the decision-making process. It lobbies members of parliament and influential bodies to create specific social structures and institutions for the establishment of effective policies and conditions "by which our aims may be achieved"; and it works together with other national, regional, and international organizations that share its aims.[6] Resolutions passed by the members at the annual meetings are forwarded to parliaments by the executive board.

Among its activities have been petitions to end violence in Bosnia; the sale of Palestinian women's crafts in the United States; joint activity by Jewish and Palestinian women against Israeli aggression; the initiation of dialogue between Greek Cypriot women and Turkish Cypriot women; joint activity among women in Zagreb, Sarajevo, and Belgrade; a visit by Italian delegates to Albania in support of women's rights; raising awareness within various Mediterranean countries of the plight of Algerian women in the 1990s; a 1997 petition for Education for Peace in the Mediterranean; protests against the 1999 NATO bombing of Yugoslavia; petitions calling for an end to sanctions against Iraq; petitions (sent to governments) deploring U.S. preparations for war against Iraq. The association puts out a newsletter, publishes the proceedings of its annual conferences, and sends copies of its resolutions to governments and to the UN. It has consultative status with the Committee on Palestine and the Committee on the Environment, although it only occasionally has a representative attending meetings in New York.[7]

Board members, and other AWMR members, have been active in various progressive causes, and some have been members of left-wing political parties.

This common political background often has allowed for the agreement and cooperation of women across different conflict regions. For example, at one point during the 1998 conference in southern Italy I was asked by delegates from Serbia and Albania to help draft a resolution on the Kosovo conflict. I was impressed by the principled and civil nature of the differing views expressed, and by the capacity of the women to agree on a statement condemning violence on both sides and calling for negotiations. This civility apparently broke down at the 1999 conference in Athens, when emotions overtook reason and principle, but it was restored at the conference in Cyprus in July 2000. Indeed, at that conference the Albanian women extended an invitation to the Serbian women delegates to visit them in Tirana to discuss peace, security, and cross-border collaborations.[8]

More than any other TFN, the AWMR issued a number of very strong statements against the NATO bombing of Yugoslavia in 1999. The war in Kosovo and the bombing of Yugoslavia, of course, fell within the regional purview of the AWMR, but the organization was also motivated by its longstanding political stance against militarism, war, and intervention. It issued three appeals calling for an immediate end to the NATO bombing, the exploration of all peaceful paths to reconciliation, the demilitarization of the Mediterranean as a whole, the removal of all foreign bases, and equality for all citizens and immigrants.[9]

One characteristic of the AWMR that distinguishes it from other transnational feminist networks is its strongly political and left-wing character. Rather than identify itself as feminist, the AWMR prefers to define itself as a women's political organization. Ninetta Pourou-Kantzasis pointed out, "Our political nature is what makes us distinctive."[10] Indeed, individual members are not necessarily feminist in the strict sense of the word. Women's equality, autonomy, and empowerment are not always at the center of every member's analyses or actions. For example, it was clear at the 2000 conference that the central concern of the Palestinian and Israeli members was "real independence" for Palestine; a few other members pointed to the gender dynamics of the conflict and argued that women and gender issues needed to be integrated into any resolution. Moreover, many members are not familiar with feminist scholarship (whether in its Marxist, socialist, radical, liberal, or postmodernist variants) and do not deploy the concepts and categories of feminist theory. However, if feminism is understood in its broader sense—that is, in terms of discourses and actions by women that implicitly or explicitly further the advancement of women—then AWMR members may rightly be called feminist. They are de facto if not self-defined feminists. Indeed, this post-ideological praxis of women activists seen around the world may be one characteristic of global feminism.

Organizational Structure

The AWMR has a three-tiered membership of individuals and women's organizations from the Mediterranean region. The membership consists of founder members (those in attendance at the inaugural conference in Malta in September 1992), full members (nongovernmental Mediterranean women's organizations and individual women from the Mediterranean region), and observer members (other women's NGOs and individual women). Members pay dues, agree with the aims of the organization, and participate in the annual conferences. AWMR officers—members of the executive board who are elected from among the full members—consist of a president, two vice-presidents, one general secretary, one assistant general secretary, one financial secretary, and one assistant financial secretary.

The AWMR has a twenty-person board of directors, one from each of the Mediterranean countries, elected for a period of three years, who are "dedicated to justice, equality, and peace."[11] The core activists have been mainly from Malta and Cyprus. In 2003, the president (and founding member) was Yana Mintoff-Bland, daughter of the late Dom Mintoff, the veteran socialist leader of Malta whose early support for the Palestinian cause set him apart from other European leaders. The general secretary, Ninetta Pourou-Kantzasis, is from Limassol, Cyprus, and has been a member of the Political Bureau of the United Democrats, a liberal-left party. Another member of the executive, Maroulla Vassiliou, is with POGO, the women's organization affiliated to the Cypriot Communist Party. Other AWMR members have been similarly prominent or well-known activists in their own countries, and have been elected or appointed to legislative positions. For example, the Moroccan human rights activist Aicha Belarbi, who had been an AWMR board member, was in 1998 appointed to a cabinet post by the new socialist prime minister, Abdelrahman Yousoufi, and in 2000 was named Morocco's ambassador to the EU. As mentioned above, the left-wing background of most AWMR members and officers allows for consensus and cooperation in what is a very politically contentious and divided region. Thus members can agree on such resolutions as: "We condemn the use of embargoes and military intervention against defenseless populations. These actions deprive children of their basic human right to health."[12]

The AWMR has the appearance of a formal organization, but it is in reality fluid and nonhierarchical. The annual conferences are very participatory, interactive, and democratic. All decisions are made by consensus; Mintoff-Bland remarked, "I don't think we have ever had to vote on an issue."[13] At times during the annual conferences, discussions can be lively and sometimes heated, with little intervention by the executive. Roberts Rules of Order are rarely used to bring discussions under control or to return to the main issue at hand, but the executive may intervene to issue a political opinion. In response to my question as to what kind of direction, management, or leadership was offered by the executive, the president said, "I think we provide political direction." She described the AWMR and its structure as "very organic."[14]

In fact, the executive provides more than political direction and leadership, although this is what it sees as its most important task. The executive maintains the network through its newsletter (circulation 900), occasional e-mail messages and appeals to individual and organizational members, the establishment of a website by the Italian branch, activities that promote the AWMR as a whole, fund-raising, and of course the annual conference. This is important, given that most members are engaged primarily in local and national-level activities. Moreover, members of the executive have the institutional memory that newer members do not have, and are able to remind new members that suggested resolutions, for example, have been adopted at previous conferences. Members of the executive also explain procedure. For instance, at the Cyprus conference in July 2000, one new member raised a question about the position statements being made by the Israeli delegates on Palestine and by the Italian delegates on the Kurdish question. In response, the general secretary explained, "This is an occasion for members to raise burning political questions and to obtain solidarity from other members."[15] Position statements are offered by delegates for endorsement by the AWMR. The executive, therefore, maintains the regional and global focus of the association, as well as its procedural coherence, organizational continuity, and political orientation.

Due to funding limitations, the AWMR has not actively participated in global conferences. For example, Cypriot members attended the Fourth World Conference on Women, but they did so in their capacity as members of Cypriot NGOs. However, in 2000 the AWMR took steps to enhance its global visibility by taking part in the planning of the World March of Women, which culminated in several days of transnational action in October 2000 (see chapter 3). Four AWMR members were part of its international liaison committee, including board members Farida El-Nakkash of Egypt and Maroulla Vassiliou of Cyprus. The AWMR was formally part of the organizing body, which included representatives of sixty women's organizations.[16] The association then established links with WEDO, and in early 2000, members of the executive were invited by WEDO to New York. This also provided them with the opportunity to take part in preparatory meetings for ICPD + 5 and Beijing + 5.

As of 2004, the AWMR had no paid positions and was based entirely on volunteer work. For the first few years of its existence it received funding from the generous private source and from the governments of Cyprus and Malta, and with some of its revenues trickling in from membership fees (individual and organizational) and from the sale of books. Local women's branches raise funds locally and nationally to organize the national conferences; for example, the Italian branch organized the 1998 conference, which focused on women, work, and social policies, while the Greek branch organized the 1999 conference, which focused on women, children, and environmental protection. In 2000, the conference was held in Cyprus and the theme was Children in the Mediterranean in the Context of the Convention on the Rights of the Child. At the business meeting in Cyprus, discussions were held on the future of the association and its financial viability. It was decided that several members would form a committee to prepare grant proposals. The committee never convened, however, and thus funds were unavailable for the 2001 conference. In addition, the newsletter was not distributed during 2001, and members were not contacted for annual fees.[17] The matter of financial viability and more effective communications was discussed again at the 2002 annual meeting in Marrakesh. As Mintoff-Bland confided regarding the work of keeping the network together, "We have the raw energy and the commitment. But the economics of it has been really hard. We try to be independent. But we can't accomplish much without real funding."[18]

Most AWMR members are active in various women's organizations or progressive movements in their own countries. The Israeli members, for example, have been active in Women in Black, the anti-occupation women's protest group, the Israeli Communist Party, and other left-wing organizations. The Albanian members are members of WILPF. In 1998, one invited speaker and new member, the Turkish sociologist Yildiz Ecevit, brought along a pamphlet describing a new women's group with which she was involved, whose name translates into Flying Broom. In 2000, the Palestinian delegation was from the Working Women's Society, which operates in the West Bank and Gaza. Others were active in various women's groups. Two delegates were from the Tunisian Mothers' Association while the Moroccans were with HERD, a network devoted to human development and environmental protection. Organizational members of the AWMR are WILPF-Italy, POGO (Cyprus), and the Union of Democratic Women (Cyprus). In 2003 the AWMR had branches in several countries—"those without strong women's movements or organizations," according to Vassiliou, such as southern Italy and Albania—and planned to establish additional ones in Greece, Israel, and Palestine.

Annual Conferences

Despite the growing importance of the use of the Internet, many TFNs continue to hold annual meetings, even though they are costly. This sets them apart from web-based groups whose form of communication is principally cybernetic. Thematically organized, the AWMR's annual meetings are held in different countries in the region—Malta, Cyprus, Italy, Greece, Morocco—and have focused on women's rights, colonialism, militarism, health, refugees and immigrants, education for peace, the environment, children, and globalization. Each conference has a formal opening and includes cultural events as well as panels, country analyses, and political discussions. The local organizing committee makes all the arrangements, including the social events and presentations by local or national officials. Each conference ends with a set of resolutions and is followed by a conference report; some conferences have resulted in the publication of a book. Resolutions are forwarded to parliamentary committees and to the United Nations secretariat in New York.

For example, the fifth annual conference of the AWMR, held in Limassol, Cyprus, focused on the problems of refugees and immigrants, and drew attention to "political conflicts which create refugees, social problems arising from immigration, and the health, social security and housing rights of immigrants and refugees." Participants had a firsthand look at refugees at the partition line in Nicosia as well as other sites. The conference called on countries to recognize and implement basic human rights for women refugees and immigrants as provided for by international human rights instruments, and to ensure that there was no discrimination on the basis of sex, ethnic identity, religion, sexual orientation, or race. Conference resolutions called for job opportunities for refugees and immigrants; the right to education (with respect for the cultural identity of immigrants and their right to participate in curriculum planning); immigrant rights to healthcare and a healthy environment; the right to reside in adequate housing; and the right to political participation. The conference papers and resolutions asked that governments institute and support programs for women immigrants and refugees and their families on the prevention of violence within and outside the home. It was suggested that immigrant and refugee women participate in planning so that counseling services and women's shelters would be culturally sensitive.

Based on the experiences in Palestine, Cyprus, Yugoslavia, and elsewhere, the conference issued an appeal to governments to recognize and implement family reunification rights for immigrants and refugees; it was recommended that registered and unregistered refugees from the former Yugoslavia be allowed to stay at their places of refuge until they could return safely to their place of origin and be assured of a decent livelihood. The conference urged that governments and responsible NGOs implement and support economic initiatives of immigrants, refugees, and displaced persons; give economic support and humanitarian aid to NGOs; and facilitate short- and long-term financial aid to immigrants and refugees. Speakers stressed the important role of the media in making visible the situation of immigrants and refugees. In keeping with the value that the network places on national-level action and working toward changes in state policies, an AWMR statement read: "Our priority must be to transmit recommendations about the rights for social security and the protection of human rights to our own governments, rather than only to the UN and European boards. Each woman is responsible to fight for human rights and the protection of refugees and immigrants in her own country and make that her focus above petitioning the UN and other European boards."

Last but not least, the AWMR conference called on governments and women's organizations to "take all appropriate measures against all forms of sex slavery, trafficking of women and forced prostitution," and urged that governments guarantee full protection and anonymity to witnesses who gave evidence and testimonies of rape as a war crime in The Hague War Crimes Tribunal.[19] The issues discussed at Limassol were revised at the 1997 Malta conference, which focused on peace, conflict resolution, and demilitarization in the Mediterranean region. Presentations by women from Algeria, Cyprus, Yugoslavia, Palestine, Israel, Lebanon, Malta, Greece, and Tunisia described the wars, partition, civil conflict, and fundamentalist movements that produced refugees, asylum seekers, and immigrants, and that brought about distinctive hardships for women. For example, a position statement on Israel/Palestine critically assessed the provisions of the Oslo Agreement and pointed out that "the question of refugees has been wiped off the negotiation's agenda by Israel and through quiet PLO consent." It added: "As women, we are concerned by the militarization of Palestinian society. This trend is blocking the growth of democratic institutions and a civil society, which is the only guarantee for the development of women and society as a whole." This statement was included in the post-conference book *In Search of Peace.*[20]

Women's perspectives on the environment in the Mediterranean region constituted the theme of the 1998 annual conference in Athens. The conference examined environmental degradation and risks in the region, and ways of developing "common action to achieve a Mediterranean Region free of pollution, to halt wanton environmental destruction, to safeguard our sea, air, soil, and water, and to press for measures for sustainable urban development."[21] The conference also issued a position statement on Yugoslavia that stressed the environmental destruction caused by the NATO bombing and its use of depleted uranium. It called for an end to all foreign military intervention, an immediate end to war, and the use of peaceful resolution of conflict by diplomatic means.[22] In the conference's final resolution, it was deemed that "the forces of capitalist production, especially the military-industrial complex, are primarily responsible" for environmental degradation in the region and elsewhere. Specific measures agreed upon by the conference were: cooperation with environmental networks and NGOs and partnerships with regional organizations such as MedForum and UNEP-MAO; equal representation on the Medbank Watch; the establishment of a committee called WomensMedWatch; empowerment of women-led community groups; and analyses of best practices, health studies, and scientific studies of pollution to build strong alliances and lobbies.[23]

In keeping with the association's concern for local issues, national priorities, and state policies, resolutions were passed on the violence in Algeria; on a parliamentary proposal in Greece to introduce military conscription for women; on the Oslo Agreement and the continuing problems in Israel/Palestine, including their implications for women; on the special problems of persons of mixed marriages in the former Yugoslavia; on women's rights and violence against Kurds in Turkey; on the conflict in Kosovo; and on the continuing division of Cyprus.

The theme of the ninth annual conference, Children in the Mediterranean Region, allowed members to review the status of children in their countries in light of the 1990 Convention on the Rights of the Child. Held in Cyprus in July 2000, the conference was attended by some fifty-eight participants from sixteen countries. As is usual at AWMR conferences, a formal opening ceremony was held, attended by various Cypriot officials from across the political parties. The minister of justice attended, in part because the national machinery for the rights of women as well as the welfare of children fell within his purview. Two invited guests and speakers represented the women's wing of the United Democrats and of the Communist Party, respectively. The AWMR president and general secretary also made presentations in which the World Bank and the IMF were taken to task for the dire situation of children. National inequalities were also deplored, and Yana Mintoff-Bland pointed out that "justice and equality are the basis for peace."[24]

At the conference, presentations were made by AWMR members from Israel, Italy, Palestine, Albania, Morocco, Spain, Tunisia, Serbia, Macedonia, Algeria, as well as by invited experts from the Council of Europe and from the Pan Cypriot Coordinating Committee for the Protection and Welfare of Children. At one point, a lively discussion was held in which the two Tunisian delegates were criticized, largely by the Algerian and Moroccan delegates, for an uncritical and overly rosy picture of the situation of children in Tunisia. This led to a discussion of the ways in which Tunisia's social welfare system does tackle poverty, children's needs, and the situation of low-income or under-educated women—albeit in a dirigiste manner.[25]

There was a significant presence of Arab women at the July 2000 meeting, including a delegation of four from Palestine, three from Egypt, two from Tunisia, one from Algeria, and one from Morocco. The Palestinians were from the Working Women's Society, a new NGO based in the West Bank and Gaza. The Jewish and Arab Israeli women were from Bat Shalom and from the Communist Party (the latter included a member of the Knesset who chaired the Committee on Children's Rights). The delegates from Albania and from Italy were members of WILPF. The Yugoslav delegation, which consisted of five women involved with two feminist groups in Belgrade, was fiercely anti-nationalist and made a number of strongly worded statements in opposition to the Milosevic government. Nevertheless, among the resolutions passed at the annual meeting, one concerned the removal of all economic sanctions against Yugoslavia. The Palestinians and the Israeli CP delegates jointly prepared a resolution protesting the continued building of Jewish settlements and calling for the shared governance of Jerusalem. A resolution was also passed calling for an immediate end to sanctions against Iraq. These resolutions were subsequently forwarded by the executive to national parliaments, regional bodies, and the United Nations secretariat.

Women, Work, and Globalization: The 1998 and 2002 Annual Meetings

Although the AWMR takes on a relatively wide array of issues, including the status of women in the Arab countries, it shares with other TFNs studied in this book a concern with capitalist inequities and the diminution of social rights. These concerns run across all the annual conferences, but they were most explicitly addressed at the 1998 and 2002 meetings, which focused on women's work conditions, poverty, social rights, and the contradictions of globalization.

Organized by the Italian branch in Lecce, southern Italy, the seventh annual conference in 1998 focused on "Women and Work in the Mediterranean." The main panel discussions were on the right to work in the context of women's human rights; exploitation, unemployment, and ways to organize; and country analyses of women and work. There was also a workshop on globalization, the presentation of position papers and resolutions, and a general assembly. Panel presentations were on immigrant working women in Italy and elsewhere; women, work, and the changing political economy in the Middle East and North Africa; the problems and prospects of women and work in Algeria; women and structural adjustment in Turkey; women and the legal profession in Italy; economic empowerment of women victims of domestic violence and war refugees; and women and work in Cyprus, Greece, Israel, Serbia, and Bulgaria. Short papers on the above subjects were available to the participants.

A paper on the peace process and Arab/Palestinian women argued that the textile industry—where approximately one-third of the work force was female—held a bleak future for Arab women. The paper explained that both Jewish-owned businesses in northern Israel and foreign-vested firms sought cheap labor and offering low wages, and it described the sweatshop conditions and low wages endured by male and female workers alike. Drawing attention to the implications of capital mobility, the paper showed that when manufacturers could find cheaper labor costs elsewhere (for example, Jordan, Turkey, China, Bangladesh), they move away from Israel, which has minimum wage laws. In such an environment, the paper argued, Arab women's employment and income security could only be described as precarious.

A panel discussion on globalization argued that the process in its present form was a massive movement of capital in search of the highest profits and an unregulated movement of speculative capital that was destabilizing economies, lowering real wages, increasing unemployment, and forcing mass migration. It argued, too, that many political agreements and various "peace processes" in the Mediterranean region were in reality a pretext for the entry of private capital and for the extension of U.S. domination. Privatization, destruction of welfare, and subcontracting were causing further unemployment and increasing women's poverty, the panel concluded.[26]

The final conference resolution—subsequently sent to government bodies of the region and to the UN—consisted of four paragraphs on the economic and political situation of the region, and a list of twelve "minimum conditions necessary to safeguard women's right to work." The introductory paragraphs highlighted the adverse effects of globalization on national economies, the feminization of poverty in countries of the region, rising unemployment, and the growing inequalities within and between countries. The minimum conditions emphasized the state's responsibility to provide work opportunity for the unemployed, "the right to work in dignity and safety and without sexual harassment," good wages, an end to huge income inequalities, an end to child labor, conducive social policies for working mothers, and "the right of all women workers, including home-workers, agricultural workers, and housewives, to pensions and benefits in their own name."[27]

The 2002 conference focused on "Reinventing Globalization" and included, in addition to addresses by AWMR members, presentations by Moroccan specialists, who noted the varied and contradictory effects of globalization on women, social classes, states, and national economies. For example, Khadijah al-Feddy (an AWMR board member as well as head of the local organizing committee) pointed out that globalization's effects on women may be positive or negative, depending on social class, race, "intellectual level," and other factors. "If globalization has positive effects upon a certain number of women in terms of the increase in job opportunities, access to up-to-date technologies, and consumption capability, it is, however, for most women, synonymous with hard labour, insecurity, suppression of social services, privatization of companies, and suppression of jobs." She went on to explain: "We are thoroughly and without any reservations for a globalization that is fair, more human, and wherein the individual's needs are taken into account; a globalization that protects the individual's dignity, cultural identity, and universal human rights. We are, however, opposed to a globalization that rests on multinational and greedy firms whose main objective is profit-making." Al-Feddy ended by saying, "The world keeps on changing, and I believe that it is high time we had a say in the matter. The era of globalization, the deep social disparities, and the weakening of the power of local authorities galvanize women into thinking about solutions and designing new models."[28]

The final conference statement described globalization as a historic process that is "both top-down and bottom-up" but whose main force is "unrestrained capitalist expansion" led by the United States and institutions such as multinational corporations, the World Bank, the IMF, and the WTO. Other features are that "strategic resources are no longer under local control, welfare services are eroded, [and] poverty and economic justice increase." Addressing the governments of the region "at this crossroads between capitalism and fundamentalism, [and] between war and peace," the statement called for a "comprehensive system of rights that will advance the status of women and eliminate discrimination between genders, races, and classes; cooperate to end imperialism in the Mediterranean and in the world and respect the sovereignty of each nation; reduce the role of MNCs and advance sustainable local development, education, and welfare; reduce state expenditure on arms and increase state expenditure on education." The statement also called on governments to "make the state a tool for progress and protection of human rights rather than a tool of political, military, and economic oppression" and to "demand democratic regional and international institutions and full compliance with UN resolutions, in particular by Israel, Turkey, and the United States." The North African delegates emphasized the following demand, which was also included in the final conference statement: "promote the role of women in decision-making and recognize women as an essential and integral part of development. Women's rights must encompass all fields and women must [obtain] all rights hitherto restricted to men."[29]

Nationalism or Internationalism?

Although there was consensus on issues pertaining to globalization, the 2002 conference in Marrakesh highlighted the continuing role of nationalist politics and the ways in which local political cultures or agendas can disrupt transnational solidarity and cooperation. The conference began, as is typical with AWMR conferences, with a formal opening ceremony and speeches. The head of the local organizing committee included among her salutations a note of congratulations to Morocco's King Mohammad VI on the occasion of his marriage. This raised a few eyebrows on the part of the republican left-wing women from Arab countries and Europe, but it was perhaps more a sign of the imperatives of local/national political culture than a monarchist sentiment. More worrisome was the relatively limited participation by AWMR members, especially those from the Middle East. Because of the Israeli military incursions and closures, the Palestinian women associated with AWMR were unable to travel; only one Palestinian woman was able to attend the conference, and that was because she carried a Jordanian passport.[30] None of the AWMR's Israeli members and officers attended, because the Moroccan government refused to extend visas to Israeli citizens as a protest against the Israeli military incursions into the West Bank during 2002. The irony of the matter was that Israeli members of AWMR were themselves strongly opposed to the continuing occupation of the West Bank and Gaza, to the building of settlements, and to the imbalances of the Oslo Agreement. Some AWMR European members expressed dismay that the local organizing committee did not lobby its government (or Minister Belarbi, for example) on the matter of visas for the Israeli AWMR members.

The 2002 conference also illustrated the lingering political tensions between Moroccans and Algerians over the disputed Western Sahara territory. Claimed by Morocco, the territory has been the site of longstanding conflict involving the Sahrawi rebels and their Algerian supporters on one side, and the Moroccan state on the other. A proposed resolution on Sahrawi women led to a heated debate between the Moroccan and Algerian members, although eventually a compromise resolution was agreed upon.

In a third example of local and nationalist politics, banners and a photo display on the Palestinian uprising included images and words endorsing suicide bombings and hailing such action by Palestinian women. This did not sit well with some of the AWMR members, and there was much discussion during breaks and lunches over the implications of such signs and statements. Because of deference to the local committee, the banners and photo displays remained, but the AWMR president made a point of issuing a statement deploring the killing of civilians, whether by the Israeli military, armed settlers, or suicide bombers. As she stated: "You cannot fight terrorism with terrorism. You cannot fight injustice with unjust means. Violence begets violence." She went on to describe two responses to globalization: those by women, workers, and young people who take "the high road," and those who were responsible for September 11, along with various religious fundamentalists. She deplored "the war on terrorism," whether by the United States in Afghanistan or the Israeli military incursions in the Palestinian territories. "It is our responsibility as women," she said, "to raise our voices and insist that we have to break the cycle of violence." Quoting Aicha Belarbi, she said, "Our reason must rule our passion." Mintoff-Bland went on to make a distinction between the Israeli government and Israeli people, and called for an end to "demonization and racism." She ended by appealing for "a long-term vision in the Mediterranean, which will come from women and young people, that will build trust among countries in the region."[31]

Despite the tensions emanating from nationalist politics, the conference was able to agree unanimously on resolutions pertaining to Palestine, Cyprus, and Iraq.

Conclusions

Transnational feminist networks have used the opportunities afforded by globalization processes, such as the information and computer technologies, to network, extend solidarity, build organizations and movements—and address themselves to inequalities, crises, and other negative entailments of globalization. The AWMR is a TFN with a focus on the problems and prospects of the Mediterranean region and a belief that the women of the region can work effectively to draw attention to gender and social inequalities and to promote demilitarization, peace education, and citizen rights. Local- and national-level action is important to the AWMR, partly because it continues to respect national sovereignty and oppose external intervention, and partly because the network believes that citizen action is the most effective and legitimate source of progressive change, which international or regional solidarity can assist. In this sense it engages in the kind of "internationalism" associated with the left-wing politics of the pre-globalization era, but it also shows characteristics of the transnational advocacy networks described by Keck and Sikkink. For example, AWMR resolutions and actions at the transnational level are meant to support local and national struggles and increase the political leverage of local activists.

The AWMR also has characteristics in common with other transnational feminist networks. The network is comprised of women who promote women's autonomy, equality, and empowerment; who believe that women can be more effective agents of social and political change; and who argue that women should take part in or lead decision-making processes at national and global levels. As such, the AWMR is not only de facto feminist according to Misciagno's definition, but is feminist according to the criteria developed by Ferree and Hess (see chapter 4). Moreover, their praxis contributes to what I have been calling global feminism, a set of claims and activities by movement intellectuals and activists around the world that has been in the making since the mid-1980s. Global feminism is encapsulated in documents such as the Cairo Declaration, the Beijing Platform for Action, and the World March of Women, and in the proliferating literature on women's human rights and on gender justice and economic justice.

The AWMR functions as a very loose network and prioritizes local and national action. It plays an important role not only in providing international solidarity for local and national struggles but also, and perhaps most importantly, in providing political direction, as seen in the discussion of the 2002 conference in Marrakesh.

But this chapter also has shown that while the AWMR is a transnational feminist network with much potential, it is also beset with organizational and funding obstacles to growth and influence, as well as seemingly intractable political conflicts. One member expressed the view that "at the beginning of the nineties the organization was still unique and radical. I put a lot into the organization, especially politically." But she has been disappointed with the network's lack of focus and direction, and the nationalisms that are sometimes on display: "I felt that everyone is stuck with the 'national issue' when it wasn't the issue."[32] The president, Mintoff-Bland, candidly described some of the problems facing the organization: "We need a whole new leadership. We also need to not just analyze things, but make a difference." In early 2002, she and some other AWMR members felt incapacitated by the cycle of violence in Israel and Palestine. As she explained: "It's not burnout. It's just that I can't see beyond the horror of what's happening in Israel and Palestine. If we could have a way of coping with what's going on."[33] In light of the organizational, financial, and political crises facing the AWMR, the invasion of Iraq by U.S. and British forces in March 2003 could have led to its collapse. Instead, the Italian branch energetically began preparations for an annual meeting to focus on peace, justice, and demilitarization in the Mediterranean region.

CHAPTER EIGHT

The Specter that Haunts the Global Economy?

The Challenge of Global Feminism

Male-dominated monetary, trade and financial policies are gender blind,
resulting in serious costs to all. [Doris Mpoumou, of WEDO, 2000]

Vigorous global feminism is perhaps the single most effective form of resistance to the systematic degradation of human rights standards worldwide,
which makes possible the worst ravages of the transnational economy.
[Margaret Spillane, in *The Nation*, 2001]

Another world is possible and women are building it! [Women's caucus at
the Monterrey conference, 2002]

We have seen how the twin processes of global economic restructuring and religious fundamentalisms galvanized women around the world, led to a convergence of previously divergent perspectives, and resulted in the formation
of transnational feminist networks. In the latter part of the 1980s, the world's
women were ready for such mobilization and forms of organization, in part
due to sociodemographic changes such as rising educational attainment and
employment among women. Since then, women have formed networks and
have joined forces with other advocacy networks, civil society groups, and social movement organizations to challenge the neoliberal corporate agenda
and to advance the cause of women's human rights. Along with other organizations and networks that are working for an alternative globalization or are
engaging with global public policies, TFNs have contributed to the transnational social movement infrastructure and are helping to construct global civil
society.

Female labor and women's organizations are integral elements of globalization in its economic, cultural, and political dimensions. The capitalist world-

economy functions by means of the deployment of labor that is waged and non-waged, formal and informal, male and female. In recent decades, the involvement of women in various kinds of labor arrangements has been striking. Capitalist accumulation is achieved through the surplus-extraction of labor, and this includes the paid and unpaid economic activities of women, whether in male-headed or female-headed households. The various forms of the deployment of female labor reflect asymmetrical gender relations and patriarchal gender ideologies. Global accumulation as the driving force of the world-system not only hinges on class and regional differences across economic zones, but it is also a gendered process, predicated upon gender differences in the spheres of production and reproduction. In an era of economic globalization, the pressure for greater competitiveness through lower labor and production costs has encouraged the demand for and supply of female labor.

However, in a reflection of the contradictions of capitalism, the incorporation of women in the global economy and in national labor forces has also served to interrogate and modify gender relations and ideologies. Women have been organizing and mobilizing against the hegemonic and particularistic aspects of globalization. Organized and mobilized women—locally, nationally, and transnationally—are raising questions about social and gender arrangements and making demands on employers, governments, patriarchal movements, and international financial institutions. Many feminist organizations have been middle-class and elite, but class lines are increasingly blurred as women professionals and women proletarians find common cause around personal, economic, and social issues, including violence against women, poverty, job security, land rights, the redistribution and socialization of domestic work, reproductive health and rights, and women's roles in decision-making. The transnational feminist networks examined in this book show also that the social movement of women has a more radical and transformative vision of the socioeconomic and political order than do many of the "new social movements" that have been the focus of much sociological research.

Organizational Dynamics, Strengths, and Weaknesses

The case-study chapters have illustrated some of the observations that were made in chapter 4 concerning women's organizations in general and transnational feminist networks in particular. First, women's organizations reflect women's collective consciousness, identity, experiences, and aspirations.

These are forged in labor processes, in domestic experiences, and in political struggles, and give rise to feminist organizations, women's caucuses, and participation in unions. We have seen that some feminist movements and their organizations have grown out of left-wing organizations, national liberation movements, labor movements, and other struggles. Disillusionment with male-dominated organizations and movements or the marginalization of women's movements and concerns often has been the impetus for women's organizations. But feminist networks emerge and make interventions in policy dialogues and debates on national and global levels also because women are convinced that their own, feminist perspectives have value and can make a difference.

When activists form organizations, they may build on preexisting organizations and networks of women. This pattern has been noted in the social movements and women's movements literatures, and has been confirmed by the case studies here. All the TFNs examined in this book have grown out of personal, professional, and political networks, and many of the founders of the networks had worked together in other organizations or movements. Women's organizations, and TFNs in particular, are not exclusivist; we have seen that they join in coalitions with unions, political parties, and other civil society organizations or advocacy networks as well as with other feminist networks. And like some other civil-society or social-movement organizations, women's organizations may face state repression and resource constraints. Limited budgets are a perennial problem, but harassment or intimidation are not unknown and are more serious. Of the TFNs examined in this book, WLUML has been the most security-conscious, mainly due to the sensitive nature of its work, whereby it opposes fundamentalists, criticizes regimes, and objects to patriarchal interpretations and applications of Islamic law.

In her study of the Women's International League for Peace and Freedom, Mary Meyer contrasts the longevity of WILPF (founded in 1915) with other women's peace groups which, while often quite radical, disavowed formal organization or dissolved following specific antimilitarist campaigns. She attributes this longevity to the WILPF founders' determination to "institutionalize the international women's peace movement . . . through an organizational structure that combined both mainstreaming and disengaging political strategies."[1] Like WILPF, contemporary TFNs engage with international organizations and public policy issues while also taking a radical and at times utopian stance on the social order.

Formal organizations, however, have their tensions. Like other types of women's organizations, TFNs face issues of centralization, decentralization, institutionalization, professionalization, as well as charismatic leadership. Professionalization is a double-edged sword, as WIDE discovered and as critics of WEDO maintain. Some activists feel that WEDO's New York office has been too central, that there is a one-way relationship with the contacts in developing countries, and that its lobbying work overwhelms other worthwhile objectives, such as fostering or supporting grassroots women's organizations. The difficulties of effecting change in the global economy to establish gender justice and economic justice have led some feminists to question the strategy of participating in international conferences and lobbying delegates. One WEDO board member remarked: "International meetings are too distracting. There's no time to take care of your housekeeping. It's the same people who go the UN meetings all the time. It's a complex, labor-intensive, technical process." The focus, rather, should be on support for grassroots women's organizations and for the building of the movement. The WEDO board member continued: "There's been a little tension within the board regarding advocacy versus movement. Bella was clear; she wanted advocacy and not grassroots work. Now there's recognition of the importance of being more organically connected to grassroots movements that organize and not just advocate."[2]

Weaknesses and risks facing transnational feminists also should be acknowledged. Like many women's groups—and as we saw in particular with the AWMR—TFNs often lack the necessary financial and other resources for real growth or more effective participation and lobbying. In the absence of a mass membership base, or due to the difficulties and expenses of collecting dues in a variety of currencies, they rely on "soft money" from external grants or foundation assistance, with its attendant problems of sustainability or legitimation.

Another weakness or danger is co-optation. There is always the possibility that states or international agencies can co-opt activists and especially "experts" who work with TFNs. After all, some transnational feminist activists have become UN officials or consultants, and they consult governments as well. The question of possible co-optation has been raised especially in connection with the World Bank's outreach activities, although there is no evidence thus far that involvement with the EGCG or participation in the many gender seminars organized by the World Bank has led to dilution of the critical analysis of those feminist political economists who accept the invitations.[3]

As we have seen with the AWMR, "political purity" or a willful disengagement from multilateral organizations can attenuate the potential effectiveness of a TFN. For example, WLUML leaders have admitted that they were not as effective as they could have been with respect to an issue that has been of central importance to the network—the fate of Algerian women, and especially fellow feminists, during the terrible years of the Algerian civil conflict.[4] WLUML was quite active in supporting Algerian feminists in their encounter with Islamist groups, but the efficacy of their work was hampered by the network's reluctance to engage with UN bodies as extensively as other TFNs have done, in favor of an approach that prioritized networking, solidarity, and appeals to feminists and other progressives around the world. On the other hand, their co-authorship of a shadow report on Algeria, submitted to the CEDAW Committee, did represent a shift in their approach.

I would conclude, nevertheless, that TFN accomplishments outweigh their weaknesses or the risks that they face. Without TFN activity the world would hardly have known about the atrocities facing Algerian and Afghan women in the 1990s. Indeed, the worldwide excoriation of the Taliban, its diplomatic isolation, and the defeat of the UNOCAL oil pipeline project is a success story of transnational feminism. Here, WLUML and its Lahore branch, Shirkat Gah, played a critical role, especially in the early years. In the area of economic policy, the trenchant and sustained critiques of structural adjustment by TFNs compelled the World Bank to retreat from its earlier disregard for the social sectors and to adopt a policy of gender-sensitivity in its research and policy work. The UN, World Bank, and international development agencies recognize the role of women's organizations in the development process and in the making of civil society, and they have adopted transnational feminist concepts such as gender approach, gender equality, empowerment, and autonomy.

In fact, the study of TFNs shows that women's organizations have become major nonstate political actors on the global, regional, and national scenes. They are in a dynamic relationship with states, the media, intergovernmental organizations, and other TSMOs and TANs. They use the global, intergovernmental arena and the transnational public sphere to accomplish national priorities in the areas of women's human rights (such as violence against women and the rights of women in Muslim societies) and economic policies (such as structural adjustment and the new global trade agenda), as well as to influence international norms and conventions. As such they challenge and engage with the state and global forces alike. They also refute stereotypical notions that women's organizations are exclusively local, or that they are concerned primarily with issues of identity and sexuality, or that they do not engage with economic policy issues.

The TFNs that I have described offer a critique of neoliberal capitalism and advocate for the welfare state and for global Keynesianism. They have actively responded to adverse global processes, including economic restructuring and the expansion of fundamentalism, and are offering alternative frameworks. In order to realize their goals of equality and empowerment for women and social justice and democratization in the society and globally, TFNs engage in information exchange, mutual support, and a combination of lobbying, advocacy, and (at times) direct action. In so doing they take advantage of other global processes, including the development and spread of information and computer technologies.

TFNs confirm the importance of networks for women—whether in the form of micro-level personal relations that spawn formal groups and organizations, or macro-level organizations that operate transnationally. Transnational feminists have devised an organizational structure that consists of active and autonomous local/national women's groups but that transcends localisms or nationalisms. And as we have seen with all case-study TFNs, including those working on Muslim or Mediterranean women's human rights, their discourses are not particularistic but universalistic; they emphasize solidarity and commonality rather than difference. This finding runs counter to some arguments that have been made by feminist scholars situated in postmodernist or postcolonialist frames.

Feminism, Labor, and Human Rights

The global women's movement, and in particular transnational feminist networks, may offer lessons to other social movements and their organizations, not least the labor movement. According to two analysts, "no major American institution changed less than the labor movement. At the end of the twentieth century, American unions are as poorly adapted to the economy and society of their time as were the craft unions of iron puddlers and corwainers to the mass production industries of seventy years ago."[5] This can hardly be said of transnational feminist networks, who have become remarkably ICT-savvy. At the dawn of the new millennium, transnational feminist networks evince the organizational form and supranational solidarities that socialists had expected of the labor movement in the early twentieth century.

In fact, just as the labor movement historically emerged from the involvement of workers in social production and the exploitation they experienced, so has the feminist movement emerged from women's involvement in the labor force and from the exploitation and inequality they experience at the workplace and in society more broadly.

Historically, trade unions and communist and socialist parties were the organizational expressions of the labor movement. The social movement of women has produced women's organizations; moreover, in a reflection of their incorporation in the paid labor force, women are becoming increasingly involved in unions. If the emergence of the workers' movement represented the contradictions of early capitalism, the emergence of the global women's movement and of transnational women's organizations are indicative of the contradictions of late capitalism in an era of globalization. It is worth pointing out that in the early 1990s, when the labor movement and left parties alike were in retreat, it was the emerging transnational women's movement, and specifically a number of TFNs, that were consistently critical of economic globalization. Since then, labor unions have become increasingly skeptical of the neoliberal capitalist agenda; the participation of U.S. unions in the Battle of Seattle and in various antiwar protests could represent the beginnings of "social movement unionism." But it remains to be seen whether the labor movement as a whole—within the United States and across the world-system—will follow the lead of the women's movement in its approach to globalization and collective action.

Indeed, it is my view that a formidable alliance would be one between feminism and labor—that is, between the social movement of women and social movement unionism—along with other elements of the global justice movement. Such an alliance is entirely possible, given global feminism's concern with the exploitation of female labor in the global economy, and given the growing participation of women in trade unions. Trade union women, and especially feminists within trade unions, could bridge the divide between the feminist movement and the labor movement. Such an alliance would call for a more activist and transnational labor movement than we have been accustomed to seeing in recent decades—although a number of commentators feel that social movement unionism and transnational alliances are now on the agenda. There is increasing recognition that unions, social movement organizations, and NGOs will need to work together to counter the dominance of neoliberal economic policies, as a roundtable held in Bangkok concluded.[6]

Many trade union activists "are able to recognize their affinity and resemblance to other social movements, while links particularly with women's and democratic movements are now common, accepted and welcomed."[7] Dan Gallin refers to the need for unions and NGOs to coalesce around "a program of radical democracy diametrically opposed to the currently hegemonic neoliberalism," and to "reconstitute the social movement worldwide, with the means provided by globalization and its technologies."[8] A formal alliance among the women's, environmental, and labor movements could help move forward the project of global Keynesianism or transnational socialism.

This is not to say that there are no tensions between the women's movement and other social movements, or tensions within the global women's movement. As we have seen, Mahnaz Afkhami of SIGI and WLP has indicated that human rights organizations do not consistently take gender issues on board; there is sometimes distance and distrust between women's human rights organizations and the nonfeminist human rights organizations. DAWN has voiced concern that women's reproductive rights could be sidelined in a broad progressive movement that includes religious groups that are against abortion. DAWN also has raised concerns about divisions between feminist groups in the South and the North concerning trade and labor standards.[9] In 2003, as the global justice movement morphed into a global justice and peace movement and as dozens of Muslim groups in some countries joined antiwar mobilizations in the wake of the American and British invasion of Iraq, secular feminists from Muslim countries and communities began to wonder if women's issues would again be glossed over. Ideally, transnational social movement organizations and the global justice and peace movement will recognize that women's rights are human rights and that the demands, objectives, and methods of the women's movement and of global feminism—encapsulated by the passage below by Peggy Antrobus of DAWN—are essential to the broader project of global change:

> Feminism's tendencies to reject domination and hierarchy and its replacement of the male concept of power (power to dominate and control) with a female concept of power (power to act, or to empower others), its concern for humanistic values, and its questioning of economistic considerations—all can serve as a brake against the corruption of unchallenged male domination and greed, as expressed in the neglect of human welfare in the interest of capital; the materialism of market liberalization that negates spiritual and cultural values associated with

women; and, most importantly, the violence that has emerged with the rise of fundamentalism, often wrapped in the flags of identity politics, which has accompanied the deterioration in the quality of life and the threats of globalization to national identity.[10]

Globalization, the State, and Gender Justice

This book has shown that TFNs contribute several new ideas to current discussions of, and collective action around, globalization. One idea pertains to understandings and definitions of globalization. We have seen that transnational feminists are not, strictly speaking, anti-globalization. They are anti-neoliberal capitalism, but they view globalization as a multifaceted phenomenon whose most positive feature is its opportunities for transnational networking and solidarity. They would like to help reinvent globalization and reorient it from a *project of markets* to a *project of peoples*. Their literature is replete with condemnations of the ills of neoliberal capitalism. But their stated solutions and strategies are to remake (*democratize* and *engender*) global governance, not to destroy it. After all, they frequently engage with institutions and norms of global governance in order to influence policymakers or affect legal frameworks at the state level. Thus they endorse redistributive mechanisms and global social policies because these would lead to greater investments in human development, increase the likelihood of gender budgets, reduce social and gender inequalities, and redirect globalization. It is worth pointing out that in late February 2004, the ILO released a report entitled *A Fair Globalization: Creating Opportunities for All*, which noted the inequalities, exclusions, and imbalances resulting from globalization's focus on the market. In calling for a shift in emphasis on people's well-being, it echoed a prominent transnational feminist theme. Many of the ILO report's recommendations—a democratic and effective state, sustainable development, solidarity and partnerships, greater accountability to people, an effective United Nations—have been among the objectives of the transnational feminist networks examined in this book.[11]

A second idea pertains to the state. For transnational feminists, the state remains a key institutional actor—even though they eschew nationalist politics in favor of internationalism and transnational solidarity. The state matters because of women's stakes in the areas of reproductive rights, family law, and social policy; and because transnational feminists oppose the neoliberal and patriarchal state and favor the welfare or developmental form of the state

that is also democratic and woman-friendly. I have called this the critical realist approach to the state. Thus the focus of TFN activity is simultaneously the
state, the region (e.g., Latin America, the European Union, the Mediterranean), and the global economy and institutions of global governance.

A third distinctive idea pertains to the transnational feminist call for
women's human rights and for "gender justice." At the UN's international
conference on human rights in 1993, feminists popularized the slogan
"women's rights are human rights," thereby rejecting the idea that women's
rights may be subject to cultural or religious conditions. Since then, they have
consistently opposed fundamentalist views on women and gender. Representative of the global feminist view of women and human rights is the following
statement by the Association for Women's Rights in Development (AWID):
"Women should be able to actualize their rights, to celebrate their cultures,
and to live in freedom and security. No tradition, cultural practice or religious
tenet can justify the violation of a fundamental human right. . . . The human
rights of women are indivisible, interdependent and universal, not subject to
a religious veto. We must oppose all fundamentalisms and the erosion of
women's enjoyment of their rights."[12] This call was first made in the context
of cooperation with the broader global economic justice movement and campaigns such as Jubilee 2000. To be sure, transnational feminists do not want
women's rights, including reproductive rights, to be placed on the back
burner or postponed until after the triumph of the antiglobalization movement, as has been the case with so many national political movements. But
they also believe that global justice is rendered a meaningless, abstract concept without consideration of the gendered (and racial) makeup of working
people—or of "working families."[13] Without due consideration of the sexual
division of labor and the care economy, of the traffic in women's bodies, of
working women's human rights (including rights to bodily integrity and reproductive rights), and of their social rights (e.g., paid maternity leaves, pater-
nity leaves, and quality child care), there can in fact be no economic justice
for women. As such, the slogan "gender justice *and* economic justice" may be
understood as a variation of the slogan "women's rights *are* human rights"—
both of which are key concepts of global feminism that have been developed
and disseminated by transnational feminist networks.

These are still early days in the study of gender and globalization, of transnational social movements, and certainly of transnational feminist networks.
This book has drawn on globalization studies, social movements research, and

the scholarship on women's organizations to examine global change and the role of transnational feminist networks. I have argued that in an era of globalization, the capitalist world-system is comprised not only of a global economy and unequal nation-states, but also of transnational movements and networks—including transnational feminist networks. By analyzing several representative feminist networks, I hope to have generated a more powerful understanding of their structure and their agency, along with their links to globalization processes. And by discussing the ideas, activities, strategies, and goals of TFNs, I hope to have elucidated what I have called global feminism.

A Women's Appeal

Women Living under Muslim Laws

Alert for Action / Algeria, 1992

We women, for whom Islam is a faith, a culture, or a memory, we now have nothing but words. But let these words awake us. South of the Mediterranean, women are in danger. Nowadays fundamentalism has made a caricature of and has seized our heritage of a tolerant and progressive Islam. Its harmful action is constantly spreading. In some countries, it has transformed what was a collective revolt against autocracy into state religious terror. In some others, a pseudo-rigorism, nurtured by petrodollars and Western arms, has imposed a segregation of the sexes which is as backwards as the worst racial segregations, and is aiming at exporting its model.

The struggle for emancipation of women in Islam, which began in the 1920s in Egypt, Turkey and the Middle East, is thus becoming even more necessary today. This year, 1992, in the heart of a multicultural Maghreb, in the heart of a people whose daughters, wives and mothers fought the colonizers only yesterday, there is an immediate risk that Algerian women may lose their most basic liberties.

We therefore call on all women and men willing to join and support us, to take solidarity action and to set up in every town, every country, everywhere you have the freedom to do so, an ACTION WATCH COMMITTEE FOR THE DEFENCE OF WOMEN'S RIGHTS IN ALGERIA AND FOR THE RESPECT OF DEMOCRATIC LIBERTIES.

15th January 1992

Women's Caucus Declaration

Third Ministerial Meeting of the World Trade Organization,
Seattle, Washington, 30 November–3 December 1999

The Women's Caucus is comprised of women's organisations from the South and North attending the Third Ministerial Meeting of the World Trade Organisation (WTO) in Seattle, Washington, USA. We are concerned that the rule-based system created by the WTO has produced increasing levels of inequality in both the North and South. This system privileges corporate interests over community and national interests. Trade liberalisation is not gender-neutral and has a different impact on women and men, similar to the different impact it has on developed and developing countries.

While some women may gain from opening up of trade, the majority of the world's women and girls are adversely affected by the unequal power relations created at the national, regional and international levels by the new trade regime. We firmly believe that the trade policies should ensure gender equality and equity and people-centered sustainable development.

We believe that the WTO undermines major international agreements that women have worked hard to get their governments to commit to, including the UN Conference on Environment and Development, the World Conference on Human Rights, the World Summit for Social Development, the Fourth World Conference on Women, and Habitat II.

We further believe that all WTO agreements and policies should be bound by international human rights standards including the International Covenant on Economic, Social and Cultural Rights and the Convention on the Elimination of All Forms of Discrimination Against Women. The Women's Caucus urges the Members of the WTO to consider the following concerns clustered around the following critical areas of discussion at the Seattle meeting:

SYSTEMIC AND IMPLEMENTATION ISSUES

- Ensure transparency and open participation of all member states in every negotiation process. Green Room by invitation-only meetings clearly violate principles of both transparency and inclusiveness as well as the integrity of the consensus process.
- Ensure that women's and other non-governmental organisations (NGOs) have equal access to information. Institute dialogue that allows substantial exchange between trade officials and NGOs.

- We recommend a comprehensive gender, social, and environmental assessment of the implementation of the Uruguay Round agreements before undertaking a new round. Such a review should address the negative impacts and correct the deficiencies and imbalances in the agreements. This review and assessment should involve consultations with women's and other non-governmental organisations. (NGOs).

- Democratise the WTOs dispute settlement system to ensure impartiality, equitable access and a final appeal process outside of the WTO. Introduce and implement mechanisms to reduce the costs of dispute settlement for developing countries.

- Ensure gender and regional balance in all WTO decision-making bodies including expert and scientific panels.

- We urge developed countries to uphold the principle of special and differential treatment for developing countries. Developed countries must fulfill their commitments in this area, especially for net food-importing countries and least-developed countries.

AGRICULTURE

- A review of the Agreement on Agriculture (AoA) must include the experience of consumers, farmers, indigenous peoples, women, civil society groups, and research non-government organisations as well as multilateral organisations that have been critical of the existing rules governing agriculture.

- Ensure food security based on self-sufficient, small-scale, diverse agriculture instead of corporate export-oriented, agro-industrial mono-cultures.

- Ensure that southern and small farmers, particularly women, are not undermined by competitive pressures resulting from the rapid removal of tariff and non-tariff barriers and subsidised agricultural products from northern countries.

- Adopt the Convention on Biodiversity. Ban the patenting of living organisms and protect the knowledge, practices and livelihoods of indigenous peoples.

GENERAL AGREEMENT ON TRADE AND SERVICES (GATS)

- Ensure that public services such as health, education, social welfare, water, energy, among others are affordable and accessible.

- Promote symmetry in the treatment of the international mobility of capital and labour. Liberal entry of multinational service corporations must be matched by market-opening measures for labour in developed countries.

- Provide women with capital, skills, training and technology that would allow them to take advantage of opportunities that increased trade in services provides.

- Ensure that trade policy does not overturn domestic regulations on consumer protection, public safety, public health and education, food safety and environmental protection, among others.

Seattle Declaration

Diverse Women for Diversity

Seattle, 1 December 1999

We, Diverse Women for Diversity, diverse in culture, race, religion, socio-economic conditions, have one common goal: biological and cultural diversity as the foundation of life on earth. Therefore we stand for self-sufficiency, self-reliance and solidarity, locally and globally. For this reason we have gathered in Seattle in November 1999 to struggle against the WTO.

The WTO was created to further and stabilise the freedom of trade and profit on behalf of a few multinationals. Going far beyond this goal, however, it acts as a new World Government. The WTO is a non-elected institution, based on secrecy and non-representation. It erodes the substance of democracy in our countries. Through its rules it imposes economic policies in favour of gigantic global corporate interests. The WTO promises to create growth and wealth for all, equality, jobs, ecological sustainability through a "free" globalised market. The reality, however, is that the free market mechanisms have led to increased poverty, to more unemployment, more ecological destruction, and to more violence against women, children and minorities.

Our food and agricultural systems have been brought under corporate control of global grain merchants like Cargill and ADM through the WTO Agreement on Agriculture. This has robbed women and peasant producers of their livelihood and has denied consumers worldwide access to sufficient, safe and healthy food. The WTO rejects any precautionary principle and thus allows corporations like Monsanto (USA), Novartis (Switzerland), DuPont (USA), Astrazeneca (UK/Netherlands) and Aventis (Germany) to spread genetically modified seeds and foods without people's knowledge and consent, thus creating unprecedented ecological and health hazards. These corporations are a danger to life on earth.

For thousands of years, indigenous people, women and men have protected, nurtured and sustained the biodiversity of food, crops and medicinal plants. This rich biodiversity is now being stolen by monopolistic "life science" corporations, under the legal protection of the Agreement on Trade-Related Intellectual Property Rights (TRIPs). TRIPs forces countries to introduce patents on life and promotes the piracy of millennia of innovation and creativity, by millions of women and peasants through the privatisation of traditional knowledge.

After the Multilateral Agreement on Investment was defeated by worldwide citizens' resistance in December 1998, the same proponents of unlimited free market are now pushing for a new round of negotiation on the same issue in WTO. They also include new areas for liberalisation, namely, TRIMs, Services, Investment, Public Procurement and Competition. All these areas, if further liberalised, will have further negative effect, particularly on women. In summary, this so-called "free-market" system is indeed a global war system, based on violence against nature, humanity, especially women and children. Together with the thousands of children, women and men gathered here in Seattle, we, Diverse Women for Diversity, reject this global war system and the WTO. We pledge to build an economy and a society where nature and human beings can live and prosper in peace and happiness.

Notes

ONE. Globalization and Its Discontents

Epigraph: WIDE, 1995, p. 3

1. See, for example, Molyneux 1979; Beneria and Sen 1981; Hartmann 1981; Barrett 1989; Safa 2000. The terms *private sphere* and *public sphere* refer, respectively, to the family (long identified with women) and the domain of politics (long identified with men). The sphere of production is where goods, commodities, and materials are produced for the market or personal use. This sphere has long had a masculine association, even though women across cultures and historical periods have been active within it. By contrast, the sphere of (biological, social, and symbolic) reproduction tends to be associated with women, largely because of the central role of the family, and of the provision of care, in this sphere.

2. See, e.g., Gill 1995; Castells 2000; Mittelman 1997; Schaeffer 1997; Sassen 1996; Lechner and Boli 2000; Boswell and Chase-Dunn 2000, Scholte 2000; Sklair 2002.

3. See Korten 1995; Edwards and Hulme 1992, Boli and Thomas 1997; Smith, Chatfield, and Pagnucco, 1997; Smith 1998; Janoski 1998; Florini 2000; Guidry, Kennedy, and Zald 2000; Hamel et al., 2001; Edwards and Gaventa 2001; Smith and Johnston 2002; Broad 2002; Khagram, Riker, and Sikkink, 2002.

4. Keck and Sikkink 1998; O'Brien et al. 2000; Cohen and Rai 2000.

5. See Katzenstein and Mueller 1987; Staggenborg 1988a 1998b; Chafetz and Dworkin 1986; Margolis 1993; Stienstra 1994; Ferree and Martin 1995; Miles 1996; Moghadam 1996a, 2000; Rupp 1998; Lycklama, Vargas, and Wieringa 1998; Berkovitch 1999; Meyer 1999; Ray 1999; Wichterich 1999; Safa 2000; Marchand and Runyan 2000; Alvarez 2000; Naples and Desai 2002; Ehrenreich and Hochschild 2003.

6. Other known terms for the division of the world into unequal parts are "developing and developed countries," "post-industrial and industrializing countries," "the global North and the global South," and—at least until the decline of communism in the late 1980s—"First World" (the rich capitalist countries), "Second World" (the communist bloc countries), and "Third World" (the developing countries of Africa, Asia, and Latin America). In world-systems analysis, core countries are those with a concentration of economic and political resources and include a hegemonic power, which since the end of World War II has been the United States; peripheral countries function as sources of raw materials and sometimes cheap labor; semiperipheral countries occupy a space in between core and periphery and include many of the developing and industrializing countries. The Middle Eastern and Muslim countries mentioned in this book are mostly semiperipheral countries.

7. See Guidry, Kennedy, and Zald (2000: 3).

8. The Palestinian question also divided participants, especially at the Copenhagen NGO Forum. See Fraser 1987.

9. See, for example, Brenner 1998.

10. Structural adjustment policies are market-friendly policies intended to put economies on a growth path and increase "competitiveness" for international trade and foreign investments through liberalization of prices, commerce and labor markets, denationalization of public sector enterprises, elimination of subsidies, and reductions in public expenditure.

11. Beneria and Feldman 1992; Chant 1995; Tanski 1994; Moghadam, 1997.

12. See, for example, INSTRAW/ILO 1985. Women-in-development (WID) began in the early 1970s and sought to bring attention to the problems facing women in the development process, including their marginalization from productive activities. (See, for example, Boserup 1970.) Women-and-development (WAD) emerged as a more critical turn, and researchers raised questions about the nature of the development process into which women were to be integrated. (See Beneria and Sen 1981; Elson and Pearson 1981.) The gender-and-development (GAD) approach grounded itself more explicitly in feminist theorizing. (See Young 1992.)

13. Standing 1989, 1999.

14. For an elaboration of various types of fundamentalism, their gender dynamics, and their impacts on women's legal status and social positions, see contributions in Moghadam 1994a, and Moghadam 1994b.

15. See Moghadam 2002b, 2003a.

16. I have adopted Chadwick Alger's observation (in Smith et al., 1997, table 15.1, p. 262) that transnational social movement organizations do the following: create and activate global networks to mobilize pressure outside states; participate in multilateral and intergovernmental political arenas; act and agitate within states; enhance public awareness and participation.

17. See, for example, *WIDE News* no. 2 (2002), which discusses its participation, along with the International Gender and Trade Network, the second World Social Forum (WSF) at Porto Alegre. That issue also includes the Statement of Social Movements, "Resistance to Neoliberalism, War and Militarism: For Peace and Social Justice," February 2002. See also *DAWN Informs*, March 2002, on the WSF 2002.

18. The proposed Tobin Tax, named after the late economics professor and Nobel laureate James Tobin, would reduce volatility and instability of financial markets by taxing international currency transactions (e.g., foreign exchange speculation). The global justice movement—and those TFNs that focus on economic policy matters—have suggested that the proceeds of that tax be placed at the disposition of the United Nations to help finance the UN's development agenda.

19. Since 1990 the United Nations Development Program's Human Development Report Office has produced an annual *Human Development Report.* The concept of human development is meant to be an alternative to the conventional emphasis on economic growth as the principal measure of development; the UNDP argues that the enlargement of people's choices through health, education, income, and women's equality are more adequate measures.

20. "Global Keynesianism" or "transnational socialism" has been mentioned as a desirable alternative to global neoliberalism. It would include full employment, improve-

ment of global income distribution, worldwide social security, sustainable economic growth, ecological sustainability, and global democracy. See Kohler 1999.

21. For other references to global feminism, see Catagay, Grown, and Santiago 1986; Bunch and Carillo, 1990; Afkhami, 1995, 2001.

22. Information from WIDE newsletters, 2002, and personal communication from Lina Abou-Habib, coordinator of the Beirut-based Machrek-Magreb Gender Link Information Project, 21 August 2003.

23. Boli and Thomas, 1997: 172.

24. Such as Keck and Sikkink, 1998.

TWO. Globalization and Its Discontents

1. For example, Frobel et al. 1980; Chase-Dunn 1989. Marx was correct, however, in predicting the ever-growing concentration and global expansion of capital.

2. For example, Melucci 1996; McAdam, McCarthy, and Zald 1996.

3. Cox 1992; Moghadam 1993; Hopkins and Wallerstein 1996; Boswell and Chase-Dunn 2000.

4. Moghadam 1994b.

5. Smith et al. 1997; Keck and Sikkink 1998; Guidry, Kennedy, and Zald 2000.

6. Marchand and Runyan 2000; Moghadam 2000a; Stienstra 2000.

7. Hoogvelt 1997, esp. chap. 6; Sklair 1991, 2001.

8. Shiva 1996; Wallerstein 1991; Chase-Dunn 1998; Wood 1997; Hirst and Thompson 1996.

9. World Bank 1995; Qureshi 1996; Slaughter and Swagel 1997.

10. Bello 2000; Khor 2000; Korten 1995; Mander 1996.

11. Jordan 2000; Burrow 2000. Professor James Tobin, winner of the 1981 Nobel Prize for Economics, proposed in 1978 a tax on international currency transactions (e.g., foreign exchange speculation) to reduce volatility and instability of financial markets. In 1994 he reiterated his proposal, suggesting that the proceeds of that tax be placed at the disposition of international organizations for development purposes. James Tobin died in March 2002.

12. Bonvin 1997; UNDP 1999; Mandle 2000; Oxfam 2002.

13. See the summary of Maddison's research in UNDP 1999. See also Atkinson 2001; Korzeniewicz and Moran 1997; Taylor 2000; Bornschier 2001; Ghose 2000; Bhagwati 2002.

14. Petras and Brill 1995; Kuttner 1998; Steger 2002.

15. Robertson 1992; Giddens 1990; Harvey 1990; Sklair 1991, 2002; Castells 2000.

16. Cox 1992; Gray 1998; Sklair 1991, 2001; Chase-Dunn 1998. Mathews (1997: 50) writes that "the absolutes of the Westphalian system," including "territorially fixed states," are all dissolving. Sklair (2001: 1) argues that "the transnational capitalist class has transformed capitalism into a globalizing project," while Robinson and Harris (2000: 20) state that "the transnationalization of the capital circuit implies as well the transnationalization of the agents of capital."

17. Hirst and Thompson 1996; Berger and Dore 1996.

18. Scholte 2000: 46; Pieterse 1998. See also Held 2000.

19. Catagay, Elson, and Grown 1995; Dickinson 1997; Moghadam 1998a; Sen 1997; Dunaway 2001.

20. Grewal and Kaplan 1994: 17.

21. Marchand 2000: 135, 139.

22. Bergeron 2001: 983, 992, 996.

23. Ling 2002: 37; Connell 1998; Hooper 2000. See *The Economist,* 2 February 1997, "In Praise of the Davos Man." J. K. Gibson-Graham (1996) is a pseudonym for two feminist scholars who co-authored the book. Like other socialist-feminists, Gibson-Graham calls for the valorization of women's involvement in the care economy as an alternative to hegemonic masculinity, and draws attention to the importance of feminine values of connectivity, peace, and so on. It should be noted that Bergeron (2001) and Marchand (2000) criticize the focus on women's caring, peace-loving, and relational roles as a false and dangerous essentialism that reinforces the maternalist trap.

24. Marchand and Runyan 2000: 14.

25. Peterson 2003: 1.

26. Brigitte Holzner, WIDE president, in a personal communication with the author, 4 April 2003. See also WIDE 2003.

27. Rojas and Caro (2003) provide an interesting discussion of four conceptual approaches to gender and the state: the state as a reproducer of gender relations; the relative autonomy of the state; the state as a constituent part of gender relations; and the state as an institutionalized interpretive system. Rojas and Caro conclude that the state is a vehicle for change; states are not really neutral with respect to gender; representations are contestable; the state "is simply there"; and states are not homogeneous. In their more empirical discussion, Geske and Bourque (2001: 256) note that Latin American feminists have sought to "find a new entry point to the state, secure legislation for gender equity, and promote democratic values within the state."

28. Aziz 1995; Brecher, Costello, and Smith 2000; Falk 1993; Waterman 2000.

29. Cerny 1995.

30. It is worth registering that the head of the Workers' Party, Luiz Inácio "Lula" da Silva, was elected president of Brazil in November 2002.

31. Various news reports, e.g., Tom Hundley, "Anti-Globalization Groups Gear Up," *Chicago Tribune,* 15 July 2001; Ben White, "An Elite Cast Debates Poverty," *Washington Post,* 3 February 2002; Leslie Crawford, "Huge Protest March Passes off Peacefully," *Financial Times,* 18 March 2002.

32. Smith, Chatfield, and Pagnucco 1997; Cohen and Rai 2000.

33. Keck and Sikkink 1998.

34. Boswell and Chase-Dunn 2000.

35. Guidry, Kennedy, Zald 2000

36. Boli and Thomas 1997; Edwards and Gaventa 2001; Florini 2000; Smith 1998.

37. Keck and Sikkink 1998: x, 31, 16; Kriesberg, in Smith et al. 1997: 14

38. Keck and Sikkink 1998: 171.

39. Rape was first defined as a crime against humanity in 1996, in the statutes of the Yugoslav war crimes tribunal. This new definition makes rape a prosecutorial offense. Rape is also listed in the category of "genocide," considered by women's groups to be a less limiting concept than "crime against humanity." See UNDP 2002: 107.

40. Boswell and Chase-Dunn 2000: 196.

41. Ibid., 245.

42. Chase-Dunn 1998: 50–53; Dickinson and Schaeffer 2001.

43. Kaldor, Anheier, and Glasius 2003.

44. Barber 2001.

45. On "sex, maids, and export processing," see Pyle 2001.

46. Flexible labor markets in neoliberal parlance refer to those without government or trade union regulations on hiring and wages, which are regarded as "distortions."

47. Handoussa and Potter 1991; Karshenas 1994; Walton and Seddon 1994; Moghadam 1998c; Pfeiffer 1999.

48. Cornia, Jolly, and Stewart 1987.

49. Pfeiffer 1999: 26.

50. Sen and Grown 1987; Commonwealth Secretariat 1989; Elson 1991; Sparr 1995.

51. Beneria and Feldman 1992; Chant 1995; Tanski 1994; Moghadam 1997.

52. Walton and Ragin (1990: 877) write that most participants of food riots, demonstrations, and strikes were "drawn from the urban poor (shantytown dwellers, unemployed youth, street vendors) and the working class (unions)." Walton and Seddon (1994: 49) write: "When austerity protests responded to internationally prescribed market reforms, . . . crowds from Rio to Rabat crying out 'Out with the IMF!' demanded a restoration of food and transportation subsidies, employment, and wages."

53. Marglin and Schor 1990.

54. UNCTAD 1997; UNDP 1999; Taylor 2000; Bornschier 2001; Atkinson 2001; Goesling 2001; Wade 2001; Milanovich 1998, 2002.

55. UNDP 1999.

56. Goesling 2001: 745, 757; UNDP 2002b: 19.

57. Dickson 2000.

58. El-Ghonemy 1998; Moghadam 1997, 2003; UNDP 2002b.

59. Taylor 2000: 25, 26.

60. Huntington 1993.

61. There is, for example, a dynamic democratic movement in the Islamic Republic of Iran, but its success has been checked by the conservative power elite.

62. UNDP 2002b.

63. Some scholars have argued that the third wave of democratization has diminished the possibilities for the type of revolutions that were characteristic of most of the twentieth century. See, for example, Jeff Goodwin (2000).

64. Brecher, Costello, and Smith 2000: 20.

65. Information on worker strikes may be found on the websites of the International Confederation of Free Trade Unions (ICFTU) and the U.S. Department of State's Bureau of Democracy, Human Rights, and Labor, among other sources. See www.icftu.org and www.state.gov/g/drl/rls/hrrpt/2003.

66. The economist Robert Samuelson (2002) called the Argentine crisis "a cautionary tale for globalization."

67. Klein 2003.

68. Salamé 1994. See also Kamrava 1998; Butterworth and Zartman, 2001.

69. One of the freedoms Islamists in Turkey call for is the right of religious women to wear the Islamic head scarf in public places such as universities and government agencies. For years, this has been banned in staunchly secular Turkey. Feminists in Turkey are sharply divided on the question of veiling and the public space; transnational feminists find it to be a complicated issue.

70. Barber 2001: 232.

71. Ibid., i.

72. See Cooley 1999. See also Hélie-Lucas 1994: 398; Moghadam 2003b, chap. 5.

73. The analogy would be to class conflict or race conflict, when subordinate groups are making social and political demands and the privileged groups are resisting change.

74. Much to the disappointment of feminist groups, the fundamentalist movement initially forced the government to put aside the proposed plan of action. But in October 2003 a royal decree had revived it, and in January 2004 the Moroccan parliament voted to adopt the plan.

75. See contributions in Moghadam 1994a.

76. El-Mikawy 1999: 88.

THREE. Female Labor, Regional Crises, and Feminist Responses

1. Evans 2000; Baudot 1999.

2. In this book, I use the term *professionalization* in two ways: in this chapter to refer to the entry of middle-class women into the professions and in the next chapter to refer to a choice made by movement organizations.

3. See Boserup 1970.

4. Mies 1986.

5. See Pampel and Tanaka 1986 for a discussion of the "feminization U" and test of the hypothesis regarding the curvilinear relationship between economic development and female labor force participation.

6. Elson and Pearson 1981; Nash and Fernandez-Kelly 1983; Lim 1985.

7. Pearson 1992: 231.

8. Joekes/INSTRAW 1987: 81.

9. UN 1999.

10. Chandler 2001.

11. Gallin 2000: 19.

12. Moghadam 1998b

13. Nathan 2000.

14. Duff-Brown 2001.

15. ICFTU, "The New Economy Is Dominated by Women in Precarious Employment," 5/11/2001.

16. See Stalker 2000.

17. See Zachary 2001. On domestic workers, see G. Chang (2000) and K. Chang and L. H. M. Ling (2000).

18. Chang 2000; Stalker 2000: 72; Chang and Ling 2000.

19. Kofman 2000.

20. On patterns of labor migration see Serageldin, Socknat, and Birks 1983; on return migration and unemployment see Shaban, Assaad, and al-Qudsi 1995.

21. OECD 1994: 11–14.

22. UN 1991: 190.

23. UN 2000.

24. Data from EuroStat 2001. See also UNDP 2002b, table 18.

25. See, e.g., UNDP 1995; Charmes 1999.

26. UN 1999; Charmes 1999; CAWTAR 2001.

27. Beneria and Roldan 1987; Cinar 1994.

28. Boris and Prugl 1996.

29. For example, in a controversial study that disputes notions of gender discrimination and emphasizes women's own preferences, Hakim (1998) provides a detailed analysis of part-time work and homework in Britain, among other types of employment. She argues that women's lower wages and concentration in female-dominated occupations shows their "preference" for family and for part-time work.

30. UNDP 1995: 36.

31. World Bank 1995: 45.

32. Pearson and Mitter 1993: 50.

33. Hopkins and Wallerstein 1996: 4.

34. UN 1999; Moghadam 1995; CAWTAR 2001.

35. Sklair 2002.

36. On the other hand, the proletarianization of women was an integral part of early industrialization in England, France, and parts of the United States (e.g., the textile mills of Lowell, Massachusetts).

37. On women and unionization, see Hastings and Coleman 1992; Cobble 1993; Martens and Mitter 1994; Chhachhi and Pittin 1996; Needleman 1998; Dannecker 2000.

38. See, for example, "The ILO's on-line conference on organized labour in the 21st century," www.ilo.org/public/english/bureau/inst/papers/2000/dp125, accessed 30 May 2001.

39. ICFTU 2002.

40. Ibid.

41. The union contract had been won at the Camisas Modernas Phillips-Van Heusen plant in 1996. Early in 1999 Phillips-Van Heusen closed the factory.

42. See www.jca.ax.apc.org/ajwrc.

43. ICFTU 2000.

44. Gabriel and Macdonald (1994) described its role in new forms of cooperation among women from Mexico, the United States, and Canada who were critical of NAFTA.

45. Franklin2001; "STITCH-ing across Borders," *Off Our Backs*, March 2001.

46. Gallin 2000: 17.

47. Briskin 1993.

48. The Danish Women Workers Union was formed in the early 1900s because the General Workers' Union refused to admit women workers. See Gallin 2000: 17.

49. Eaton 1992; Hastings and Coleman 1992.

50. AFL-CIO Fact Sheet: "Facts about Working Women," http://aflcio.org/women/wwfacts.htm, accessed 15 April 2002.

51. Spillane 2001: 6.

52. Franzway 1994.

53. Briskin 1998a.

54. Briskin 1998b: 24

55. Briskin 1998a: 7.

56. Warskett 2001: 4.

57. See Hastings and Coleman 1992; Klausen 1997.

58. ICFTU, "After Beijing: Progress Sketchy," 15 June 2000, www.icftu.org, accessed 10 April 2002.

59. Gallin 2000: 19.
60. UNDP 1999.
61. Blustein 2002; Samuelson 2002; Faiola 2002.
62. Oxfam 2000; Lustig 1999.
63. Goering 2000.
64. Ibid.
65. ILO 1999b.
66. Mikhalev 1999; UNDP 2002b.
67. ILO 1999b; Moghadam 2001a.
68. Layachi 2001.
69. Ibid., 11.
70. Ibid., 18.
71. Al-Feddy 2000.
72. Layachi 2001: 25.
73. "Working without a Net: Women and the Asian Financial Crisis," *Gender Matters Quarterly,* January 2000, p. 6.
74. Stiglitz 2000: 58. See also Sachs 1998.
75. "The Situation of Women Workers in Asia," excerpts from *Asian Women Workers Newsletter* [The Committee for Asian Women, Bangkok]. The article reported on country papers circulated in CAW's regional consultation, held in Bangkok 23–26 January 2000.
76. "Working without a Net," p. 2.
77. Ibid.
78. Ibid.
79. Ibid., 4, 6.
80. Soriano 1998. Zenaida Soriano is with AMIHAN, the National Federation of Peasant Women, Philippines. She delivered her statement at a regional forum entitled "Asian Regional Crisis: Impact on Women and Children," in Manila on 20 August 1998. Other statements compiled in the proceedings were from Indonesia and Thailand. The forum was sponsored by the National Federation of Peasant Women, the Asian Peasant Women Network, the Children's Rehabilitation Center, and Gabriela.
81. "Women's Labor: A Key Factor in Globalization," *Economic Justice News* [50 Years Is Enough].
82. Petchesky 2000: 6.
83. Cited in WIDE newsletter, "From Copenhagen to Beijing," March 1995, p. 19.
84. WIDE newsletter, November 1993, p. 4.
85. "How IMF/World Bank Policies Damage Women Worldwide," summarized in *WIN News* 25, no. 4 (Autumn 1999): 19–20.
86. Cited in *EcoFeminist Journal* [Feminists for Animal Rights], 12, nos. 1–2 (Spring–Summer 2000): 1, 10.
87. Hilkka Pietila, "Women's Human Rights in the World of Disparity and Distress," WIDE-Finland, mimeo, February 2000.
88. *Declaration for Economic Justice and Women's Empowerment,* Economic Justice Caucus, Beijing Plus Five PrepCom March 2000. See www.wicej.addr.com/declaration.htm.
89. Smith 2000: 6.
90. ICFTU 2002.
91. Tiano 1994; Kim 1997; Safa 1996.

FOUR. The Women's Movement and Its Organizations

1. Jaquette 1994; Basu 1995; Ray 1999; Al-Ali 2000; Moghadam 1998b.

2. See contributions in Basu 1995; Mikell 1997.

3. These are: (1) women are a special category of people with certain characteristics in common, whether owing to biology or socialization; (2) only women should define what is feminine; (3) recognition of and dissatisfaction with living in a man's world; (4) radical change: to end men's unjust power and claim for women what is rightfully theirs. See Ferree and Hess 1995: 32–33.

4. Misciagno 1997 on "de facto feminism"; the definition is from Ferree and Risman, 2001: x.

5. Chafetz and Dworkin 1986; Dahlerup 1987; Margolis 1993; Moghadam 1994; Jaquette and Wolchik 1998; Ray 1999.

6. Ferree and Hess 1995; Staggenborg 1998b. On Latin America see Safa 2000.

7. On the U.S. see Evans 1980; on Algeria see Moghadam 2000; on Iran see Shahidian 1996, 1997; on Palestine see Abdulhadi 1998; on Latin America see Jaquette 1994, Alvarez 2000, Safa 2000.

8. See, for example, *Gender and Development* (1997).

9. See Ferree and Hess 1994; Ferree and Martin 1995; Staggenborg 1998a, 1999.

10. Gerlach 1999: 95.

11. An example from the Middle East might be criticism of the leadership style of Egyptian feminist physician and writer Nawal Saadawi, who founded the Arab Women's Solidarity Association.

12. As we shall see, this distinction characterizes differences between some of our case-study TFNs, such as WIDE (a formal and professionalized organization) and WLUML and especially AWMR (informal networks).

13. Staggenborg 1988a; 1999: 129.

14. Freeman 1999.

15. Castells 2000: 695. Castells has written extensively about social networks—including what he calls the network society and the network economy—and he argues that networks constitute the social structure of the information age, an imperative of the era of globalization. My use of the term *network* is more limited, referring to a type of social movement organization or advocacy group.

16. In their study of Indian women's transnational activism, Subramanian, Gupte, and Mitra (2002) show how networks may be usefully seen not only as structures but also as actors in a web of ties across geographical boundaries spanning local, national, and global sites.

17. See Rupp 1998; Berkovitch 1999; Meyer 1999; Stienstra 1994; Rupp and Taylor 1999.

18. Berkovitch 1999: 81–82.

19. Boxer and Quataert 1978. Kennedy and Tilly (1987: 25, 34) cite Charles Sowerwine to the effect that the socialist parties generally organized women in much smaller numbers than men. The German Social Democratic Party reached the highest female enrollment, at 16 percent (175,000 women) in 1914, while the French socialist movement trailed with an estimated 23 percent women, reaching a high of about 1,500 members in 1914. The women's suffrage groups were relatively large; the National

Union of Women's Suffrage Societies, in Britain, was founded in 1897 and grew to over four hundred branches with a membership of 30,000 in 1913 (Kennedy and Tilly 1987: 10). The socialist movement organized predominantly working-class women, such as textile workers, while the feminist organizations were largely middle-class and reformist.

20. Jayawardena 1986.

21. Although WILPF has national sections that in turn have local branches, it sees itself as "not a federation of national organizations, but an international community of women," as cited by Meyer (1999: 114).

22. Stienstra 1994: 100.

23. Ibid., 101.

24. See Pietila and Vickers 1994: 80–83. See also Zinsser 2002.

25. Fraser 1987: 61.

26. Peter Waterman (1998: 154) has made the same point.

27. Both quotes in Bunch and Carillo 1990: 73.

28. Mair 1986: 590.

29. Lycklama, Swiebel, and Vargas 1998: 30.

30. Zinsser 2002: 166.

31. See, for example, Davis 1996: 42–47. Davis was the executive director of WEDO.

32. Sen and Grown 1987: 22.

33. WIDE 1995: 3.

34. Lycklama à Nijeholt, Swiebel, and Vargas 1998: 34.

35. Gittler 1996: 86. See also Moghadam 1996a, 2000a; Miles 1996; Stienstra 1994, 2000; Harcourt 1999.

36. See, for example, Harcourt 1999.

37. Arizpe 1999: xvi.

38. Author's interview with Nadia Johnson, WEDO, New York, 1 March 2002.

39. WIDE bulletin: "From Copenhagen to Beijing," March 1995, p. 6

40. WIDE newsletter, April 1995, 3

41. WIDE bulletin: "From Copenhagen to Beijing," March 1995, p. 11

42. *Bridges,* SID vol. 3–4, 1998, p. 19.

43. *Bridges,* SID vol. 3–4, 1998, pp. 19–20.

44. IWTC Global Net 27 January 1999.

45. Sen and Grown 1987: 89.

46. Gal and Kligman 2000.

47. AWSA was closed down because it took a position critical of the bombing of Iraq in 1991, which the Egyptian government endorsed. Egyptian sociologist and civil society activist Professor Saadeddin Ibrahim was arrested and tried on spurious charges of accepting external funding for his Ibn Khaldun Center for Development Studies. After a lengthy trial and imprisonment, he was finally released in fall 2002.

48. Mahnaz Afkhami, formerly of SIGI, now of the Women's Leadership Partnership, personal interview, 10 April 2002, Bethesda, Maryland.

49. Buechler 2000.

50. Stienstra 1994: 146.

51. Author's interview with Bénédicte Allaert, WIDE project officer for ACP NGOs, Brussels, 7 January 2000.

52. Mahnaz Afkhami has pointed out that many of the leaders of women's organizations in MENA countries, for example, are elite women who would consider it embarrassing to seek a salary, although some members of their staff may be salaried. She feels that this type of voluntarism is a strength but also a drawback in some cases. Personal interview, Bethesda, Maryland, 10 April 2002.

53. Bénédicte Allaert of WIDE, in an interview with the author, Brussels, 7 January 2000.

54. Sen and Grown 1987: 10.

55. Interview with Marieme Hélie-Lucas, Vienna, January 2001.

56. Ibid.

57. This statement draws in part on my own experience in the Iranian student movement from the mid-1970s until the early 1980s.

58. Interview with Mahnaz Afkhami, Bethesda, Maryland, 10 April 2002.

59. Brigitte Holzner, personal communication with the author, 4 April 2003.

60. Marilee Karl 1986: 1, cited in Stienstra 1994: 102.

61. Shaheed 1995: 324.

62. Interview with Hélie-Lucas, Vienna, 20 January 2000.

63. Ibid.

64. WLUML, *Plan of Action, Dhaka 1997*, p. 23. See also Farida Shaheed 1994.

65. The South Asia office is coordinated by Shirkat Gah, a women's resource center based in Lahore, which produces the *News Sheet*. Leading figures there are Farida Shaheed and Khawar Mumtaz. Another leading figure, based in Bangladesh, is Salma Sobhan, a well-known lawyer and activist long associated with WLUML. In Lagos, sociologist and activist Ayesha Imam runs Baobob, a women's NGO which also coordinates WLUML's work in Africa.

66. WLUML, Plan of Action, Dhaka, p. 24.

67. *DAWN Informs,* no. 1, 1999, p. 10.

68. Francisco 1999: 6–8.

69. Kriesberg 1997: 14; Keck and Sikkink 1998: 16.

70. See, for example, Kriesi 1996.

FIVE. From Structural Adjustment to the Global Trade Agenda

Epigraphs: WIDE newsletter, April 1995, p. 3; WIDE bulletin: "From Copenhagen to Beijing," March 1995, p. 19; *WEDO News & Views* 11, no. 2 (June 1998): 15.

1. *DAWN Informs,* no. 1, 1999, p. 2.

2. Author's interview with Caren Grown, MacArthur Foundation, Chicago, 14 December 1999.

3. Ibid.

4. Ibid.

5. Lycklama à Nijeholt, Swiebel, and Vargas 1998: 30.

6. Sen and Grown 1987: 80.

7. Author's observations and discussions at the NGO forum and the FWCW, September 1995.

8. See *World Development* 23, no. 11 (November 1999) and 28, no. 7 (July 2000). The 1995 issue included articles by Lourdes Beneria on integrating gender into economics

and Diane Elson on gender awareness in modeling structural adjustment and DAWN's vision of social development.

9. *DAWN Informs,* no. 1, 1999.

10. Ibid.

11. Gita Sen and Sonia Correa, "Gender Justice and Economic Justice: Reflections on the Five Year Review of the UN Conferences of the 1990s." Paper prepared for UNIFEM in preparation for the five-year review of the Beijing Platform for Action. (Mimeo, no date.) The themes of this paper have appeared in various issues of *DAWN Informs.*

12. Author's participant observation. I was also a speaker at that conference, and I discussed the impact of the postsocialist transitions in Eastern Europe on women workers.

13. Author's observation at the Beijing conference.

14. Author's interview with Bénédicte Allaert, WIDE, Brussels, 7 January 2000.

15. WIDE newsletter, April 1995, p. 3.

16. Ibid.

17. Quoted in *Women's International Network News,* no. 22–23, summer 1997.

18. *WEDO News & Views* 12, no. 1 (May 1999).

19. *WEDO News & Views* 12, no. 3 (November 1998): 1.

20. *WEDO News & Views* 8, no. 3–4 (January 1995): 4.

21. Ibid.

22. *WEDO News & Views* 1 7, no. 3 (January 1995): 8.

23. Ibid., 1.

24. Author's observations at the Beijing conference.

25. *WEDO News & Views* 11, no. 2 (June 1998): 11.

26. "At CSD, Women Say 'No' to War," *WEDO News & Views* 12, no. 1 (May 1999): 5.

27. Diederich 1999: 4.

28. Petchesky 2000: 7.

29. Petchesky 2000: 6.

30. *WEDO News & Views* 12, no. 2 (November 1998): 1.

31. Leni Silverstein, in an interview with the author, MacArthur Foundation, Chicago, 14 December 1999.

32. *WEDO News & Views* 4, no. 3 (December 1994): 4.

33. Bowen 1997: 177.

34. *WEDO News & Views* 4, no. 3 (December 1994): 3.

35. WIDE newsletter, December 1994, p. 3.

36. A short version of *Challenging the Given: DAWN's Perspectives on Social Development* was reprinted in the journal *World Development.* See DAWN 1995.

37. Ibid., 1.

38. WIDE newsletter, December 1994, p. 3.

39. *WEDO News & Views* 8 (June 1995): 3.

40. WIDE newsletter, December 1994, p. 2.

41. WIDE newsletter, April 1995, p. 3.

42. Ibid., 3.

43. *WEDO News & Views* 7, no. 3 (January 1995): 6.

44. WIDE newsletter, April, 1995, p. 2.

45. WIDE newsletter, July 1995, p. 5. At the time, Spain held the (rotating) EU presidency.

46. Author's observations at the Beijing conference, and various interviews.

47. WIDE newsletter, July 1995, p. 4.

48. WIDE newsletter, July 1995, p. 4, and interview with Bénédicte Allaert.

49. *WEDO News & Views* 8, no. 3–4 (December 1995): 1.

50. WEDO also took part in the World Food Summit (Rome, November 1996) and the Earth Summit + 5 (June 1997).

51. WIDE bulletin: "From Copenhagen to Beijing," March 1995, p. 29.

52. WIDE newsletter, May 1996, p. 1.

53. WIDE 1998.

54. Information from WIDE-Osterreich. The annual conference took place in Vienna on 22–25 May 2003.

55. Author's observations at the WIDE annual meeting, Brussels, May 2000.

56. WIDE, 2002b.

57. WEDO *News & Views* 13, no. 1 (March 2000): 8.

58. Ibid., 1.

59. *WEDO News & Views* 12, no. 3 (November 1998): 6–7, 14.

60. *WEDO News & Views* 7, no. 3 (January 1995): 3.

61. *WEDO News & Views* 12, no. 3 (November 1998): 13.

62. *WEDO News & Views* 10, no. 2 (September 1997): 8.

63. See, for example, *WEDO News & Views* 9, no. 3–4 (December 1996).

64. *ARROWS for Change* 5, no. 1 (May 1999): 9–10.

65. WEDO, "Gender Breakdown of Boards of Directors at World Financial Institutions," *News &Views* 15, no. 1 (2002).

66. Author's interview with Nadia Johnson, Program Associate, Economic and Social Justice, WEDO, New York, 1 March 2002.

67. See www.awid.org/monterreyflstatement.html.

68. WIDE 2002a: 5.

69. Petchesky 2000, p. 7.

70. Ibid.

71. Nadia Johnson, WEDO, New York, 1 March 2002.

72. Caren Grown, in an interview with the author, MacArthur Foundation, Chicago, 14 December 1999.

73. According to Leni Silverstein, "the Latin American network is the most articulate and well-organized" of the networks that make up DAWN. Chicago, 14 December 1999.

74. In 1999, Leni Silverstein, then senior program officer at the MacArthur Foundation in charge of population issues, said that "DAWN's work on reproductive health and rights is the best organized."

75. Josefa (Gigi) Francisco, "Gender in the Campaign for Tax Reform in the Philippines," *DAWN Informs*, no. 1, 1999, pp. 6–8.

76. *DAWN Informs*, no. 1, 1999, p. 10.

77. Personal observation, annual WIDE meeting, Brussels, May 1995, May 2000.

78. WIDE 2003:31.

79. Personal communication from Brigitte Holzner, WIDE president, 4 April 2003.

80. Author's interview with Bénédicte Allaert, WIDE, Brussels, 7 January 2000.

81. Author's interview with Nadia Johnson, program officer, WEDO, New York, 1 March 2002.

82. Ibid.

83. Author's interview with Nadia Johnson, program officer, WEDO, NYC, 1 March 2002.

84. Cited in Mary Thom, "Promises to Keep: Beijing and Beyond" [interviews with Florence Butegwa, Gita Sen, Charlotte Bunche, and Jecelyn Dow]. *Ford Foundation Report*, Winter 2000, p. 32.

85. Brigitte Holzner, WIDE president, personal communication, 4 April 2003.

86. Personal observation. Ms. Nguyen visited Helsinki, Finland, while I was a staff member of UNU/WIDER, to promote a new World Bank publication on gender and development and to try to counter criticisms of the World Bank's structural adjustment policies and their impacts on working women.

87. This has been raised in a number of meetings, and in private conversations.

88. Goetz 2000: 47.

89. Zenebeworke Tadesse, in a talk entitled "Beyond the Magic Bullet: African Women and Their Long and Complex Quest for Gender Justice," delivered at the Woodrow Wilson International Center for Scholars, Washington, D.C., 19 February 2002.

90. Ibid.

91. Ibid.

92. Caren Grown, in an interview with the author, Chicago, 14 December 1999.

93. Author's interview with Nadia Johnson, Program Associate, Economic & Social Justice, WEDO, New York, 1 March 2002

SIX. Feminists versus Fundamentalists

Epigraphs: Shaheed 1995: 306; Afkhami 1995: 5–6.

1. In a number of its position papers, DAWN has noted that the neoliberal turn in economic globalization has been accompanied by the rise of patriarchal religious fundamentalism and of violence against women. They argue that "both feed on men's defensive responses to restructured masculinities." See *DAWN Informs*, November 2001, p. 24. See also statement by Peggy Antrobus in chapter 8 (Antrobus 1996: 66–67).

2. "I was against it," Hélie-Lucas has stated with characteristic frankness, "because the UK harbors fundamentalists." Personal interview, Amherst, Mass., 7 March 2002.

3. On the women's movement in Algeria, see Moghadam 2001b.

4. Kazi 1997: 141.

5. Hélie-Lucas 1993a: 225.

6. This was stated at a conference I organized on comparative fundamentalisms and women, which took place at UNU/WIDER (The World Institute for Development Economics Research, of the United Nations University) in Helsinki, Finland, in October 1990. See Moghadam 1993a.

7. See Boix 2001: 6.

8. www.sigi.org, accessed December 1999.

9. Ibid.

10. "Letter from the President," *SIGI News* 7, nos. 1 & 2 (Spring/Summer 1999): 12.

11. Letter from Mahnaz Afkhami, 9 December 1999.

12. Mahnaz Afkhami, personal interview, 10 April 2002, WLP offices, Bethesda, Maryland.

13. See www.sigijordan.org and www.amanjordan.org.

14. Interview with Mahnaz Afkhami, outgoing president, the Sisterhood Is Global Institute (SIGI) Washington, D.C., 21 November 1999.

15. Personal communication from Marieme Hélie-Lucas, 3 July 2003. For details on Algerian women's organizations, see Moghadam 2001b and Moghadam 2003a. Khalida Messaoudi (now Toumi) later became a member of parliament and a cabinet minister.

16. Interview with Hélie-Lucas, Vienna, Austria, 20 January 2000.

17. WLUML, Plan of Action, Dhaka 1997.

18. Sisters in Islam are believing women who are opposed to the Islamic laws that are in place in many Muslim countries, particularly family laws that place women in subordinate positions vis-à-vis husbands and male kin. Sisters in Islam, and other "Islamic feminists," seek reform of the family laws, are opposed to fundamentalism, and favor separation of religion and the state while identifying themselves as Muslim women. As a network, WLUML includes believing and nonbelieving women, as well as women born into different religious communities in the Muslim world.

19. Shaheed 1994: 7–8.

20. See www.whrnet.org.

21. WLUML, *Publications* [catalog], p. 3.

22. The two books are Marfua Tokhtakhodjaeva, *Between the Slogans of Communism and the Laws of Islam: The Women of Uzbekistan* (Lahore: Shirkat Gah Women's Resource Center, 1995), and Marfua Tokhtakhodjaeva and Elmira Turgumbekova, eds., *The Daughters of Amazons: Voices from Central Asia* (Lahore: Shirkat Gah Women's Resource Center, 1996).

23. See, for example, *News Sheet* 15, no. 1 (April 2003).

24. Hélie-Lucas 1993a: 227.

25. Ibid.

26. "Their Culture, Our Culture," Dossier 14/15, 1996.

27. WLUML, Plan of Action, Dhaka, 1997, p. 6.

28. Hélie-Lucas 1993b: 62.

29. For an elaboration, see Moghadam 2001b.

30. "Shadow Report on Algeria to the Committee on the Elimination of All Forms of Discrimination against Women," submitted by the International Women's Human Rights Law Clinic and Women Living under Muslim Laws (January 1999). WLUML, February 2000.

31. Full disclosure: I was asked to write an expert-witness affidavit in support of the civil suit, in August 2002.

32. For an elaboration, see Moghadam 2002b, 2003b, chapter 7.

33. Boix 2001: 7.

34. "SIGI's Center in Jordan Provides Women Access to New Resources," *SIGI News* 6, no. 2 (Fall/Winter 1998): 4.

35. Letter from Mahnaz Afkhami, 9 December 1999.

36. "SIGI's Field Coordinators Report on Workshops," *SIGI News* 6, no. 2 (Fall/Winter 1998): 5.

37. Ibid.

38. Mahnaz Afkhami, personal interview, Washington, D.C., 21 November 1999.

39. "SIGI Publishes *Safe and Secure,*" *SIGI News* 6, no. 2 (Fall/Winter 1998): 10.

40. Ibid.

41. Ibid., 10–11.

42. Ibid., 11–12.

43. "SIGI Publishes in Our Own Words," *SIGI News* 7, nos. 1 & 2 (Spring/Summer 1999): 12.

44. "1998 State of the World Forum," *SIGI News* 7, nos. 1 & 2 (Spring/Summer 1999): 8.

45. Interview with Mahnaz Afkhami, Bethesda, Maryland, 10 April 2002.

46. Interview with Marieme Hélie-Lucas, Vienna, 20 January 2000.

47. Personal communication from Marieme Hélie-Lucas, 3 July 2003.

48. Interview with Hélie-Lucas, Vienna, 20 January 2000.

49. Shaheed 1994: 7.

50. Interview with Hélie-Lucas, Vienna, 20 January 2000.

51. WLUML, Plan of Action, Dhaka 1997, p. 23. See also Shaheed 1994.

52. The Asia office is coordinated by Shirkah Gah, a women's resource center based in Lahore, which produces the *News Sheet.* Leading figures there are Fareeda Shaheed and Khawar Mumtaz. Another leading figure, based in Bangladesh, is Salma Sobhan, a well-known lawyer and activist long associated with WLUML. In Lagos, sociologist and human rights activist Ayesha Imam runs Baobob, a women's NGO which also coordinates WLUML's work in Africa. Note that Shirkat Gah and Baobob are separate organizations, some of whose members devote time to WLUML.

53. Kazi 1997: 145.

54. Shaheed 1995: 320.

55. Shaheed 1994: 9.

56. Van Bruinessen 2002.

57. Hélie-Lucas, interview with the author, Vienna, 20 January 2000.

58. Hélie-Lucas 1993b: 226.

59. Interview with Mahnaz Afkhami, Washington, D.C., 21 November 1999.

60. Ibid.

61. Interview with Afkhami, Bethesda, Maryland, 10 April 2002.

62. For example, in October 2002 Asma Khader was working on the case of a young Yemeni woman accused of adultery and sentenced to death; the man involved in the case was sentenced to only one and a half years in prison. See WLP eNews i1 (October 2002), www.learningpartnership.org, accessed 1 November 2002.

63. Interview with Afkhami, Bethesda, Maryland, 10 April 2002.

64. Interview with Afkhami, Washington, D.C., 21 November 1999.

65. Ibid.

66. Interview with Afkhami, Bethesda, Maryland, 10 April 2002.

67. Ibid.

68. Ibid.

69. Ibid.

70. Ibid.

71. Interviews and observations at SIGI-Jordan, Amman, 15 October 2003.

72. Interview with Hélie-Lucas, Vienna, 20 January 2000.

73. Interview with Mahnaz Afkhami, Washington, D.C., 21 November 1999.

74. Interview with Afkhami, 10 April 2002.

SEVEN. The Travails of Transnational Feminist Organizing

1. See Freeman 1999; Staggenborg 1998a, 1999.

2. Madhu Kishwar has discussed this matter in a number of essays in the magazine *Manushi,* and in a 1998 seminar at Illinois State University. For her views on women's self-determination and gender justice in India, see Kishwar 1999.

3. From its brochure and mission statement.

4. Author's interview with AWMR president Yana Mintoff and general secretary Ninetta Pourou-Kantzasis, 16 July 2000.

5. From the AWMR statutes.

6. From the AWMR statutes, approved 20/9/92 and amended on 29/7/97.

7. Author's interview with Ninetta Purou-Kantzasis, Limassol, Cyprus, 16 July 2000.

8. Author's observations at annual meetings in Italy, July 1998, and in Cyprus, July 2000.

9. Appeal sent via e-mail, 26 March 1999.

10. Author's interview, 16 July 2000.

11. From its mission statement.

12. A resolution of the 1994 conference on Militarism in the Mediterranean, held in Malta.

13. Author's interview with Yana Mintoff-Bland, Limassol, 16 July 2000.

14. Ibid.

15. Ninetta Pourou-Kantzasis, Limassol, 15 July 2000. A position statement that elicited much discussion (and was twice revised before it was accepted by the membership) was one prepared by the Italian delegation strongly protesting the imprisonment in Turkey of Abdullah Ocalan, leader of the (outlawed) Kurdish revolutionary party, the PKK.

16. Author's interview with Maroulla Vassiliou, Marrakesh, July 2002.

17. I am a member of the AWMR, and thus some of this information comes from personal experience and observation.

18. Yana Mintoff-Bland, in a telephone conversation with the author, 17 February 2002.

19. Information from the conference report, 1997.

20. Mintoff-Bland 1998: 143–44.

21. AWMR Newsletter, no. 7 (Winter 1998): 8.

22. Ibid., position statement on Yugoslavia.

23. Eighth Annual AWMR Conference, "Mediterranean Environment—The Women's Perspective," Athens, Greece, 26–30 May 1999, Final Resolution.

24. Address by Yana Mintoff-Bland, 12 July 2000.

25. Author's observations at the July 2000 conference in Cyprus.

26. AWMR Newsletter, no. 7 (Winter 1998): 1.

27. From AMWR, Final Resolution, Gallipoli, Italy, 11 July 1998.

28. Khadijah al-Feddy, Opening Speech, Tenth Annual AWMR Conference, Marrakesh, 12 July 2002. The address was in French, the translation mine.

29. Tenth Annual AWMR Conference, Final Statement and Recommendations, 14 July 2003. Available at http://digilander.libero.it/awmr/int.

30. The high cost of travel to Morocco was also a factor. As a result of its fiscal crisis, the AWMR could not offer adequate subsidies for participants, and the cost of the hotel stay in Marrakesh was unusually high.

31. Yana Mintoff-Bland, opening remarks, tenth annual conference, Marrakesh, 12 July 2002.

32. Personal communication from a former board member, 17 July 2003.

33. Yana Mintoff-Bland, in a telephone conversation with the author, 17 February 2002.

EIGHT. The Specter that Haunts the Global Economy?

Epigraphs: Mpoumou 2000: 6; Spillane 2001; statement by the Women's Caucus, United Nations International Conference on Financing for Development, Monterrey, Mexico, issued 19 March 2002.

1. Meyer 1999:108. Meyer notes that while the radical feminist peace groups of the 1980s lost their focus and energy or largely disappeared, WILPF's formal organizational structure allowed it to adapt to new times (p. 119).

2. Personal interview with Rosalind Petchesky, WEDO board member, New York, 3 March 2002.

3. This statement pertains also to the present author.

4. Marieme Hélie-Lucas, in a conversation with the author, Vienna, January 2000.

5. Brecher and Costello 1998: 25.

6. The Bangkok International Roundtable of Unions, Social Movements, and NGOs was organized by Focus on the Global South and the Friedrich Ebert Stiftung, in Bangkok on 11–13 March 2001.

7. Cohen and Rai 2000: 11, citing the works of Sarah Ashwin, Ronaldo Munck, Peter Waterman, and others.

8. Gallin 2000: 30–31.

9. See, for example, various articles in *DAWN Informs,* 1999, 2000, 2001, 2002.

10. Antrobus 1996: 66–67.

11. ILO 2004.

12. www.awid.org/campaign/globalizethis.html, accessed 28 March 2004.

13. "Justice for working families" is the motto of the AFL-CIO of the United States.

References

Abdulhadi, Rabab. 1998. "The Palestinian Women's Autonomous Movement: Emergence, Dynamics, and Challenges." *Gender & Society* 12, no. 6: 649–73.

Afkhami, Mahnaz. 1995. "Introduction." In Mahnaz Afkhami, ed., *Faith and Freedom: Women's Human Rights in the Muslim World*. Syracuse, N.Y.: Syracuse University Press.

———. 2001. "Gender Apartheid, Cultural Relativism, and Women's Human Rights in Muslim Societies." in Marjorie Agosín, ed., *Women, Gender, and Human Rights: A Global Perspective*. New Brunswick: Rutgers University Press.

Al-Ali, Nadje. 2000. *Secularism, Gender, and the State in the Middle East: The Egyptian Women's Movement*. Cambridge: Cambridge University Press.

al-Feddy, Khadijah. 2000. Country Report on Morocco, AWMR annual meeting, Limassol, Cyprus (14 July).

Alvarez, Sonia E. 2000. "Translating the Global: Effects of Transnational Organizing on Local Feminist Discourses and Practices in Latin America." *Meridiens* 1, no. 1 (Autumn).

Antrobus, Peggy. 1996. "Bringing Grassroots Women's Needs to the International Arena." *Development* (June 1993: 3): 65–67.

Arizpe, Lourdes. 1999. "Freedom to Create: Women's Agenda for Cyberspace." In Wendy Harcourt, ed., *Women@Internet: Creating New Cultures in Cyberspace*. London: Zed Books.

Atkinson, Anthony. 2001. "Is Rising Inequality Inevitable? A Critique of the Transatlantic Consensus." WIDER Annual Lectures 3. Helsinki: UNU/WIDER (November).

Aziz, Nikhil. 1995. "The Human Rights Debate in an Era of Globalization: Hegemony of Discourse." *Bulletin of Concerned Asian Scholars* 27, no. 4: 9–15.

Barber, Benjamin. 2001. *Jihad vs. McWorld*. New York: Times Books. 2nd ed.

Barnet, Richard, and John Cavanagh. 1994. *Global Dreams: Imperial Corporations and the New World Order*. New York: Touchstone.

Barrett, Michèle. 1989. *Women's Oppression Today: The Marxist/Feminist Encounter*. London: Verso Books.

Basu, Amrita, ed. 1995. *The Challenge of Local Feminisms: Women's Movements in Global Perspective*. Boulder, Colo.: Westview Press.

———. 2000. "Globalization of the Local/Localization of the Global: Mapping Transnational Women's Movements." *Meridiens* 1, no. 1 (Autumn).

Baudot, Jacques. 1999. *UNRISD News* 20, no. 1.

Bello, Walden. 2000. "Building an Iron Cage: Bretton Woods Institutions, the WTO, and the South." In Sarah Anderson, ed., *Views from the South: The Effects of Globalization and the WTO on Third World Countries*. Chicago: Food First Books.

Beneria, Lourdes, and Martha Roldan. 1987. *The Crossroads of Class and Gender: Industrial Homework, Subcontracting, and Household Dynamics in Mexico City*. Chicago: University of Chicago Press.

Beneria, Lourdes, and Gita Sen. 1981. "Accumulation, Reproduction and Women's Role in Development: Boserup Revisited." *Signs* 8, no. 2 (Winter).

Beneria, Lourdes, and Shelley Feldman, eds. 1992. *Unequal Burden: Economic Crises, Persistent Poverty, and Women's Work*. Boulder, Colo.: Westview Press.

Berger, Suzanne, and Ronald Dore, eds. 1996. *National Diversity and Global Capitalism*. Ithaca, N.Y.: Cornell University Press.

Bergeron, Suzanne. 2001. "Political Economy Discourses of Globalization and Feminist Politics." *Signs: Journal of Women in Culture and Society* 26, no. 4 (Summer): 983–1006.

Berkovitch, Nitza. 1999. *From Motherhood to Citizenship: Women's Rights and International Organizations*. Baltimore, Md.: Johns Hopkins University Press.

Bhagwati, Jagdish. 2002. *Free Trade Today*. Princeton, N.J.: Princeton University Press.

Blustein, Paul. 2002. "IMF, White House Fumble for a Strategy as Argentina Founders." *Washington Post*, 18 January.

Boix, Monserrat. "Women's Networks: Islamists' Violence and Terror." *WLUML News Sheet* 13, no. 4 (November–December 2001).

Boli, John, and George M. Thomas. 1997. "World Culture in the World Polity." *American Sociological Review* 62, no. 2 (April): 171, 190.

Bonvin, Jean. 1997. "Globalization and Linkages: Challenges for Development Policy." *Development* 40, no. 2 (June): 39–42.

Boris, Eileen, and Elisabeth Prugl, eds. 1996. *Homeworkers in Global Perspective*. Totawa, N.J.: Rowman and Littlefield.

Bornschier, Volker. 2001. "Changing Income Inequality in the Second Half of the 20th Century: Preliminary Findings and Propositions for Explanations." Paper presented at the 42nd annual meetings of the International Studies Association, Chicago, 20–24 February.

Boserup, Ester. 1970. *Women and Economic Development*. New York: St. Martin's.

Boswell, Terry, and Christopher Chase-Dunn. 2000. *The Spiral of Capitalism and Socialism: Toward Global Democracy*. Boulder, Colo.: Lynne Rienner.

Bowen, Donna Lee. 1997. "Abortion, Islam, and the 1994 Cairo Population Conference." *International Journal of Middle East Studies* 29, no. 2 (May): 161–84.

Boxer, Marilyn, and Jean Quataert, eds. 1978. *Socialist Women: European Socialism Feminism in the Nineteenth and Early Twentieth Century*. Westport, Conn.: Greenwood Publishers.

Brecher, Jeremy, and Tim Costello. 1998. *Global Village or Global Pillage*. Boston: South End Press. 2nd ed.

Brecher, Jeremy, Tim Costello, and Brendan Smith. 2000. "Globalization from Below." *The Nation* (4 December 4): 19–22.

Brenner, Robert. 1998. "The Economics of Global Turbulence. *New Left Review* 229.

Briskin, Linda. 1993. "Union Women and Separate Organizing." In Linda Briskin and Patricia McDermott, eds., *Women Challenging Unions: Feminism, Democracy, and Militancy*. Toronto: University of Toronto Press, 1993.

———. 1998a. "Unions and Women's Organizing in Canada and Sweden." Paper presented at the World Congress of Sociology, Montreal (26 July–1 August). Forthcoming in Linda Briskin and Mona Eliasson, eds., *Women's Organizing, Public Policy and*

Social Change in Canada and Sweden. Montreal: McGill-Queen's University Press, 1999.

———. 1998b. "Autonomy, Diversity and Integration: Union Women's Separate Organizing in North America and Western Europe in the Context of Restructuring and Globalization." Paper presented at the World Congress of Sociology, Montreal, 26 July–1 August.

Broad, Robin, ed. 2002. *Global Backlash: Citizen Initiatives for a Just World Economy.* Lanham, Md.: Rowman and Littlefield.

Buechler, Steven M. 2000. *Social Movements in Advanced Capitalism: The Political Economy and Cultural Construction of Social Activism.* New York: Oxford University Press.

Bunch, Charlotte, and Roxanna Carillo. 1990. "Feminist Perspectives on Women in Development." In Irene Tinker, ed., *Persistent Inequalities: Women and World Development.* New York: Oxford University Press.

Burrow, Sharan. 2000. "Globalization, Yes, but Be Sure to Focus on People." *International Herald Tribune,* 13 September.

Butterworth, Charles, and William I. Zartman, eds. 2001. *Between the State and Islam.* Washington, D.C.: Woodrow Wilson Center Press and Cambridge University Press.

Castells, Manuel. 2000. 2nd ed. 3 vols. *The Information Age: Economy, Sociology, and Culture.* Oxford: Blackwell.

Catagay, Nilufer, Diane Elson, and Caren Grown. 1995. "Introduction." In "Gender, Adjustment and Macreconomics," special issue of *World Development* 23, no. 11: 1827–36.

Catagay, Nilufer, Caren Grown, and Aida Santiago. 1986. "The Nairobi Women's Conference: Toward a Global Feminism?" *Signs* 12, no. 2 (Summer): 401–12.

CAWTAR. 2001. *Globalization and Gender: Economic Participation of Arab Women.* Tunis: CAWTAR Arab Women's Development Report.

Cerny, Philip G. 1995. "Globalization and the Changing Logic of Collective Action." *International Organization* 49, no. 4 (Autumn): 595–625.

Chafetz, Janet S., and Gary Dworkin. 1986. *Female Revolt: Women's Movements in World and Historical Perspective.* Totowa, N.J.: Rowman and Allanheld.

Chandler, Clay. 2001. "A Factory to the World: China's Vast Labor Pool, Low Wages Lure Manufacturers." *Washington Post,* 25 November.

Chang, Grace. 2000. *Disposable Domestics: Immigrant Women Workers in the Global Economy.* Boston: South End Press.

Chang, Kimberly, and L. H. M. Ling. 2000. "Globalization and Its Intimate Other: Filipina Domestic Workers in Hong Kong." In Anne Sisson Runyan and Marianne Marchand, eds., *Gender and Global Restructuring: Sightings, Sites and Resistances.* London: Routledge.

Chant, Sylvia. 1995. "Women's Roles in Recession and Economic Restructuring in Mexico and the Philippines." In Alan Gilbert, ed., *Poverty and Global Adjustment: The Urban Experience.* Oxford: Blackwell.

Charmes, Jacques. 1999. "Gender and the Informal Sector." Background Paper for the World's Women 2000: Trends and Statistics. New York: United Nations.

Chase-Dunn, Christopher. 1998. 2nd ed. *Global Formation: Structures of the World-Economy.* Rowman and Littlefield.

Chhachhi, Amrita, and Renee Pittin, eds. 1996. *Confronting State, Capital, and Patriarchy: Women Organizing in the Process of Industrialization.* New York: St. Martin's.

Cinar, Mine. 1994. "Unskilled Urban Migrant Women and Disguised Employment: Homeworking Women in Istanbul, Turkey." *World Development* 22, no. 3: 369–80.

Cobble, Dorothy Sue. 1993. *Women and Unions: Forging a Partnership*. Ithaca, N.Y.: ILR Press.

Cohen, Robin, and Shirin M. Rai, eds. 2000. *Global Social Movements*. London: Athlone Press.

Commonwealth Secretariat. 1989. *Engendering Adjustment for the 1990s*. London: Commonwealth Secretariat.

Connell, R. W. 1998. "Masculinities and Globalization." *Men and Masculinities* 1, no. 1: 1–20.

Cooley, John. 1999. *Unholy Wars: Afghanistan, America and International Terrorism*. London: Pluto Press.

Cornia, Giovanni A., Richard Jolly, and Frances Stewart, eds. 1987. *Adjustment with a Human Face*. Oxford: Clarendon.

Cox, Robert W. 1992. "Global Perestroika." In Ralph Miliband and Leo Panitch, eds., *Socialist Register 1992*. London: Merlin Press.

da Gama Santos, Margarida. 1985. "The Impact of Adjustment Programmes on Women in Developing Countries." *Public Enterprise* 5, no. 3 (May): 287–97. Ljubljana: International Center for Public Enterprises in Developing Countries.

Dahlerup, Drude, ed. 1987. *The New Women's Movement: Feminism and Political Power in Europe and the USA*. London: Sage.

Dannecker, Petra. 2000. "Collective Action, Organization Building, and Leadership: Women Workers in the Garment Sector in Bangladesh." *Gender & Development* 8, no. 3: 31–39.

Davis, Susan. 1996. "Making Waves: Advocacy by Women NGOs at UN Conferences." *Development* (3 June): 42–47.

DAWN 1991. *Alternatives, Volume 1: The Food, Energy, and Debt Crises in Relation to Women, and Alternatives; Volume 2: Women's Visions and Movements*. Rio de Janeiro.

———. 1995. "Rethinking Social Development: DAWN's Vision." *World Development* 23, no. 11: 2001–4.

Dickinson, Torry. 1997. "Selective Globalization: The Relocation of Industrial Production and the Shaping of Women's Work." *Research in the Sociology of Work* 6: 109–29. JAI Press.

Dickinson, Torry, and Robert Schaeffer. 2001. *Fast Forward: Work, Gender, and Protest in a Changing World*. Lanham, Md.: Rowman and Littlefield.

Dickson, Martin. 2000. "Gap between the Rich and the Poor Is Increasing." *Financial Times*, 22 September, p. 24.

Diederich, Ellen. "Bombs Are Good for Business, for Some," *WEDO News & Views* (May 1999): 4.

Duff-Brown, Beth. 2001. "Services Boom in India, but Some See Sweatshops." *Chicago Tribune*, 9 July.

Dunaway, Wilma. 2001. "The Double Register of History: Situating the Forgotten Woman and Her Household in Capitalist Commodity Chains." *Journal of World-Systems Research* 7, no. 1 (Spring): 2–29.

Eaton, Susan C. 1992. "Women Workers, Unions and Industrial Sectors in North America." Geneva: International Labour Office, IDP Women Working Paper 1 (October).

Edwards, Michael, and John Gaventa, eds. 2001. *Global Citizen Action*. Boulder, Colo.: Lynne Rienner.

Edwards, Michael, and David Hulme, eds. 1992. *Making a Difference: NGOs and Development in a Changing World*. London: Earthscan Publications.

Ehrenreich, B., and A. Hochschild. 2003. *Global Woman: Nannies, Maids, and Sex Workers in the New Economy*. New York: Metropolitan Books.

El-Ghonemy, M. Riad. 1998. *Affluence and Poverty in the Middle East*. London: Routledge.

El-Mikawy, Noha. 1999. "The Informal Sector and the Conservative Consensus: A Case of Fragmentation in Egypt." In Haleh Afshar and Stephanie Barrientos, eds., *Women, Globalization and Fragmentation in the Developing World*. London: Macmillan.

Elson, Diane, ed. 1991. *Male Bias in the Development Process*. London: Macmillan.

Elson, Diane, and Ruth Pearson. 1981. "Nimble Fingers Make Cheap Workers: An Analysis of Women's Employment in Third World Export Manufacturing." *Feminist Review* (Spring): 87–107.

Employment Observatory: Trends. 1994. Bulletin of the European System of Documentation on Employment, no. 19.

Evans, Peter. 2000. "Fighting Marginalization with Transnational Networks: Counter-Hegemonic Globalization." *Contemporary Sociology* (March): 230–241.

Evans, Sara. 1980. *Personal Politics: The Roots of Women's Liberation in the Civil Rights Movement and the New Left*. New York: Vintage.

Faiola, Anthony. 2002. "Argentina Signals Shift away from U.S." *Washington Post*, 16 January.

Falk, Richard. 1993. "The Making of Global Citizenship." In Jeremy Brecher, John Brown Childs, and Jill Cutler, eds., *Global Visions: Beyond the New World Order*. Boston, Mass.: South End Press.

Featherstone, Mike, ed. 1990. *Global Culture: Nationalism, Globalization, and Modernity*. London: Sage.

Ferree, Myra Marx, and Beth B. Hess. 1994. *Controversy and Coalition: The New Feminist Movement across Three Decades of Change*. Rev. ed. New York: Twayne.

Ferree, Myra Marx, and Patricia Yancey Martin, eds. 1995. *Feminist Organizations: Harvest of the New Women's Movement*. Philadelphia: Temple University Press.

Ferree, Myra Marx, and Barbara Risman. 2001. "Constructing Global Feminism: Transnational Advocacy Networks and Russian Women's Activism." *Signs* 26, no. 4.

Florini, Ann M., ed. 2000. *The Third Force: The Rise of Transnational Civil Society*. Tokyo and Washington, D.C.: Japan Center for International Exchange and Carnegie Endowment for International Peace.

Francisco, Josefa (Gigi). 1999. "Gender in the Campaign for Tax Reform in the Philippines." *DAWN Informs* 1: 6–8.

Franklin, Stephen. 2001. "Organizing Workers against Fear." *Chicago Tribune*, 27 March.

Franzway, Suzanne. 1994. "Women Working in Australian Unions." Paper prepared for the International Sociological Association, RC44, Bielefeld, Germany, 18–23 July.

Fraser, Arvonne. 1987. *The U.N. Decade for Women: Documents and Dialogue*. Boulder, Colo.: Westview Special Studies on Women in Contemporary Studies.

Freeman, Jo. 1999. "A Model for Analyzing the Strategic Options of Social Movement Organizations." In Jo Freeman and Victoria Johnson, eds., *Waves of Protest: Social Movements since the Sixties*. Lanham, Md.: Rowman and Littlefield.

Frobel, Folker, Jurgen Jeinrichs, and Otto Kreye. 1980. *The New International Division of Labor*. Cambridge: Cambridge University Press.

Gabriel, Christina, and Laura Macdonald. 1994. "NAFTA, Women and Organising in Canada and Mexico: Forging a 'Feminist Internationality.'" *Millennium: Journal of International Studies* 23, no. 3: 535–62.

Gal, Susan, and Gail Kligman. 2000. *The Politics of Gender after Socialism*. Princeton, N.J.: Princeton University Press.

Gallin, Dan. 2000. "Trade Unions and NGOs: A Necessary Partnership for Social Development." Civil Society and Social Movements Programme, Paper No. 1 (June). Geneva: UNRISD.

Gender and Development. [Oxfam journal.] Vol. 5, no. 1. February 1997. Issue on Organizational Culture.

Gerlach, Luther. 1999. "Social Movements as Segmentary, Polycentric, and Reticulate." In Jo Freeman and Victoria Johnson, eds., *Waves of Protest: Social Movements since the Sixties*. Lanham, Md.: Rowman and Littlefield.

Geske, Mary, and Susan C. Bourque. 2001. "Grassroots Organizations and Women's Human Rights: Meeting the Challenge of the Local-Global Link." In Marjorie Agosín, ed., *Women, Gender, and Human Rights: A Global Perspective*. New Brunswick, N.J.: Rutgers University Press.

Ghose, Ajit K. 2000. "Trade Liberalization, Employment and Growing Inequality." *International Labour Review* 139, no. 3: 281–305.

Gibson-Graham, J. K. 1996. *The End of Capitalism (as We Knew It): A Feminist Critique of Political Economy*. Oxford: Blackwell.

Giddens, Anthony. 1990. *The Consequences of Modernity*. Stanford, Calif.: Stanford University Press.

Gill, Stephen. 1995. "Theorizing the Interregnum: The Double Movement and Global Politics in the 1990s."I In Bjorn Hettne, ed., *International Political Economy: Understanding Global Disorder*. London: Zed Books.

Gittler, Alice Mastrangelo. 1996. "Taking Hold of Electronic Communications." *Journal of International Communication* 3, no. 1.

Goering, Laurie. 2000. "Mexican Anomaly: Boom Sees More Poor." *Chicago Tribune*, 7 September.

Goesling, Brian. 2001. "Changing Income Inequalities within and between Nations: New Evidence." *American Sociological Review* 66 (October): 745–61.

Goetz, Anne Marie. 2000. "The World Bank and Women's Movements." In O'Brien, Robert, Anne Marie Goetz, Jan Aart Scholte, and Marc Williams, *Contesting Global Governance: Multilateral Economic Institutions and Global Social Movements*. Cambridge, UK: Cambridge University Press.

Goodwin, Jeff. 2000. "Is the Age of Revolutions Over?" In Mark N. Katz, ed., *Revolution: International Dimensions*. Washington, D.C.: Congressional Quarterly Press.

Gray, John. 1998. *False Dawn: The Delusions of Global Capitalism*. London: Granta Books.

Grewal, Inderpal, and Caren Kaplan, eds. 1994. *Scattered Hegemonies: Postmodernity and Transnational Feminist Practices*. Minneapolis: University of Minnesota Press.

———. 1994. "Introduction." In Grewal and Kaplan, eds., *Scattered Hegemonies*.

Guidry, John A., Michael D. Kennedy, and Mayer N. Zald, eds. 2000. *Globalizations and Social Movements: Culture, Power, and the Transnational Public Sphere*. Ann Arbor: University of Michigan Press.

Hakim, Catherine. 1998. *Social Change and Innovation in the Labour Market: Evidence from the Census SARs on Occupational Segregation and Labour Mobility, Part-time Work and Student Jobs, Homework and Self-Employment.* New York: Oxford University Press.

Hamel, Pierre, Henri Lustiger-Thaler, Jan Nederveen Pieterse, and Sasha Roseneil, eds. 2001. *Globalization and Social Movements.* Basingstoke and New York: Palgrave.

Handoussa, Heba, and Gillian Potter, eds. 1991. *Employment and Structural Adjustment: Egypt in the 1990s.* Cairo: American University of Cairo Press.

Harcourt, Wendy, ed. 1999. *Women@Internet: Creating New Cultures in Cyberspace.* London: Zed Books.

Hartmann, Heidi. 1981. "The Unhappy Marriage of Marxism and Feminism: Toward a More Progressive Union." In Lydia Sargent, ed., *Women and Revolution.* Boston: South End Press.

Harvey, David. 1990. *The Condition of Postmodernity.* Oxford: Blackwell.

Hastings, Sue, and Martha Coleman. 1992. "Women Workers and Unions in Europe: An Analysis by Industrial Sector." IDP Working Paper 4. Geneva: International Labour Office.

Held, David, et al., eds. 2000. *A Globalizing World? Culture, Economics, Politics.* London: Routledge.

Hélie-Lucas, Marie-Aimee. 1993a. "Women Living under Muslim Laws." In Joanna Kerr, ed., *Ours by Right: Women's Rights as Human Rights.* London: Zed Books, in association with the North-South Institute.

———. 1993b. "Women's Struggles and Strategies in the Rise of Fundamentalism in the Muslim World: From Entryism to Internationalism." In Haleh Afshar, ed., *Women in the Middle East: Perceptions, Realities, and Struggles for Liberation.* London: Macmillan.

———. 1994. "The Preferential Symbol for Islamic Identity: Women in Muslim Personal Laws." In Moghadam, ed., *Identity Politics and Women: Cultural Reassertions and Feminisms in International Perspective.* Boulder, Colo.: Westview.

Hirst, Paul, and Grahame Thompson. 1996. *Globalization in Question: The International Economy and the Possibilities of Governance.* Cambridge, U.K.: Polity Press.

Hopkins, Terence K., and Immanuel Wallerstein. 1996. "The World System: Is There a Crisis?" In Wallerstein et al., eds., *The Age of Transition: Trajectory of the World-System 1945–2025.* London: Zed.

Hoogvelt, Ankie. 1997. *Globalization and the Postcolonial World: The New Political Economy of Development.* Baltimore: The Johns Hopkins University Press.

Hooper, Charlotte. 2000. "Masculinities in Transition: The Case of Globalization." In Marchand and Runyan, *Gender and Global Restructuring.*

Huntington, Samuel. 1993. *The Third Wave: Democratization in the Late Twentieth Century.* Norman: University of Oklahoma Press.

ICFTU. 2000. "International Survey of Violation of Trade Union Rights, 2001." www.icftu.org, accessed 10 April 2002.

———. "Three Thousand Trade Unionists March in Protest at Poverty and Violence against Women in Durban on April 5." www.icftu.org, accessed 15 April 2002.

ILO. 1999a. *Decent Work and Protection for All: Priority of the Americas.* Geneva: ILO.

———. 1999b. *Key Indicators of the Labour Market* CD-ROM. Geneva: ILO.

———. 2004. *A Fair Globalization: Creating Opportunities for All.* Geneva: International Labor Organization. www.ilo.org/public/english/wxsdg/docs.

INSTRAW/ILO. 1985. *Women in Economic Activity: A Global Statistical Survey 1950–2000*. Santo Domingo: INSTRAW.

Janoski, Thomas. 1998. *Citizenship and Civil Society: A Framework of Rights and Obligations in Liberal, Traditional, and Social Democratic Regimes*. Cambridge, Mass.: Cambridge University Press.

Jaquette, Jane, ed. 1994. *The Women's Movement in Latin America: Participation and Democracy*. 2nd ed. Boulder, Colo.: Westview.

Jaquette, Jane S., and Sharon L. Wolchik, eds. 1998. *Women and Democracy: Latin America and Central and Eastern Europe*. Baltimore, Md.: Johns Hopkins University Press.

Jayawardena. Kumari. 1986. *Feminism and Nationalism in the Third World*. London: Zed.

Joekes, Susan, and INSTRAW. 1987. *Women in the Global Economy: An INSTRAW Study*. New York: Oxford University Press.

Jordan, Bill. 2000. "Yes to Globalization, But Protect the Poor." *International Herald Tribune*, 21 December.

Kaldor, Mary, Helmut Anheier, and Marlies Glasius, eds. 2003. *Global Civil Society*. Oxford: Oxford University Press.

Kamrava, Mehran. 1998. *Democracy in the Balance: Culture and Society in the Middle East*. New York: Chatham House.

Karshenas, Massoud. 1994. *Macroeconomic Policies, Structural Change and Employment Policies in the Middle East and North Africa*. Geneva: ILO.

Katzenstein, Mary Fainsod, and Carol McClurg Mueller. eds. 1987. *The Women's Movements of the United States and Western Europe: Consciousness, Political Opportunity, and Public Policy*. Philadelphia: Temple University Press.

Kazi, Seema. 1997. "Muslim Laws and Women Living under Muslim Laws." In Mahnaz Afkhami and Erika Friedl, eds., *Muslim Women and the Politics of Participation*. Syracuse, N.Y.: Syracuse University Press.

Keck, Margaret E., and Kathryn Sikkink. 1998. *Activists beyond Borders: Advocacy Networks in International Politics*. Ithaca, N.Y.: Cornell University Press.

Kennedy, Marie, and Chris Tilly. 1987. "Socialism, Feminism and the Stillbirth of Socialist Feminism in Europe, 1890–1920." *Science & Society* 51, no. 1 (Spring): 6–42.

Khagram, Sanjeev, James V. Riker, and Kathryn Sikkink, eds. 2002. *Restructuring World Politics: Transnational Social Movements, Networks, and Norms*. Minneapolis: University of Minnesota Press.

Khor, Martin. 2000. "How the South Is Getting a Raw Deal at the WTO." In Sarah Anderson, ed., *Views from the South: The Effects of Globalization and the WTO on Third World Countries*. Chicago: Food First Books.

Kim, Seung-Kyung. 1997. *Class Struggle or Family Struggle? The Lives of Women Factory Workers in South Korea*. Cambridge, UK: Cambridge University Press.

Kishwar, Madhu. 1999. *Off the Beaten Track: Rethinking Gender Justice for Indian Women*. New Delhi: Oxford University Press.

Klausen, Jytte. 1997. "The Declining Significance of Male Workers: Trade Unions' Responses to Changing Labor Markets." In Peter Lange et al., eds., *Crisis and Conflict in Contemporary Capitalism*. Cambridge: Cambridge University Press.

Klein, Naomi. 2003. "Snapshot of a Nation: How Argentina's New President Deals with the Occupied Factories Will Be Hugely Significant." *The Guardian*, 23 April.

Kofman, Eleonore. 2000. "Beyond a Reductionist Analysis of Female Migrants in Global European Cities: The Unskilled, Deskilled, and Professional." In Anne Sisson Runyan and Marianne Marchand, eds., *Gender and Global Restructuring: Sightings, Sites and Resistances*. London: Routledge.

Kohler, Gernot. 1999. "Global Keynesianism and Beyond." *Journal of World-Systems Research* 5, no. 2: 253–74. http://csf.colorado.edu/jwsr (accessed 5/9/01).

Korten, David. 1995. *When Corporations Rule the World*. San Francisco: Kumarian.

Korzeniewicz, Roberto P., and Timothy P. Moran. 1997. "World-Economic Trends in the Distribution of Income, 1965–1992." *American Journal of Sociology* 102: 1000–39.

Kriesberg, Lawrence. 1997. "Social Movements and Global Transformation." In Jackie Smith, Charles Chatfield, and Ron Pagnucco, eds., *Transnational Social Movements and Global Politics*. Syracuse, N.Y.: Syracuse University Press.

Kriesi, Hanspeter. 1996. "The Organizational Structure of New Social Movements in a Political Context." In McAdam Doug, John McCarthy, and Meyer Zald, eds., *Comparative Perspectives on Social Movements: Political Opportunities, Mobilizing Structures, and Cultural Frames*. Cambridge: Cambridge University Press.

Kuttner, Robert. 1998. "Globalism Bites Back." *American Prospect* 37 (March–April): 6–8.

Layachi, Azzedine. 2001. "Reform and the Politics of Inclusion in the Maghrib." *Journal of North African Studies* 53 (Autumn): 15–47.

Lechner, Frank J., and John Boli. 2000. *The Globalization Reader*. Malden: Blackwell Publishers.

Ling, L. H. M. 2002. *Postcolonial International Relations: Conquest and Desire between Asia and the West*. UK: Palgrave.

Lim, Linda. 1985. *Women Workers in Multinational Enterprises in Developing Countries*. Geneva: ILO.

Lustig, Nora. 1999. "Containing the Human Impact of Economic Crisis." *WIDER Angle* 1, no. 99: 5–6.

Lycklama à Nijeholt, Geertje, Joke Swiebel, and Virginia Vargas. 1998. "The Global Institutional Framework: The Long March to Beijing." In Geertje Lycklama À Nijeholt, Virginia Vargas, and Saskia Wieringa, eds., *Women's Movements and Public Policy in Europe, Latin America, and the Caribbean*.

Lycklama À Nijeholt, Geertje, Virginia Vargas, and Saskia Wieringa, eds. 1998. *Women's Movements and Public Policy in Europe, Latin America, and the Caribbean*. New York: Garland Publishing.

Mair, Lucille Mathurin. 1986. "Women: A Decade Is Time Enough." *Third World Quarterly* 8, no. 2 (April): 583–93.

Mander, Jerry. 1996. "The Dark Side of Globalization: What the Media Are Missing." *The Nation*, 15/22 July: 9–29.

Mandle, Jay R. 2000. "Trading Up: Why Globalization Aids the Poor." *Commonweal*, 2 June: 15–18.

Marchand, Marianne. 2000. "Reconceptualizing 'Gender and Development' in an Era of "Globalization.'" In Sarah Owen Vandersluis and Paris Yeros, eds., *Poverty in World Politics: Whose Global Era?* Basingstoke: Macmillan.

Marchand, Marianne, and Ann Sisson Runyan, eds. 2000. *Gender and Global Restructuring*. London: Routledge.

Marglin, Stephen, and Juliet Schor, eds. 1990. *The Golden Age of Capitalism*. Oxford: Clarendon Press.

Margolis, Diane. 1993. "Women's Movements around the World: Cross-Cultural Comparisons." *Gender & Society* 7, no. 3 (September): 379–99.

Marshall, C., and G. B. Rossman. 1995. *Designing Qualitative Research.* 2nd ed. Thousand Oaks: Sage.

Martens, Margaret Hosmer, and Swasti Mitter, eds. 1994. *Women in Trade Unions: Organizing the Unorganised.* Geneva: ILO.

Mathews, Jessica. 1997. "Power Shift." *Foreign Affairs* 76, no. 1 (January–February): 50–66.

McAdam, Doug, John D. McCarthy, and Mayer N. Zald, eds. 1996. *Comparative Perspectives on Social Movements.* Cambridge: Cambridge University Press.

Melucci, Alberto. 1996. *Challenging Codes: Collective Action in the Information Age.* Cambridge: Cambridge University Press.

Meyer, J., J. Boli, G. Thomas, and F. Ramirez. 1997. "World Society and the Nation-State." *American Journal of Sociology* 103:144–81.

Meyer, Mary K. 1999. "The Women's International League for Peace and Freedom: Organizing Women for Peace in the War System." In Mary K. Meyer and Elisabeth Prugl, eds., *Gender Politics in Global Governance.* Lanham, Md.: Rowman and Littlefield.

Mies, Maria. 1986. *Patriarchy and Accumulation on a World Scale.* London: Zed Books.

Mikell, Gwendolyn, ed. 1997. *African Feminism: The Politics of Survival in Sub-Saharan Africa.* Philadelphia: University of Pennsylvania Press.

Mikhalev, Vladimir. 1999. "Transition's Social Costs." *WIDER Angle* 2, no. 99 (December): 8.

Milanovich, Branko. 1998. *Income Inequality and Poverty during the Transition from Planned to Market Economy.* Washington, D.C.: World Bank.

———. 2002. "On Income Inequality." *Economic Journal.* (January).

Miles, Angela. 1996. *Integrative Feminisms: Building Global Visions, 1960s–1990s.* New York: Routledge.

Miliband, Ralph, and Leo Panitch, eds. 1994. *Socialist Register 1994: Between Globalism and Nationalism.* London: Merlin.

Mintoff-Bland, Yana, ed. 1998. *In Search of Peace.* Austin, Tex.: AWMR.

Misciagno, Patricia S. 1997. *Rethinking Feminist Identification: The Case for De Facto Feminism.* Westport, Conn.: Praeger.

Mittelman, James H. 1997. *Globalization: Critical Reflections.* Boulder, Colo.: Lynne Rienner Publishers.

Moghadam, Valentine M., ed. 1993. *Democratic Reform and the Position of Women in Transitional Economies.* Oxford: Clarendon Press.

———, ed. 1994a. *Identity Politics and Women: Cultural Reassertions and Feminisms in International Perspective.* Boulder, Colo.: Westview Press.

———. 1994b. "Women and Identity Politics in Theoretical and Comparative Perspective." In V. M. Moghadam, ed., *Identity Politics and Women: Cultural Reassertions and Feminisms in International Perspective.* Boulder, Colo.: Westview Press.

———. 1994c. "Women in Societies." *International Social Science Journal* 139 (February): 94–115.

———. 1995. "Gender Aspects of Employment and Unemployment in a Global Perspective." In Mihaly Simai, ed., *Global Employment: An Investigation into the Future of Work.* London: Zed Books; Tokyo: United Nations University Press.

———. 1996a. "Feminist Networks North and South: DAWN, WIDE and WLUML." *Journal of International Communication* 3, no. 1 (July): 111–26.

———. 1996b. "The Fourth World Conference on Women: Dissension and Consensus." *Indian Journal of Gender Studies* 3, no. 1: 93–102.

———. 1997. "The Feminization of Poverty? Notes on a Concept and Trends." Illinois State University Women's Studies Program, Occasional Paper No. 2 (August).

———. 1998a. "Gender and the Global Economy." In Myra Marx Ferree, Judith Lorber, and Beth Hess, eds., *Revisioning Gender*. London: Sage.

———. 1998b. "The UN Decade for Women and Beyond." In Nellie Stromquist, ed., *Women in the Third World: An Encyclopedia of Contemporary Issues*. New York: Garland Publishing.

———. 1998c. *Women, Work, and Economic Reform in the Middle East and North Africa*. Boulder, Colo.: Lynne Rienner Publishers.

———. 1999. "Gender and Globalization: Female Labor and Women's Mobilizations." *Journal of World-Systems Research* 5, no. 2 (Spring): 301–14.

———. 2000a. "Transnational Feminist Networks: Collective Action in an Era of Globalization." *International Sociology* 15, no. 1 (March): 57–86.

———. 2000b. "Transnational Feminism: Notes from the Field." *Women's Voice* [Illinois State University Women's Studies Program] 6, no. 2 (September): 1–2.

———. 2001a. "Globalization and Women's Unemployment in the Arab Region." Background Paper prepared for the CAWTAR Report *Globalization and Gender: Economic Participation of Arab Women*.

———. 2001b. "Organizing Women: The New Women's Movement in Algeria." *Cultural Dynamics* 13, no. 2: 131–54.

———. 2002a. "Enhancing Women's Economic Participation in the Middle East and North Africa." In Heba Handoussa and Zafiris Tzannatos, eds., *Employment Creation and Social Creation in the Middle East and North Africa*. Cairo: American University in Cairo Press.

———. 2002b. "Patriarchy, the Taleban, and the Politics of Public Space in Afghanistan." *Women's Studies International Forum* 25, no. 1: 19–31.

———. 2003a. "Global Feminism, the State, and Women's Citizenship in the Muslim World: The Cases of Iran, Algeria, and Afghanistan." Prepared for the conference "Citizenship, Borders, and Gender: Mobility and Immobility," Yale University (8–10 May).

———. 2003b. *Modernizing Women: Gender and Social Change in the Middle East*. 2nd ed. Boulder, Colo.: Lynne Rienner Publishers.

———. 2003c. "Population, Urbanization, and the Challenges of Unemployment and Poverty." In Deborah Gerner, ed. *Understanding the Middle East*. Boulder, Colo.: Lynne Rienner Publishers.

Molyneux, Maxine. 1979. "Beyond the Domestic Labor Debate." *New Left Review* 116.

Morgan, Robin, ed. 1985. *Sisterhood Is Global*. New York: Anchor Books.

Mpoumou, Doris. 2002. "The Proof Is in the Numbers, the Power Is in the Women." *WEDO News & Views* 15, no. 1 (March): 6–7.

Naples, Nancy, and Manisha Desai, eds. 2002. *Women's Activism and Globalization*. London: Routledge.

Nash, June, and Maria Fernandez-Kelly, eds. 1983. *Women, Men, and the International Division of Labor*. Albany, N.Y.: SUNY Press.

Nathan, Debbie. 2000. "Sweating Out the Words." *The Nation,* 21 February: 27–30.

Needleman, Ruth. 1998. "Women Workers: Strategies for Inclusion and Rebuilding Unionism." In Gregory Mantsios, ed., *A New Labor Movement for the New Century.* New York: Garland.

O'Brien, Robert, Anne Marie Goetz, Jan Aart Scholte, Marc Williams. 2000. *Contesting Global Governance: Multilateral Economic Institutions and Global Social Movements.* Cambridge: Cambridge University Press.

OECD. 1994. *Employment Observatory 1994.* Paris: OECD.

Oxfam. 2000. "Poverty at Work Has a Human Face." *Links* (March): 2.

————. 2002. *Rigged Rules and Double Standards: Trade, Globalization, and the Fight against Poverty.* Oxford: Oxfam.

Pampel, Fred C., and Kazuko Tanaka. 1996. "Economic Development and Female Labor Force Participation: A Reconsideration." *Social Forces* 64, no. 3 (March): 599–620.

Pearson, Ruth. 1992. "Gender Issues in Industrialization." In Tom Hewitt, Hazel Johnson, and David Wield, eds., *Industrialization and Development.* Oxford: Oxford University Press.

Pearson, Ruth, and Swasti Mitter. 1993. "Employment and Working Conditions of Low-skilled Information-processing Workers in Less-developed Countries." *International Labour Review* 132, no. 1: 49–64.

Petchesky, Rosalind P. 2000. "WSSD+5 Gains for Women." *WEDO News & Views* 13, no. 2 (August).

Peterson, V. Spike. 2003. *A Critical Rewriting of Global Political Economy: Integrating Reproductive, Productive, and Virtual Economies.* London: Routledge.

Petras, James, and Henry Brill. 1995. "The Tyranny of Globalism." *Journal of Contemporary Asia* 15, no. 4: 403–20.

Pfeiffer, Karen. 1999. "How Tunisia, Morocco, Jordan and even Egypt became IMF 'Success Stories' in the 1990s." *Middle East Report* (Spring): 23–27.

Pieterse, Jan Nederveen. 1998. "Hybrid Modernities: Mélange Modernities in Asia." *Sociological Analysis* 1, no. 3: 75–86.

Pietila, Hillka, and Jeanne Vickers. 1994. *Making Women Matter: The Role of the United Nations.* London: Zed Books. 2nd ed. Pyle, Jean. 2001. "Sex, Maids, and Export Processing: Risks and Reasons for Gendered Global Production Networks." *International Journal of Politics, Culture and Society* 15, no. 1 (September): 55–76.

Qureshi, Zia. 1996. "Globalization: New Opportunities, Tough Challenges." Washington, D.C.: The World Bank. www.worldbank.org/fandd/english/0396/articles/050396.htm, accessed 26 November 1997.

Ray, Raka. 1999. *Fields of Protest: Women's Movements in India.* Minneapolis: University of Minnesota Press.

Robertson, Roland. 1992. *Globalization: Social Theory and Global Culture.* London: Sage.

Robinson, William I. 2001. "Social Theory and Globalization: The Rise of a Transnational State." *Theory and Society* 30, no. 2 (April): 157–200.

Robinson, William I., and Jerry Harris. 2000. "Towards a Global Class? Globalization and the Transnational Capitalist Class." *Science & Society* 64, no. 1 (Spring): 11–54.

Rojas, Maria Cristina, and Elvia Caro. 2003. "Gender and the State: Between Disenchantment and Hope." In Martha Gutiérrez, ed., *Macroeconomics: Making Gender Matter.* London: Zed Books and GTZ.

Rupp, Leila. 1998. *Worlds of Women: The Making of an International Women's Movement.* Princeton, N.J.: Princeton University Press.

Rupp, Leila J., and Verta Taylor. 1999. "Forging Feminist Identity in an International Movement: A Collective Identity Approach to Twentieth-Century Feminism." *Signs: Journal of Women in Culture and Society* 24, no. 21: 363–86.

Sachs, Jeffrey. 1998. "The IMF and the Asian Flu." *American Prospect* (March–April): 16–21.

Safa, Helen. 1996. "Gender Inequality and Women's Wage Labor: A Theoretical and Empirical Analysis." In V. M. Moghadam, ed., *Patriarchy and Development.* Oxford: Clarendon Press.

———. 2000. "Women's Social Movements in Latin America." In Maxine Baca Zinn, Pierrette Hondagneu-Sotelo, and Michael A. Messner, eds., *Gender through the Prism of Difference.* 2nd ed. Boston: Allyn and Bacon.

Salamé, Ghassan, ed. 1994. *Democracy without Democrats: The Renewal of Politics in the Muslim World.* London: I. B. Taurus.

Samuelson, Robert J. 2002. "Do Cry for Argentina." *Washington Post,* 16 January.

Sassen, Saskia. 1996. *Losing Control? Sovereignty in an Age of Globalization.* New York: Columbia University Press.

Schaeffer, Robert K. 1979. *Understanding Globalization: The Social Consequences of Political, Economic, and Environmental Change.* Lanham, Md.: Rowman and Littlefield.

Scholte, Jan Aart. 2000. *Globalization: A Critical Introduction.* London: Palgrave.

Seidman, Gay. 1999. "Gendered Citizenship, South Africa's Democratic Transition, and the Construction of a Gendered State." *Gender and Society* 13, no 3 (June): 287–307.

Sen, Gita. 1997. "Globalization, Justice and Equity: A Gender Perspective." *Development* 40, no. 2 (June): 21–26.

Sen, Gita, and Caren Grown. 1987. *Women, Crises, and Development Alternatives.* New York: Monthly Review Press.

Serageldin, Ismail, James A. Socknat, and John S. Birks. 1983. "Human Resources in the Arab World: The Impact of Migration." In I. Ibrahim, ed., *Arab Resources: The Transformation of a Society.* London: Croom Helm; Washington, D.C.: Center for Contemporary Arab Studies.

Shaban, Radwan A., Ragui Assaad, and Sulayman S. Al-Qudsi. 1995. "The Challenge of Unemployment in the Arab Region." *International Labour Review* 134, no. 1: 65–81.

Shaheed, Farida. 1994. "Controlled or Autonomous: Identity and the Experience of the Network Women Living under Muslim Laws." WLUML Occasional Paper No. 5 (July).

———. 1995. "Linking Dreams: The Network of Women Living under Muslim Laws." In Margaret A. Schuler, ed., *From Basic Needs to Basic Rights: Women's Claim to Human Rights.* Washington, D.C.: Women, Law, and Development International.

Shahidian, Hammed. 1996. "Iranian Exiles and Sexual Politics: Issues of Gender Relations and Identity." *Journal of Refugee Studies* 9, no. 1: 43–72.

———. 1997. "Women and Clandestine Politics in Iran 1970–1985." *Feminist Studies* 23, no. 1: 7–42.

Shiva, Vandana. 1996. "Democracy in the Age of Globalization." *Asian Action* (April–June).

Sklair, Leslie. 1991. *A Sociology of the Global System.* Baltimore, Md.: Johns Hopkins University Press.

———. 2001. *The Transnational Capitalist Class.* Oxford: Blackwell.

———. 2002. *Globalization: Capitalism and Its Alternatives.* 3rd ed. Oxford: Oxford University Press.

Slaughter, Matthew J., and Phillip Swagel. 1997. "Does Globalization Lower Wages and Export Jobs?" Washington, D.C.: International Monetary Fund. http://www.imf.org /external/pubs. Accessed 11/21/97.

Smith, Jackie. 1998. "Global Civil Society? Transnational Social Movement Organizations and Social Capital." *American Behavioral Scientist* 42, no. 1 (September): 3–107.

Smith, Jackie, Charles Chatfield, and Ron Pagnucco, eds. 1997. *Transnational Social Movements and Global Politics.* Syracuse, N.Y.: Syracuse University Press.

Smith, Jackie, and Hank Johnston, eds. 2002. *Globalization and Resistance: Transnational Dimensions of Social Movements.* Lanham, Md.: Rowman and Littlefield.

Smith, Jenn. "Protesting Global Economic Policies: Where are the Feminists?," *Off Our Backs* 30, no. 6 (June 2000): 6.

Soriano, Zenaida. 1998. "The Asian Crisis: Its Impact on the Lives of Women and Children." In *Proceedings of the Forum on Asian Regional Crisis: Impact on Women and Children.* Manila: AMIHAN, APWN, Gabriela, CRC.

Sparr, Pamela, ed. 1995. *Mortgaging Women's Lives: Feminist Critiques of Structural Adjustment.* London: Zed.

Spillane, Margaret. 2001. "The V-Word is Heard." *The Nation,* 5 March: 6.

Staggenborg, Suzanne. 1998a. "The Consequences of Professionalization and Formalization in the Pro-Choice Movement." *American Sociological Review* 53 (August): 585–606.

———. 1998b. *Gender, Family, and Social Movements.* Thousand Oaks: Pine Forge Press.

———. 1999. "Consequences of Professionalization on Feminist Organizations." In Jo Freeman and Victoria Johnson, eds., *Waves of Protest: Social Movements since the Sixties.* Lanham, Md.: Rowman and Littlefield.

Stalker, Peter. 2000. *Workers without Frontiers: The Impact of Globalization on International Migration.* Boulder and Geneva: Lynne Rienner Publishes and the ILO.

Standing, Guy. 1989. "Global Feminization through Flexible Labor." *World Development* 17, no. 7: 1077–95.

———. 1999. "Global Feminization through Flexible Labor: A Theme Revisited." *World Development* 27, no. 3: 583–602.

Steger, Manfred. 2002. *Globalism: The New Market Ideology.* Lanham, Md.: Rowman and Littlefield.

Stienstra, Deborah. 1994. *Women's Movements and International Organizations.* New York: St. Martin's.

———. 2000. "Dancing Resistance from Rio to Beijing: Transnational Women's Organizing and United Nations Conferences, 1992–6." In Anne Sisson Runyan and Marianne Marchand, eds., *Gender and Global Restructuring: Sightings, Sites and Resistances.* London: Routledge.

Stiglitz, Joseph. 2000. "The Insider: What I Learned at the World Economic Crisis." *New Republic,* 17 and 24 April: 56–60.

Subramaniam, Mangala, Manjusha Gupte, and Debarashmi Mitra. 2002. "Women's Organizing through Grassroots and Transnational Spaces: Evidence from India." Paper presented at the annual meetings of the American Sociological Association (August).

Tanski, Janet. 1994. "The Impact of Crisis, Stabilization and Structural Adjustment on Women in Lima, Peru." *World Development* 22, no. 11: 1627–42.

Taylor, Lance. 2000. "External Liberalization, Economic Performance, and Distribution in Latin America and Elsewhere." Helsinki: WIDER Working Papers No. 215 (December).

Tiano, Susan. 1994. *Patriarchy on the Line: Labor, Gender, and Ideology in the Mexican Maquila Industry.* Philadelphia, Pa.: Temple University Press.

UN. 1991. *World Economic Survey 1991.* New York: UN/DIESA.

———. 1996. *The Beijing Declaration and Platform for Action.* New York: UN.

———. 1999. *World Survey on the Role of Women in Development: Globalization, Women, and Work.* New York: UN.

———. 2000. *The World's Women 2000: Trends and Statistics.* New York: UN.

UNCTAD. 1997. *Trade and Development Report.* Geneva: UNCTAD.

UNDP. 1995. *The Human Development Report 1995.* New York: Oxford University Press.

———. 1999. *Human Development Report 1999* [on globalization]. New York: Oxford University Press.

———. 2002a. *Arab Human Development Report.* New York: Oxford University Press.

———. 2002b. *Human Development Report 2002* [on democracy]. New York: Oxford University Press.

Van Bruinessen, Martin. 2002. "Islam, Women's Rights, and Islamic Feminism." *ISIM Newsletter* no. 9 (January).

Wade, Robert. 2001. "Winners and Losers." *The Economist,* 26 April.

Wallerstein, Immanuel. 1991.*Geopolitics and Geoculture: Essays on the Changing World-system.* Cambridge: Cambridge University Press.

Walton, John, and Charles Ragin. 1990. "Global and National Sources of Political Protest: Third World Responses to the Debt Crisis." *American Sociological Review* 55 (December): 876–90.

Walton, John, and David Seddon. 1994. *Free Markets and Food Riots: The Politics of Global Adjustment.* Oxford: Blackwell.

Warskett, Rosemary. 2001. "Feminism's Challenge to Unions in the North: Possibilities and Contradictions." *Socialist Register 2001: Working Classes, Global Realities.* New York: Monthly Review Press.

Waterman, Peter. 1998. "Beyond Internationalism: Women, Feminism and Global Solidarity." Chapter 6 of *Globalization, Social Movements and the New Internationalisms.* London and Washington: Marshall.

———. 2000. "Social Movements, Local Places and Globalized Spaces: Implications for 'Globalization from Below.'" In Barry K. Gills, ed., *Globalization and the Politics of Resistance.* London: Macmillan.

West, Guida, and Rhoda Blumberg, eds. 1990. *Women and Social Protest.* New York: Oxford University Press.

Wichterich, Christa. 1999. *The Globalized Woman: Notes from a Future of Inequality.* London: Zed Books.

WIDE. 1995. WIDE bulletin: "From Copenhagen to Beijing." Brussels: WIDE.

———. 1998. *Trade Traps and Gender Gaps: Women Unveiling the Market.* Report on WIDE's Annual Conference held at Jarvenpaa, Finland, 16–18 May 1997. Brussels: WIDE.

———. 2002a. *Globalization, Development, and Sustainability: A WIDEr View.* Brussels: WIDE.

———. 2002b. *Women's Rights and Gender Equality in the European Union.* Brussels: WIDE.

———. 2003. *Europe Moving to the Right: Where Lie the Alternatives for Transnational Feminism?* WIDE bulletin [report on the May 2002 Consultation]. Brussels: WIDE.

Wood, Ellen Meiksins. 1997. "'Globalization' or 'Globaloney'? A reply to A. Sivanandan." *Monthly Review* 48, no. 9 (February): 21–32.

World Bank. 1995. *World Development Report 1995: Workers in an Integrating World*. New York: Oxford University Press.

World Development. 1995. Vol. 23, no. 11. Symposium on Gender and Structural Adjustment.

Young, Kate, ed. 1992. *Gender and Development Reader*. Ottawa: Canadian Council for International Cooperation.

Zachary, G. Pascal. 2001. "Shortage of Nurses Hits Hardest Where They Are Needed the Most." *Wall Street Journal*, 24 January.

Zinsser, Judith P. 2002. "From Mexico City to Copenhagen to Nairobi: The United Nations Decade for Women, 1975–1985. *Journal of World History* 13, no. 1: 139–68.

Index

Valentine M. Moghadam is Director of the Women's Studies Program and Professor of Sociology at Illinois State University. Born in Iran and educated in North America, she is an internationally known scholar of the Middle East, gender issues, and women's movements. Her first book, *Modernizing Women: Gender and Social Change in the Middle East* (2d ed. published in 2003), was a Choice Outstanding Book in 1993. In addition to her academic career, she has been a United Nations staff member and a consultant to international organizations.